The Changing Politics of Local Government

The Changing Politics of Local Government

John Gyford
Steve Leach
Chris Game

LONDON
UNWIN HYMAN
BOSTON SYDNEY WELLINGTON

© John Gyford, Steve Leach and Chris Game,
1989

Published by the Academic Division of
Unwin Hyman Ltd
15/17 Broadwick Street, London W1V 1FP, UK

Unwin Hyman Inc.,
8 Winchester Place, Winchester, Mass. 01890,
USA   1054670 7

Allen & Unwin (Australia) Ltd,
8 Napier Street, North Sydney, NSW 2060,
Australia

Allen & Unwin (New Zealand) Ltd in association
with the Port Nicholson Press Ltd,
Compusales Building, 75 Ghuznee Street,
Wellington 1, New Zealand

First published in 1989

British Library Cataloguing in Publication Data

Gyford, John
  The changing politics of local
  government
  1. Great Britain. Local government.
  Political aspects
  I. Title   II. Leach, Steve
  III. Game, Chris
  352.041
ISBN 0-04-445299-3

Typeset in 10pt Baskerville and printed by Billing
& Sons, London and Worcester

Contents

Tables and Figures

Tables

Figures

Preface

In 1985 we were commissioned, together with Arthur Midwinter of Strathclyde Business School, to carry out a research project on behalf of the Widdicombe Committee of Inquiry into the Conduct of Local Authority Business. The project focused on the political organization of local authorities and was conducted by means of a postal questionnaire to all authorities in Great Britain and an interview survey of councillors and officers in 103 authorities. The results of the project were published by Her Majesty's Stationery Office as Research Volume I concurrently with the Final Report of the Committee in 1986.

Other research was also commissioned by the Committee and duly published along with ours. Research Volume II contained a 10 per cent sample survey of councillors carried out by Jude England of Social and Community Planning Research (SCPR) and a study of members' allowances by Phillip Ramsdale and Stuart Capon of the Institute of Public Finance Ltd (IPF). In Research Volume III Ken Young dealt with public attitudes to local government and William Miller with local electoral behaviour: both authors drew on survey work conducted by NOP Market Research Ltd. Finally, Research Volume IV contained an analysis of local authority discretionary spending by Ramsdale and Capon of IPF together with four commissioned papers on topics of particular interest to the Committee. In addition to these publications the Committee had also issued an earlier Interim Report on Local Authority Publicity in 1985.

The Committee's reports and the four research volumes attracted a considerable degree of interest, not least because they provided the most comprehensive body of evidence on the political workings of local government since the Maud Committee investigation nearly twenty years earlier. More specifically one commentator was kind enough to suggest that the findings of Research Volume I merited wider circulation. He expressed the view that if the authors of that volume were to recast their findings in a more accessible form they would be performing 'a public service' (Rhodes, 1987a, p. 202). This book is an attempt to respond to that kind suggestion.

In preparing the book, rather than merely re-draft or summarize the published research report, we have returned to our original research material from the postal questionnaire and interview surveys. The questionnaire was designed by Royston Greenwood in conjunction with Jude England of SCPR and Ken Young, the research adviser to the Committee: analysis of the data was the work of Mary Davies, assisted by Annette Warner, at Birmingham University's Institute of Local Government Studies (INLOGOV). We gratefully acknowledge the help provided by the above named. We are also beholden to the 494 authorities who completed the questionnaire, thereby providing a remarkably high response rate of 95 per cent. Additionally, we owe a great debt to the 550 officers and councillors in a stratified random sample of 103 authorities who allowed themselves to be interviewed in the second half of 1985. Details of the design and execution of both the questionnaire and interview surveys, together with copies of the questionnaire itself and of the semi-structured interview topics, were published in the original Research Volume I and are not repeated here.

The questionnaire survey was designed to obtain information on the political workings of local authorities of all types and covered such topics as party representation and organization, the operation of party groups, support services for members, the co-option of non-councillors onto committees and the role of councillors in officer appointments. Not all of the 494 councils who responded provided answers to every single question: on some issues therefore the findings relate to a slightly smaller base number than 494. The interview survey explored in greater depth some of the issues raised in the questionnaire survey and also sought to gain insights into the particular experiences and attitudes of those to whom we spoke, who included chief officers, party group leaders and backbenchers. In neither survey was there any bias, whether in terms of type of authority or political control, amongst those who declined to take part: in most cases non-response was due to pressure of time and other commitments on the part of those concerned. In both surveys we undertook not to identify individual councillors, officers or authorities in any subsequent publication. This undertaking we have of course fulfilled. Accordingly, any references hereafter to named individuals or authorities are derived from sources other than our research for the Committee.

We have in fact supplemented our own Widdicombe research data by relating them where appropriate to the findings of others working in similar fields, to our own knowledge of recent developments and to the wider literature of contemporary local politics. In addition we have tried as far as possible to take account of events since the research was carried out and since the Committee itself reported in 1986. We have thus aimed to present a realistic account, and, we hope, a helpful interpretation of the state of local politics in Britain in the late 1980s.

We are grateful to the Department of the Environment and to the Controller of Her Majesty's Stationery Office for permission to reproduce certain previously published tables, whose source is identified as they occur in the text. Figure 1 on p. 7 originally appeared as Figure 4.1 on p. 79 of *Half A Century of Municipal Decline*, edited by M. Loughlin, D. Gelfand and K. Young, and we are thus also grateful to Unwin Hyman Ltd for permission to reproduce it here.

In the course of our research Arthur Midwinter gave us many valuable insights into the particular features of local government in Scotland as well as providing stimulating contributions to collective discussion of our findings. Throughout the project Ken Young was a constant source of enthusiasm, encouragement and sound advice. We thank them both, whilst also acquitting them, and all others, from any responsibility for what follows, which is ours alone. Our thanks go also to Diana Myers, Gillian Davis and Jennifer Jeynes who typed the original manuscript.

The writing of this book was completed after the birth of the new Social and Liberal Democratic Party. During and after the period of our research the ancestors of the new party were of course commonly known as the Alliance parties and we have retained that usage even though it now recedes into history.

We should perhaps clarify one other matter of usage. In the conduct of both the questionnaire and interview surveys we adopted the conventional term of 'chairman' to refer to those individuals who chair meetings of committees, party groups, etc. In some instances, particular authorities now use the term 'chair' to identify those individuals and we have deferred to their preference when making specific reference to them. This particular question of usage has occasionally provoked some lively debate and may be seen as one symbol or symptom of the current politicization of local government. If that is so then it is perhaps worth pointing out that in 1888 a Liberal councillor, Mrs Sarah Wilson, refused to become the 'chairman' of Sheffield City Council's school management committee and became its 'president' instead (Hollis, 1987, p. 167). The politicization of local government may have intensified recently but it has never been wholly absent.

John Gyford
Steve Leach
Chris Game

1
The politicization of local government

On the night of the Council meeting, when screaming and shouting started from the gallery and everybody was going bananas . . . I said to the Mayor 'I'm sorry, but there is no way in which I can clear that gallery without some heads being broken' . . . . 'What are we going to do then?' . . . . I said 'Just bore them' and we bored them till half-past three in the morning.

The meeting thus recalled by one chief executive illustrates a form of local government in which political passions run deep. Alarmed by such happenings in the town hall, some evoke a time when, as they recall, councils dealt only with such non-political tasks as street sweeping and dustbin emptying. Councillors then were not politicians but simply 'local worthies who kept an eye on one or two amenities' (Walden, 1987). However, the truth does not lie in notions of a lost golden age of routine municipal housekeeping. In one form or another politics has always existed in British local government; for as the old saying goes 'You can no more take politics out of government than you can keep sex out of procreation.'

In reflecting on the sex/procreation analogy and on the inseparability of politics and government, the chief executive of Westminster City Council, Rodney Brooke, observed that

Over the years local government has done its best to perform the impossible. Historically, the mechanics of party decision-taking have been regarded as a rather seamy and disreputable underworld, best ignored by local government officers.   (Brooke, 1982, p. 3)

It is an underworld largely by-passed too, as Brooke also observed, by the reports of such government-appointed committees as Maud (1967) and Bains (1972). The prescriptions of such committees – the Maud Committee's recommendation of a powerful but bipartisan management board is a good example – tended at best to ignore, if not to deplore, the increasing party politicization of local authorities. There has been a failure to come to terms with the fact that the reality of power in local councils is much more likely nowadays to rest with the party groups – and specifically with the majority party group – than in the formal committee structure. There has been an inability to reconcile satisfactorily the institutions and procedures of party politics with the traditional structures and processes of local authorities.

It has indeed seemed at times as though a vain attempt was afoot to remove the politics from local government – and the officer from politics – to the frustration and confusion of all concerned. Almost inevitably, tensions and frictions have arisen between elected members and officers, some of which we discuss later on in this book, notably in Chapter 4. And some officers, uncertain about what is expected of political power, have reacted by ignoring or distancing themselves from the political decision-taking process – instead of taking up what Rodney Brooke (1982, p. 6) sees as their rightful and vital place: 'firmly in the middle'.

The Widdicombe Committee Inquiry, the occasion for much of the research we shall be describing, sought quite explicitly to forestall the accusation of ignoring politics that had been levelled at some of its predecessors. True, the composition of the Committee was just as devoid of any elected councillors as the Bains Committee had been. But its emphasis and language were very different. The Widdicombe Report acknowledges, for instance, that 'politics has existed for as long as local government, the very genesis of which was political' (p. 58). And it talks of 'the need to accommodate politics in local government' (p. 62), of 'the desirability and inevitability of politics' (p. 60) and, in a particularly vivid phrase, of politics being 'the essential currency of representative democracy' (p. 60).

As will be apparent, the term 'Politics' is being used here

consistently with a 'big P' – as a shorthand of organized Party Politics. In that sense, it could be argued to be a narrow definition of politics and political activity. It certainly seems a much narrower definition than would be adopted by many political scientists, who would claim, for example, that:

politics is at the heart of *all* collective social activity, formal and informal, public and private, in *all* human groups, institutions and societies, not just some of them . . . it always has been and always will be.

politics is *not* a separate realm of public life and activity. On the contrary, politics comprises all the activities of cooperation and conflict, within and between societies, whereby the human species goes about organising the use, production and distribution of human, natural and other *resources* in the course of the production and reproduction of its biological and social life.

Wherever we live and work in groups, and whatever we do in our collective productive and social lives, we are always engaged in activities of cooperation and conflict over the use, production and distribution of resources. That is, we are constantly engaged in politics. (Leftwich, 1984, pp. 63–70, emphasis in original)

This much broader interpretation of politics would, of course, deride the notion that individual councillors – let alone whole councils – could seriously describe themselves as 'non-political'. For surely their whole *raison d'être* is the organization of the use and distribution of resources? Similarly, it would regard as both misguided and potentially threatening the efforts of either individuals or organizations to 'keep politics out' of certain debates, whether it be the local arrangements for secondary education, international sport, or Prince Charles's views on architectural design:

There is, in fact, nothing *more political* than the constant attempts to exclude certain types of issues from politics. (Leftwich, 1984, p. 144, emphasis in original)

It would have been possible, then, for the Widdicombe Committee to embrace a much more expansive conception of politics than it did – to see it as a much more universal 'small p' activity, rather than as something confined essentially to formalized parties and the institutions of government. But Widdicombe did, as we have already suggested, go a great deal further in its positive recognition of politics than had its predecessors. Indeed, some of the phrases deployed by at least one member of the Committee, Sir Lawrence Boyle – albeit outside the confines of the Report itself – come close to echoing those of Leftwich.

Sir Lawrence explains that he starts from the position

that all governments, be they central or local, have a two-fold function to perform. They have the service function and they have the political function.

The service function consists of the provision of those goods or services which for one reason or another are supplied through the public sector. The political function, on the other hand, is *the management and resolution of the conflict which arises out of the issues involved in the public provision of goods and services*. It embraces such questions as the scope, the scale and the quality of the public services and the manner in which their costs should be met. . . . If the political function is removed from local government, it ceases to be local government.   (Boyle, 1986, p. 33, our emphasis)

There is no mention at all here, it should be noted, of political parties. On the contrary, Boyle's assertion is that any government – any local council, for instance – with services to provide, resources to allocate, and decisions to take is going to be engaged in this business of conflict management and resolution, quite irrespective of whether organized and labelled political parties happen to be represented or not.

Put another way, the activities of Eden District Council in Cumbria, composed entirely of self-described 'non-political' members, are just as intrinsically 'political' as are those of Birmingham City Council, with its traditions of organized party caucuses and groupings dating back to the days of Joseph Chamberlain. The scale of services may be different in the two authorities, but the Eden councillors, like their counterparts in Birmingham, have decisions to take about their stock of council houses, their leisure amenities, their car parks and their town centre redevelopment (Penrith), as well as, of course, about their budget and rates. And those decisions are political decisions, whether they happen to emerge relatively predictably out of the machinery of organized party groups or more unpredictably out of the 'cut and thrust' of open debate in the committee room or council chamber. To return to our aphorism: politics, viewed in these terms, is indeed as inextricable a part of local government as sex is of procreation.

Keeping that discussion in mind, we should make it clear that the remainder of this chapter is concerned with the *party* politicization of local government. Even where the adjective 'party' is omitted for the sake of brevity, what is being referred to is the presence and the increasing prominence of organized parties and party systems.

The Weberian 'ideal-type' elements of the party system in local government has been usefully spelt out by George Jones (Jones, 1975). A co-biographer of Herbert Morrison, the London Labour leader in the 1920s and 1930s, Jones described the model of party politics that had been developed and refined by Morrison on the London County Council (LCC). The key elements of the model are:

1 *Candidates for the council are selected* by local ward parties, subject to some supervision . . . by the executive of the constituency or borough party.

2 *The electoral policy is decided* by the constituency or borough party: usually it is formulated by a committee consisting of leading members of the council and leading members of the party who are not on the council. This policy is adhered to by all candidates of the party in their manifestos.

3 *The members of the council* meet regularly in a party group to decide how they shall act in the council. They have the responsibility, as directly elected members of the council, to decide council policy.

4 *Each committee of the council may hold* group meetings of the members of the party to plan their action on the committee.

5 Leading the party group will be a *policy committee* or an *executive committee* of the leading members.

(Jones, 1975, p. 29, emphases in original)

Here, then, we have the basic features of an 'ideal-type' party system, or, as Jones puts it, 'an analytical model against which one can set actual systems' (p. 28). The process of party politicization could be defined as the increasingly visible presence of these features in increasing numbers of local authorities. And, if there is one generalization which can safely be made about the enormously variegated world of local government, it is that over the past century and a half – and particularly since the structural reorganizations of the early 1970s – there has been an increase in party politicization.

The process has not occurred with uniform speed in all parts of the country or in all types of authority. Nor, as we shall see, has it resulted in anything like a complete homogenization of local politics. Jones's ideal-type model leaves plenty of scope for local interpretation and variation, even among councils which would qualify as fully-fledged 'party political'. The extent of these variations and of the diversity of the present-day 'landscape of local politics' will be the focus of the final section of this chapter. First, though, we need to identify some of the principal historical stages in the process of party politicization.

The stages of party politicization

The now extensive domination of most councils by party politicians is best seen not as some sudden metamorphosis, but as the culmination of a secular, though by no means uniform, development. It reflects what has been described as 'a steady long-term trend, beginning in the nineteenth century, spreading in this century first through the major cities and then, if less evenly, to the shires' (Young, 1985, p. 81). This trend has proceeded through changing social and political circumstances since the Municipal Corporations Act of 1835 first laid down the basic outlines of nineteenth- and twentieth-century local government. At some risk of over-simplification we may conjecture that party politicization of local government has passed through some five stages in the years since 1835 (Figure 1). The stages may have varied in their occurrence somewhat from place to place and they should be seen as shading into one another rather than proceeding by abrupt succession.

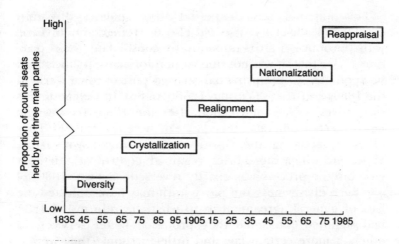

Figure 1 *Party politics in local government: five conjectural stages*
Source: Gyford, 1985

The first stage is that which began in 1835 and lasted into the late 1860s and is best characterized by *diversity*, both administrative and political. Alongside the reformed councils created by the 1835 Act there existed a complex system of Poor Law Guardians, local Boards of Health (after 1848) and improvement commissioners, not to mention the parish vestries which in some areas still retained a number of administrative functions from earlier times. Indeed the vestries themselves, despite their limited parochial concerns and their ecclesiastical origins, could sometimes prove a focus for political action. Before the 1835 Act 'Liberal vestries counter-balanced Tory oligarchies and after it artisan and working-class vestries counter-balanced bourgeois-dominated councils' (Fraser, 1976, p. 30). The complexity of administrative structures was matched by that of local politics. Tories, Whigs, Conservatives, Liberals, Radicals, Chartists, Improvers and Economizers offered varying prescriptions in different towns. Conservatives might be Economizers in one town but Improvers in another: a local party might split, as did the Leeds Liberals in the 1840s over the merits of state education; in some places political labels might mask what were essentially factions based on personalities.

This was not only a period when politics displayed considerable diversity: it could also be 'remarkably divisive' with 'incoming parties anxious to consolidate their position . . . [so that] it was not uncommon for active politicians to be appointed to the principal salaried post of town clerk' in the 1830s and 1840s (Young, 1986b, p. 86). In Colchester, in similar vein, the first election after the 1835 Act saw the newly elected Liberals make 'a clean sweep of the old Tory officers, replacing them with men of their own party'. However, when the Tories regained control at the next election 'the process was exactly reversed' (Brown, 1980, p. 43). Such divisiveness and party spirit may have reflected the lack of general agreement as to what the reforms of 1835 had signified. To some they promised better services, to others a more certain law and order; to some they were a bulwark for the propertied middle class, to others a tool with which to undermine the aristocracy and its political power. To the radical Cobden they provided a chance to 'place forever the population of our town and neighbourhood beyond the control of a booby squirearchy' (Fraser, 1979, p. 17). Perhaps for their Whig progenitors the new councils incorporated from 1835 onwards had been visualized chiefly as more effective mechanisms for urban order than their unreformed and allegedly corrupt predecessors. The fact that others might see them as suitable vehicles for other forms of public policy was to become increasingly important in the second of our five stages, during the last third of the nineteenth century and into the Edwardian era.

This period may be described as one of *crystallization* for during it the patterns both of local government structure and of local politics took on a more readily definable form. The Royal Sanitary Commission which sat between 1868 and 1871 concluded that local government was being hampered by a confusion of areas and powers: in England alone some 27,069 different authorities levied eighteen different kinds of rate upon the rate-payers. In an attempt at rationalizing the system in line with the Commission's findings a Local Government Board was set up in 1871, combining the Public Health branch of the Privy Council, the Poor Law Board and the Local Government Act department of the Home Office:

the aim was to relate more closely the administration of public health and Poor Law relief. At the local level the Public Health Acts of 1872 and 1875 provided for uniform patterns of public health administration for urban and rural areas.

Perhaps of more immediate political significance than these reforms was the creation in 1870 of a national system of locally elected school boards which 'brought a new intensity to local politics' (Young, 1986b, p. 85). Issues of religious instruction in education became matters of much public dispute and the inter-denominational conflict between Anglicans and non-conformists often paralleled the partisan division between Conservatives and Liberals, each reinforcing the other as school board and council elections became political contests between those who identified respectively with church and chapel. This crystallization of local politics into a Conservative-Liberal contest was perhaps encouraged by the Representation of the People Act of 1867 which greatly enlarged the ranks of urban working-class voters and called for a more disciplined form of electoral politics than in earlier decades.

This new form of politics was most clearly evident in the reorganized Birmingham Liberal Association in and after 1868, the so-called caucus, whose efficiency at election time made it an object of grave suspicion to *The Times* which accused it of stirring up agitation and 'manufacturing' public opinion (Briggs, 1968, p. 65). Under the leadership of Joseph Chamberlain however it proved to be effective not only at winning elections but also at initiating major changes in urban policy. It became the pioneer of a programmatic local politics based in this instance on a municipal collectivism embracing gas and water supply, slum clearance, parks and gardens and public health.

Liberals were not alone in seeing the need for paying more systematic attention to local elections as the franchise widened. The Conservative party's principal agent, Sir John Gorst, began to look upon local election results as harbingers of parliamentary results in the 1870s, and with the creation and election of the first county councils in 1889 party managers from both camps began to see such contests not merely as indicators but as useful dress rehearsals for subsequent general elections (Hanham, 1959, pp. 388–90; Young, 1975, p. 32).

The early years of this stage of politicization were thus characterized by a crystallization of the party conflict within, and the administrative structure of, local government. The later years, the 1890s and after, featured two rather different forms of crystallization, those of ideological conflict and of patterns of party organization within local councils.

As we have seen, Chamberlain's civic gospel embraced a wide measure of collectivism: but he himself was no socialist and indeed one of his arguments in favour of municipal gas supply was that its profits could reduce the burden on the ratepayers. None the less the Municipal Sanitary Conference which he convened in Birmingham in 1875 has been judged to represent 'the real beginning of the movement later known as "municipal" or "gas and water" socialism' (Cole, 1957, p. 387).

A newly enfranchised working class in the cities, a developing Labour movement and an innovative municipal collectivism proved to be a significant political combination as 'the Fabian Society. . . set [the Independent Labour Party] off to capture municipal government with the aid of using it as an instrument for the achievement of some measure of constructive socialism' (Cole, 1948, p. 289). Increasingly 'working class and socialist organisations took up the opportunities of active local government and extended it in important ways' (Blunkett and Jackson, 1987, p. 51). This in turn produced vigorous opposition from anti-socialist bodies such as the Liberty and Property Defence League, which identified municipal socialism as one of its campaign targets along with the growth of trade unionism and the spread of picketing (Soldon, 1974). By 1902 there were 'some two hundred municipal gas and water undertakings and over a hundred transport undertakings' and the columns of *The Times* were laden with correspondence and articles debating the alleged virtues and vices of municipal trading: there were it seemed some who saw such activities as not merely politically undesirable but as morally depraved, involving 'irreligion and licentiousness' (Fraser, 1979, p. 172; Shaw,

1908, p. x).

In London the municipal socialist challenge posed by the Liberal-Labour Progressive Party had called forth, in 1894, the opposition of the London Municipal Society, a body combining Conservatives and Liberal Unionists. The latter included somewhat paradoxically Joseph Chamberlain himself, the unwitting precursor of municipal socialism, now an enthusiast for dismantling its stronghold in the LCC and a 'nasty enemy' to its supporters (Young, 1975; Webb, 1983, p. 64). Yet again, however, Chamberlain was involved in a form of innovation in local politics, for the ostensibly non-party anti-socialist coalition of the London Municipal Society was to have its successors elsewhere in years to come.

The LCC, in addition to being the scene of vigorous ideological debate over the merits of municipal socialism, also witnessed what may have been the birth of party group meetings in local government, with Progressive councillors and aldermen beginning to meet in conclave in 1890 in response to an alleged, but unproven, similar practice by their opponents (Young, 1986b, p. 93).

By the beginning of the twentieth century, then, the kaleidoscopic administrative and political picture of post-1835 local government had crystallized after the 1860s into a simpler Conservative-Liberal contest. Within this framework a major ideological debate over municipal socialism had arisen, reflecting in part the rise of the enfranchised urban workers and the Labour movement, and prototypes of two new forms of local political organization had emerged – the anti-socialist non-party coalition and the party group of councillors. The latter were to continue and to flourish in the next, third stage of politicization which revolved mainly around the rise of the Labour party and a consequent *realignment* in local politics.

Labour's displacement of the Liberals as a force in local politics during the first four decades of the present century was clearly a reflection of a similar development at national level. However, Labour's advance in local government was aided by its ability to offer a distinctive municipal programme calling for better wages and conditions for council workers, the provision of work for the unemployed, public baths and laundries, and adequate housing for working-class families. The further extension of the local government franchise in 1918 and the fact that councils were becoming significant employers of manual and clerical workers widened the constituency to which Labour could reasonably make a municipal appeal. The Liberals however found it harder to maintain a distinctive stance, particularly as religious non-conformity and its preoccupations with denominational education and licensing laws went into long-term decline as a social force. Local Liberal associations also found themselves unable to attract, or unwilling to select, younger or more working-class candidates who might have re-invigorated or re-oriented the party.

Labour candidates had initially often been willing to stand for election in alliance with the Liberals, as in the case of the London Progressives. However, the emergence of a distinctive Labour party in the first decade of the century paved the way for separate local Labour campaigns, especially after the party adopted a constituency-based structure in 1918. Whereas Labour had some 420 councillors in the provincial and metropolitan (London) boroughs in 1914, the first local elections after the war in 1919 saw the figure more than double to 938 with the party taking control of twelve metropolitan boroughs out of twenty-nine, eighteen of the seventy-nine county boroughs, and four county councils, including the LCC. For the Liberals meanwhile there were continuous net losses of Liberal seats in each of the inter-war years and a gradual but consistent fall in the number of Liberal candidates standing for local office (Cole, 1948, pp. 445-58; Cook, 1975).

This sequence of events has been described as one in which 'Liberal councillors succumbed to the Tory embrace while their old following among the electorate largely drifted into the Labour camp' (Beloff, 1975, p. 8). Thus in Reading in 1919 the Liberal agent ventured to suggest to the Conservatives 'that it was desirable to arrive at an agreement to fight Labour at the forthcoming municipal elections', a proposal which met with a favourable response and led a decade later to the formation of a Reading Municipal Association uniting the anti-socialist councillors under increasingly Conservative domination (Alexander 1985, pp. 176–7).

Such an arrangement was clearly following in the steps first taken by the London Municipal Society; it was to be paralleled between the wars by a number of other anti-socialist groupings in other localities going under a variety of names such as Moderate, Progressive, Citizens', Anti-Socialist, Municipal Alliance and Ratepayers. This last title was adopted by a number of groups operating under the umbrella of the National Union of Ratepayers' Associations set up in 1921 as an extension of the London Municipal Society, from which it separated in 1935. Despite its public advocacy of an independent non-party approach to local government this ratepayer movement 'is best understood as an orchestrated response to the rise of the Labour party, prompted by the strategic calculations of Conservative party managers' (Young, 1986b, p. 82).

A process of political realignment was not the only characteristic of local government during this period. One historian suggests that 'the period from the late nineteenth century to the Second World War might be called the heyday of local government', with the inter-war years being 'called "the golden age of the shopocracy" in local government' (Stevenson, 1984, pp. 309 and 314). During these years local councils took over control of education and of Poor Law relief following the abolition of the Schools Boards and the Boards of Guardians in 1902 and 1929 respectively. Major public utilities such as gas, water, electricity and transport were also significant local government responsibilities by now, despite the earlier hostility to municipal trading in some quarters. Councils, particularly perhaps the all-purpose county boroughs, thus played a major and identifiable part in the social and economic life of their communities. They employed moreover, through their utilities, a workforce embracing large numbers of manual as well as white-collar workers and could thus be seen perhaps as something more than the preserve of middle-class professionals.

Those manual workers who did work for the council were thereby precluded from seeking election as councillors. With the break-up of many of the great landed estates after 1918 there had also occurred a 'territorial abdication' of land-owners from local politics (Cannadine, 1982, p. 5). Shop-keepers and small businessmen were thereby able to play a major role in local politics: in Wolverhampton for example over half the councillors who served between 1930 and 1940 were shopkeepers, publicans or businessmen (Jones, 1969). Their own economic interest lay in keeping rates at a low level in decades when high unemployment produced calls for greater spending on relief. This created a major and recurrent issue in local politics, particularly where both business and workers were hard hit by depression as in parts of the North East of England. Indeed the matter of relief payments for the jobless, and the government's enthusiasm for a means test in that connection, provoked in 1931-2 the 'most widespread rebellion by local govern-ment in the twentieth century' on the part of some twenty dissident authorities (Stevenson, 1984, pp. 310–11). The rebellion was unsuccessful but its eventual outcome was not without significance for the future. It persuaded the gov-ernment thereafter to remove unemployment relief from the field of local politics and to place it, in 1934, in the hands of what in later years would have been called a quango, the Unemployment Assistance Board. Such a removal of functions from local to central control was a harbinger of policies that were to become increasingly com-mon in the period after the Second World War.

The three decades after 1945 can be seen as the fourth stage in the politicization of local government, one to which the term *nationalization* may be applied. Such a description had an immediate and particular relevance to the period of the Attlee Labour government from 1945 to 1951. During those years local authorities lost much of their public utility work to new nationalized industries and their hospitals to the National Health Service: the consequent devaluation of the role of local government was later to be described as 'Labour's great mistake' (Blunkett and Jackson, 1987, p. 64). However the notion of nationalization also came to be applied to local government in a rather different usage as well. Some observers detected a trend towards the gradual assimilation of local politics into the national contest between

Labour and the Conservatives, with a certain 'ironing out of autonomous local characteristics' promoted by 'the great national parties' (Johnson, 1972, p. 53): the result was seen as 'the "nationalisation" of local politics' (Schofield, 1977).

Certainly the two major parties made great efforts in the post-war decades to secure better co-ordination of their local and national efforts with local government units being established at party headquarters and a variety of conferences, meetings and publications being launched. However it is clear that in practice neither party headquarters really possessed the necessary powers or resources actually to bend their party's councillors to the will of the national leadership (Gyford and James, 1983). Instead it seems more likely that the coming together of local and national politics during this period reflected a general measure of bipartisan agreement at both levels on the desirability of the welfare state and the mixed economy, on the respective roles of local and central government therein and on the virtues of what Rhodes (1986, p. 126) calls 'reasonably consensual' dealings between the two levels of government. This was for the most part an era of economic growth, in which not all choices were as hard as they later became, and of considerable electoral stability, in which each party was able to call on the loyalties of a large block of voters who were rarely distracted by local issues or the appeals of third parties.

Local politics in this period conveyed an air of considerable stability. Party politicization increased but it did so slowly: even as late as the early 1970s barely a half of all councils could be described as 'partisan' (Table 1). In some ways indeed this was perhaps the most stable of all the five stages under consideration and, to those who recall it, it may thereby have bequeathed an image of stability as normality in local politics. Party control of councils did have an impact on patterns of spending, with Labour tending to spend more on redistributive services than the Conservatives and to adapt council procedures and conventions so as to secure swift implementation of political decisions (Boaden, 1971; Sharpe and Newton, 1984). Yet these differing attitudes to policy and to practice were rarely expressed in detailed party manifestos at local election times: they reflected rather the general stances of the parties to which council officers adapted their own proposals. In this respect at least councils under party control shared something in common with the non-party councils which still persisted in many small towns and rural areas, namely adherence to a form of administrative politics (Hill, 1972) in which administrators rather than politicians dominated the decision-making process whilst nevertheless negotiating or consulting with, and when necessary accommodating, the latter. What did particularly distinguish the partisan from the non-partisan or Independent councils was the increasing tendency for the former to adopt highly developed and disciplined systems of party groups, in some cases underpinning the rule of strong political leaders who in turn worked very closely with their council's chief officers. Such a pattern of administrative politics, of strong group discipline, of dominant leaders and of close collaboration between leaders and chief officers did not however survive without challenge after local government reorganization in the 1970s. Reorganization was perhaps the occasion rather than the cause of such challenges but it does seem to have ushered in a new, fifth, stage of politicization, one within which we still find ourselves and which we may term one of *reappraisal.*

Both the Conservative and Labour parties saw the reorganization of local government as an opportunity to strengthen and extend their roles in local politics. On the Conservative side Central Office positively encouraged the replacement of Independents of Conservative sympathy by straightforward Conservative Party councillors, even if necessary confronting recalcitrant Independents with official party candidates. For its part the Labour Party introduced a new structure of district, county and Scottish regional party organization to parallel that of the new local authorities.

By itself however such developments might have led to little more than an extension into hitherto non-partisan authorities of the party practices common elsewhere in the three post-war decades. The outcome then would have been a quantitative change, in the extent of partisan local politics, which did indeed occur (see Table 2), rather than a qualitative change in the character of local politics. One way of characterizing the qualitative change which did also begin to develop is to see it as the emergence of an ideological politics to challenge the local administrative politics of the previous decades. In such an ideological politics 'unified political parties provide specific programmes' which they expect to be implemented by the public bodies which they control (Hill, 1972, p. 211). Typical of such an approach was that of Labour in Nottinghamshire at the first election to the new county council in 1973. The party produced a detailed policy statement of over 30,000 words: after the party's victory in the election the policies therein became official council policy and chief officers and their departments were expected to work towards their implementation. This was a style of politics which was to find many imitators in years to come, although it has yet to become universal and is still rare in rural authorities. Such an innovation might be seen as little more than an attempt to make explicit in policy terms what may always have been implicit in the general stance of a party. It may have been a refinement, or a logical escalation, of the partisan local politics of the post-war era. However it has been accompanied by the emergence of other features which in some places have changed the character or the 'feel' of local politics very markedly.

Perhaps the most modest of these changes has been the increased *formalization* of partisan politics, whereby the existence of party is accepted not as an informal reality but as a part of the formal machinery of local authority operations. This formalization may take various forms. It may include reference to party groups and their rights in a council's standing orders, provision of meeting rooms, officers, and even staffing for party groups, and arrangements for officer advice to be given to groups as well as to the council committees. The rights of party groups, and their proper relation with one another and with council officers, are most clearly spelled out in the various agreements or 'conventions' which have been adopted in a number of 'hung' councils where there is no single party with an overall majority. Hung councils can vary considerably in their nature (Table 6) but they have sometimes found it advisable to spell out exactly how such an authority should function politically in terms of the parties' rights of access to officer advice, decision-making and publicity for example.

The emergence of hung authorities reflects a further change in local politics, namely the move away from the two-party contest of the post-war era to a multi-party contest in the wake of the Liberal revival and the creation of the SDP. If this has injected greater fluidity, or even volatility, into a previously more stable system it has not been alone in doing so. The apparent decay of some traditional patterns of voting behaviour and the growth of factionalism within the Labour and Conservative parties has also contributed to a more uncertain local politics in which the number of variables capable of determining a council's political complexion has multiplied.

Internal party factionalism reflects in turn a process of ideological *polarization* to which both the Labour and Conservative parties have been subject. Within the Labour party traditional or right-wing or moderate councillors, 'soft left' and 'hard left' councillors can be and are identified by both members and officers alike. To some extent the use of such terms is almost a shorthand whose applicability varies from one group to another, and since they are relative rather than absolute terms they inevitably lack some precision. In some cases they partly reflect differences between generations or between cohorts of newer and more established councillors but in policy terms they have often crystallized around views such as how far to go in opposing rate-capping or in pursuing equal opportunities policies. On the Conservative side the 'wet' and 'dry' distinction can be a very real one with the former maintaining a strong commitment to service provision, often in rural areas in a rather paternalistic, quasi-feudal fashion: the drys for their part have emphasized the need for efficiency, 'good-housekeeping' and 'value for money', and in some cases have concluded that these are best achieved not by improved local authority management but by contracting service provision to private firms. One by-product of factionalism within the parties, and also perhaps of the influx of new, younger councillors after reorganization, has been the decline of strong political leaders and their replacement by more democratic or at least consultative leadership. Shifts of power between factions within a ruling party as well as actual changes in party control have also become important sources of policy change on occasion.

The political distance between the Conservative right-wing drys, enthusiastic for privatization, and Labour's hard left, committed to defend council services to the utmost, is such that ideological polarization can be accompanied by an intense distaste by each for the other. In one polarized authority, run by an energetic and very dry Conservative group, Labour and Conservative councillors were seen by the chief executive as 'two quite different races . . . [with] no shred of the old consensus politics'; their relations were basically 'vituperative'. Such an *intensification* of political passions can sometimes spread beyond the council into the ranks of supporters outside – and then back to the council itself.

Thus in April 1987 council meetings in the London boroughs of Westminster, Bromley, Haringey, Tower Hamlets, Waltham Forest, and Hammersmith and Fulham were the focus of varying mixtures of verbal and physical abuse involving councillors, protestors and/or supporters in the public galleries and demonstrations inside and outside the chamber. At Waltham Forest the Labour leader of the council received death threats and was the target of a fire-bomb attack after a decision to increase domestic rates by over 60 per cent. In the wake of these events the *London Daily News* asked whether the blame lay with 'the rhetoric of Labour's New Left and the Conservatives' New Right'.

Whether or not rhetoric was to blame the focusing of intense ideological passions on local government does reflect in part the emergence of radical critiques of its traditional assumptions and practices on both the Conservative New Right and the Labour New Left. Both critiques have shared a considerable hostility towards the power and influence of professional council officers and the structures within which they work: their remedies however differ sharply. The left have stressed the need for greater democratization and decentralization and for a commitment to explicitly egalitarian policies: the right have stressed efficiency and market discipline. The left have looked for support to radical community and minority groups and to the local authority trade unions: the right have looked to the business community and to the Conservative government. In the latter at least the right have found a willing ally.

Given its general commitment to reducing the size of the public sector it is no surprise that the government should have introduced legislation designed to control spending by local government and to facilitate the privatization of its services. In doing so however it incurred the opposition not only of Labour, left and right, but of the Alliance parties and many Conservative wets, particularly those in local government. As a result the political climate of central-local relations became increasingly frosty and the character of those relations changed from the 'reasonably consensual' bargaining of the post-war period to one of 'direction' and 'centralization' after 1979 (Rhodes, 1986, pp. 126–132). The vigour, indeed sharpness, of the debate between central and local government did not merely reflect the clash of particular interests. It also reflected the fact that the role, indeed some might say the very desirability, of traditional local government was being subject to a fundamental scrutiny by politicians in central government. In this sense it is true to say that while local politicians and officers were having to reappraise their hitherto established practices in the light of multi-party politics, hung councils, electoral volatility and ideological polarization the status of local government itself as a political institution was also undergoing a major and searching reappraisal in this fifth and current stage of politicization.

The new landscape of local politics

From the way in which we have presented our five conjectural stages of party politicization it will be clear that we do not conceive of it as a unidimensional process. Quite the contrary. It has, for a start, both quantitative and qualitative aspects to it.

The quantitative aspects – the gradual growth in the numbers of party-dominated authorities and the corresponding decline in the numbers of Independent councillors – are probably the most obvious and certainly the more easily recorded, as we shall see in the remainder of this chapter. But, for observers of contemporary local politics especially, it is equally important to recognize some of the qualitative aspects of the politicization process – those that we have sought to describe through concepts like 'formalization', 'polarization', and 'intensification'. Moreover, with the great majority of councils today made up very largely of party politicians representing only a small number of nationally-based parties, there is a temptation to exaggerate their uniformity.

There would, for instance, be an understandable temptation to assume, because Birmingham, Manchester, Sheffield and Wakefield City Councils are all metropolitan district authorities, with the same functions and responsibilities, and are all, at the time of writing, comfortably Labour-controlled, that their modes and styles of political operation would therefore be essentially similar. The same might be assumed of the Conservative-controlled London Boroughs of Bromley, Harrow, Merton and Wandsworth. Alternatively, there might be a temptation to assume that the style of politics in, say, Westminster or Lambeth today represents some kind of predictor of what is likely to happen in, respectively, other Conservative or Labour authorities tomorrow.

Such temptations and assumptions should, in our view, be resisted, for they are at least as likely to mislead as to enlighten. Closer observation of such authorities is likely to reveal that, below the surface similarities of their party arithmetic, there are significant differences in their operational styles. Different issues and policies will be pursued, with differing degrees of intensity, through different forms of decision-making machinery, with, hardly surprisingly, widely varying outcomes. Indeed, when one considers the diverse political histories and traditions of local authorities, their varying responsbilities, sizes and topographies, the differing demographic and socio-economic profiles of their populations and their elected memberships, the greater surprise would be to find that there *was* extensive uniformity.

There is, therefore, a balance to be struck. In purely

quantitative terms it may be true, as at least one acute observer of local politics has argued, that the process of party politicization, especially in the post-reorganization period, has contributed to 'a greater homogeneity between different authorities, reducing the diversity of local political systems' (Bristow, 1978, p. 17). But if the homogeneity is greater, it is certainly not complete; if the diversity has been reduced, it has been very far from eliminated. The landscape of local politics may appear somewhat flatter than in the past, but, like the lunar landscape, the more closely one examines it, the more uneven, unpredictable and interesting it becomes.

That is exactly what we propose to do in this final section of the chapter: to examine, with the help of a few figures, the present-day 'landscape of local politics', and to see how it has evolved over the past thirty years or so. In order to maximize comparability across that time period, we have relied on a single, consistent source: the figures drawn from the questionnaire sent out annually by the *Municipal Yearbook* to all local authorities in the country, asking for details of their political composition. Reliance on this single source, comprehensive though it is, does mean that we are left with some missing data, especially in the pre-reorganization period. There is good reason to believe, though – both from a study of the list of non-responding authorities and from the replies of some who asked specifically not to be put into any category – that the great majority of the missing councils would, for our purposes, be classifiable as 'non-partisan'. For this reason, therefore, we suggest that the figures in the final two columns of Tables 1 and 2 are likely to be the more nearly accurate.

The pre-reorganization landscape

The first of these *Municipal Yearbook* surveys was carried out in 1955, more or less in the middle of what we have termed the 'nationalization' stage of party politicization. There were at this time over 1500 local councils in England and Wales alone, and even on what might be felt to be a minimalist definition of 'partisanship' – over 50 per cent of seats held by self-proclaimed members of political parties – probably no more than about 40 per cent of them could be described as operating on party lines (see Table 1). The figure of Scotland was much lower still, at little more than 20 per cent. Probably more significant than these overall figures, though, was the urban-rural divide. In London, apart of course from the City of London Corporation, there was complete two-party domination: with the sole exception of an Independent councillor in Stepney, every single seat was held by a Labour or Conservative member. Outside London the picture was similar without being quite so extreme. The cities and all the towns of any size were entirely party political – as, indeed, many of them had been since their first municipal elections in the 1830s and 1840s. But several of the smaller non-county boroughs and many of the urban district councils had quite sizeable clutches of at least self-styled Independents, even if in practice, and in national politics, some of them may have been supporters or even members of mainstream political parties.

In the rural areas of the country, however, the picture was very different. Only about one-third of even the top-tier county councils – and these mainly the largest and most urbanized ones – could be classified as 'partisan'. Outside London and Middlesex, there was not a single county council without some representation of Independents. And among the rural district authorities, while there were examples of party dominated councils – such as Conservative Bromsgrove and Bagshot and Labour's Chesterfield and Chester-le-Street – they were, particularly outside Wales, few and far between.

Given this strong association between urbanization and formal party politicization, it is probably not surprising to find, in 1955, Labour controlling over half as many councils again as the Conservatives. In this pre-organization period the Conservatives required a succession of 'good years' – as in the late 1960s, towards the end of six years of Labour national government – if they were to reverse this situation. But if the proportion of Conservative-controlled councils, at least outside London, happened to have risen quite strikingly by the time of reorganization, the overall proportion of partisan authorities had not. There had been only a fairly gradual increase over the sixteen-year period, to around 50

	Partisan councils									
	Conserv.[a]		*Labour*		*Liberal*		*Others*[b]		*Hung*[c]	
	1955	*1971*	*1955*	*1971*	*1955*	*1971*	*1955*	*1971*	*1955*	*1971*
England and Wales										
London[f]	9	10	19	21	–	–	–	–	–	2
County councils	7	12	6	2	–	–	–	–	7	6
Municipal corporations[g]	86	138	109	58	1	–	2	2	45	56
Urban district councils	83	115	143	143	1	–	–	1	46	81
Rural district councils	15	12	27	22	–	–	–	–	3	11
Total (England and Wales)	200	287	304	246	2	–	2	3	101	156
Scotland										
County councils	–	–	2	4	–	–	–	–	–	–
Burghs	2	5	29	37	–	–	7	3	4	12
Total (Great Britain)	202	292	335	287	2	–	9	6	105	168

Source: The Municipal Yearbook (1956 and 1972)

Notes:
[a] 'Conservative' here includes Conservative-supported Independents.
[b] 'Others' includes Ratepayers' Associations and other formal groupings of non-socialist members – e.g. Progressives (Bath, Coatbridge), Moderates (Airdrie, Dumbarton), Citizen Party (Bristol). Also, in Table 2, Scottish and Welsh Nationalists.
[c] For the purposes of these tables, the terms 'partisan' and 'hung' are purely arithmetical.
'Partisan' thus refers to a situation in which over 50 per cent of the seats on the council are held by members of political parties or groups.
'Hung' refers to a situation in which no single party or formal grouping of members on a 'partisan' council holds over 50 per cent of the seats. Neither term should be taken as giving any indication of the *de facto* control or operation of a council.
[d] 'Independent' here refers to councils on which over 50 per cent of the seats are held by members describing themselves variously as 'Independents', 'non-political' or 'non-party'. No attempt has been made to exclude from this category self-styled 'Independents' who might in practice be, for instance, Conservative supporters.

Table 1   *Party politics in local government: 1) Pre-reorganization*

		Non-partisan councils				Total No. of councils			% Partisan councils		
Total Partisan[e]		*Independent*[d]		*Non-respondents*				*As % of responding councils*[e]		*As % of all councils*[e]	
1955	*1971*	*1955*	*1971*	*1955*	*1971*	*1955*	*1971*	*1955*	*1971*	*1955*	*1971*
								(%)		(%)	
28	33	1	1	–	–	29	34	97	97	97	97
20	20	31	25	11	13	62	58	39	44	32	34
243	254	118	71	41	18	402	343	67	78	60	74
273	340	228	157	61	25	562	522	54	68	49	65
45	45	351	326	78	98	474	469	11	12	9	10
609	692	729	580	191	154	1529	1426	46	54	40	48
2	4	21	19	10	10	33	33	9	17	6	12
42	57	122	112	33	28	197	197	26	35	21	29
653	753	872	711	234	182	1759	1656	43	51	37	45

[e] It is reasonable to assume, not least from some of the actual replies received by *The Municipal Yearbook,* that the great majority of the non-respondents were in fact 'Independent' or 'Non-Partisan' councils. The figures in the final two columns – giving the lower of the figures for 'partisan councils' – seems likely, therefore, to be the more nearly accurate.

[f] 'London' refers in 1955 to the metropolitan boroughs, and in 1971 to the London boroughs and the Greater London Council (GLC). Both sets of figures include the non-partisan Corporation of the City of London. In Table 2 the 1986 figure excludes the abolished GLC, but includes the directly elected ILEA.

[g] 'Municipal Corporations' were also known as 'County Boroughs' and 'Non-County Boroughs', of which there were 83 and 260 respectively in 1971.

[g] In Table 2 'County Councils' includes the six metropolitan county councils in 1974, but not in 1986, by which time they had been abolished.

per cent, mostly from among the more urbanized of the smaller authorities.

The post-reorganization landscape

It took, therefore, the structural reorganizations of the early 1970s – the boundary changes and the amalgamations of the smallest authorities with or into larger and more partisan ones – finally to extinguish much of the old-style, ostensibly non-partisan politics of the rural areas. The rapidity of this change, when it did come, can be seen from the 1974 figures in Table 2. Almost literally overnight – over the night of the first elections of the newly-created authorities – the proportion of 'partisan' authorities on our definition rose from around half to well over three-quarters. The figures for the shire county councils changed more dramatically still, from little over one-third to nearly 90 per cent, leaving in England just three counties – Cornwall, Shropshire and the Isle of Wight – where Independents remained the largest political grouping. At district level the pattern was essentially the same, although it should be noted that in the rural areas of Scotland in particular 'non-partisan' politics remained – and continues to remain – more of a force than it does in England and Wales.

There were at least two related influences at work in these first post-reorganization elections which, between them, so accelerated the process of party politicization. First, there was the reorganization itself which, as noted above, often meant the merging of one or more previously non-partisan councils with others on which there was a tradition of party activity. Then there were the activities of the major political parties. The Labour party continued its efforts to increase its representation in rural areas – to give as many potential party supporters as possible the opportunity to vote for a Labour candidate, even in the most unpromising electoral circumstances. At the same time, local Conservative parties, with the encouragement of Central Office, put their energies into persuading like-minded Independents to stand as party candidates, or else face an official Conservative opponent.

This latter campaign in particular continued throughout

the 1970s into the 1980s, contributing both to the further erosion of Independent representation and to the related growth in the number of Conservative-controlled councils. Our figures for 1974 in Table 2 – showing majority Labour administrations in over 40 per cent of partisan councils, compared to the Conservatives' 25 per cent – seemed rather to call into question the allegations that were made about the 1972 reorganization being a political gerrymander, designed to suit the Conservative party more than the public (Goldsmith and Newton, 1984; Sharpe, 1978). By 1986–7, on the other hand, with almost all the newly-partisan authorities, at least in England and Wales, apparently in Conservative hands, such ideas make rather more sense.

That second set of figures in Table 2 and those in Table 3 bring us up to date. They present a slightly revised picture of the local political environment that is described in the Widdicombe research volumes and which is worth examining here in a little detail.

In the years since reorganization the number of 'non-partisan' councils has continued gradually to fall. They now constitute just 15 per cent of the total in Great Britain, and only 12 per cent in England and Wales. Among English county councils the process of formal party politicization was completed at the 1985 elections. Only just over eighty Independent councillors were returned, out of a total of over 3000, and even on the traditionially staunchly non-partisan Cornwall County Council they were displaced by the Liberals as the largest single grouping. Out of all 515 councils in the country, those on which there are still no acknowledged party representatives at all can now be counted on the fingers (plus one thumb) of two hands: Eden DC and the City of London Corporation in England, Radnor DC and South Pembrokeshire DC in Wales, Orkney, Western Isles, Stewartry DC (Dumfries and Galloway), Sutherland DC and Tweeddale DC in Scotland.

The one guaranteed feature of any set of May local election results nowadays is that, irrespective of which of the major parties may emerge as net winners, Independent candidates will invariably end up as net losers. The 1987 local results, details of which tended to get lost in the welter

Partisan councils

	Conserv.[a]		Labour		Liberal/ Alliance		Others[b]		Hung[c]	
	1974	1986	1974	1986	1974	1986	1974	1986	1974	1986
England and Wales										
London boroughs[f]	13	11	19	16	–	2	–	–	1	4
County councils[h]	15	10	17	19	–	1	–	–	15	25
Metropolitan districts[g]	5	1	16	27	–	–	–	–	5	8
Shire district councils	57	119	94	77	1	5	1	1	80	82
Total (England & Wales)	90	141	146	129	1	8	1	1	101	119
Scotland										
Regions and islands	1	–	4	4	–	–	–	–'	1	2
District councils	2	3	16	23	–	1	1	3	8	6
Total (Great Britain)	93	144	166	156	1	9	2	4	110	127

Source: The Municipal Yearbook (1975 and 1987)
Notes: See Table 1

Table 2   *Party politics in local government: 2) Post-reorganization*

of speculation about the possibly forthcoming general election, provide a typical illustration. As can be seen in Table 4, 1987 was an indisputably bad year for Labour, and the party lost its previous overall control of a dozen district councils – including Cambridge, Darlington, Kirklees, Nottingham, Walsall, and Wolverhampton. They did, however, have some little consolation in winning control of North Tyneside, Reading, and Stockton-on-Tees. Independent councillors and candidates, however, standing as individuals, without the financial support, organization or camaraderie of a political party, had no such compensation. By losing small

	Non-partisan councils				Total No. of councils		% Partisan councils			
Total Partisan^c		Independent^d		Non-respondents				As % of responding councils^e		As % of all councils^e	
1974	*1986*	*1974*	*1986*	*1974*	*1986*	*1974*	*1986*	*1974*	*1986*	*1974*	*1986*
								(%)		*(%)*	
33	33	1	1	–	–	34	34	97	97	97	97
47	45	6	2	–	–	53	47	89	95	89	95
36	36	–	–	–	–	36	36	100	100	100	100
233	284	81	49	19	–	333	333	74	85	70	85
349	398	88	52	19	–	456	450	80	88	77	88
6	6	6	6	–	–	12	12	50	50	50	50
27	36	19	17	7	–	53	53	59	68	51	68
382	440	113	75	26	–	521	515	77	85	73	85

numbers of seats, mainly to Conservatives and Liberals, they lost their overall majority position on eleven district councils, gained control of none, and lost a net total of some 300 seats.

The survival of the Independents

But if that aspect of party politicization seems like an inexorable and irreversible process, it is important also to keep it in perspective. As our figures show, even after those 1987 results, there still remain over 2000 Independent or non-party councillors in this country and over 10 per cent of

	Conservative	Labour	Liberal/SDP Alliance (Alliance)	(Liberal)	(SDP)
England					
London boroughs	685 (36%)	956 (50%)	(205)	(41)	(3)
(ILEA)	(11)	(45)			
(Corporation of City of London)	–	–			
County councils	1,318 (44%)	959 (32%)	(436)	(170)	(9)
Metropolitan district councils	545 (22%)	1,649 (66%)	(103)	(129)	(5)
Shire district councils	6,006 (45%)	3,459 (26%)	(944)	(716)	(86)
Wales					
County councils	52 (9%)	295 (53%)	(25)	(12)	(2)
District councils	179 (12%)	622 (41%)	(45)	(26)	(8)
Total (England and Wales)	8,785 (38%)	7,940 (35%)	(1,758)	(1,094)	(113)
Scotland					
Regional and islands councils	65 (12%)	227 (43%)	(37)	(3)	–
District councils	179 (16%)	537 (47%)	(69)	(17)	–
Total (Scotland)	244 (15%)	764 (46%)	(106)	(20)	–
Total (Great Britain)	9,029 (37%)	8,704 (35%)	(1,864) (8%)	(1,114) (5%)	(113) (0)

Source: The Municipal Yearbook (1987)

Notes: 0 = less than 0.5 per cent

Table 3   *Party political composition of local councils (1986)*

Total Alliance	*Nationalists*	*Others*	*Independent/ Non-party*	*Vacant*	*Total seats*
249 (13%)	–	20 (1%)	3 (0)	1 (0)	1,914
(2)	–	–	–		(58)
–	–		(158)		(158)
615 (20%)	–	19 (1%)	81 (3%)	13 (0)	3,005
237 (10%)	–	22 (1%)	20 (1%)	8 (0)	2,481
1,746 (13%)	–	669 (5%)	1,506 (11%)	60 (0)	13,446
39 (7%)	23 (4%)	7 (1%)	143 (26%)	1 (0)	560
79 (5%)	72 (5%)	153 (10%)	390 (26%)	8 (1%)	1,503
2,965 (13%)	95 (0)	890 (4%)	2,143 (9%)	91 (0)	22,909
40 (8%)	37 (7%)	32 (6%)	123 (23%)	–	524
86 (7%)	65 (6%)	55 (5%)	230 (20%)	2 (0)	1,154
126 (8%)	102 (6%)	87 (5%)	353 (21%)	2 (0)	1,678
3,091 (13%)	197 (1%)	977 (4%)	2,496 (10%)	93 (0)	24,587

councils on which they continue to form a majority. Put another way, for every one Alliance-controlled council there are roughly seven that are dominated by Independents. And there are, of course, plenty of others where, though no longer in a numerical majority, they continue to have both a substantial presence and a significant influence.

Moreover, in addition to these Independents and listed separately in Table 3, there are the nearly one thousand 'others'. As the label suggests, this is an extremely heterogeneous group. They range, to use the loose categorization suggested by David Denver (Vallely, 1987), from disenchanted former party members who have fallen out with their colleagues and describe themselves as, say, 'Independent Labour' or 'Independent Conservative' to 'individuals who are motivated almost entirely by a single parochial issue'. The single largest group, though, comprise what could be termed 'purely local party' councillors, and in particular Ratepayers' and Residents' Association members. The heyday of the national ratepayer movement may be long past (Young, 1975 and 1986), but there are still well over 200 local Ratepayer and Residents' Association councillors, most notably in the affluent Surrey suburbs of Epsom and Ewell and Elmbridge, where they form the largest and second largest groups respectively.

Small scatterings of these purely local party councillors are to be found in all types of area, urban, suburban and rural: from Havering and Harrow in Greater London, through the South Shields-based Progressives on North Tyneside, to the affiliated members of the Shetland Movement – possibly the one 'party' in this country to produce a manifesto but *not* to contest elections. By contrast, Independent-dominated authorities tend nowadays to be most common in the remoter rural parts of the country – areas in which a political party would find it most difficult to set up and maintain an efficient organization, and where culturally there is likely to be the greatest suspicion of any outside or national intrusion into local politics (Grant, 1977). Some of these areas, particularly those in the rural counties of southern England and the Midlands have for many years returned Conservative MPs to Parliament, often with quite substantial majori-

	Councils			Councillors		
	Gains	*Losses*	*Net*	*Gains*	*Losses*	*Net*
Conservatives	18	16	+ 2	586	508	+ 78
Labour	3	12	− 9	179	399	−220
Alliance	5	2	+ 3	648	210	+438
Independents + others	–	11	−11	146	442	−296
No overall control	37	22	+15	n/a	n/a	n/a

Note: These results are based on 339 comparable councils.

Sources: The Times, 9 May 1987; Game, 1987c.

Table 4 *Changes of control and transfers of seats: district council elections, May 1987*

ties. But others – those, for instance, within what might loosely be labelled the 'Celtic fringe' – are far from being instinctively Conservative, and the same is true of their Independent local councillors, as can be seen in Table 5.

This table summarizes the responses to two questions asked in the 1985 SCPR survey of councillors carried out for the Widdicombe Committee. All councillors were asked which political party, if any, they represented last time they stood for election. The responses produced a profile of party membership that matches quite closely, though not precisely, our own figures in Table 3. Labour and Alliance members would appear to be slightly under-represented in the SCPR sample, and Conservatives and Independents slightly over-represented. The 15 per cent self-styled Independents were then also asked if they were members of any political party. Over one-third were, and while the Conservative party accounted for by far the largest group, it is worth noting that over 10 per cent of these 'Independents' were members of other political parties. It would appear, then, that Stanyer's observations of more than a decade ago are still as relevant today:

in most non-partisan areas the Conservative Party is the dominant one, but . . . in the case of north and west Devon and central and

north Cornwall many of the Independents are Liberals rather than
Conservatives, whilst in parts of Wales, where the Conservative
Party is very weak, Independents are likely to be Labour, Liberal or
Nationalist in national political orientation.   (Stanyer, 1976, p. 85)

	Party stood for last time elected %	Independents: membership of political party %
Conservative	40	26
Labour	33	2
Liberal	9	5
SDP	1	0
SNP	0	2
Plaid Cymru	0	1
Independent	15	62
Other	1	0
Base	1,491	241

Source: Widdicombe Committee, Research Vol. II, 1986, p. 38.

Note: 0 = less than 0.5 per cent

Table 5   *Political party membership of Independents (1985)*

	%
Low partisanship	2
Formal coalitions	8
Minority administrations	51
'Knife-edge' control	6
No administration	7
Base	105

Source: Leach and Stewart, 1987, p. 22.

Table 6   *Categories of hung authorities (July 1986)*

The spread of hung authorities

As the figures in Tables 2 and 3 show, under 60 per cent of this country's councils are controlled by majority Conservative or Labour administrations, and well under three-quarters of all councillors are members of these two major parties. Two-party dominance, in other words, is considerably more diluted in contemporary local politics than it is at the parliamentary level. One reason for this lies in the survival of the relatively large numbers of Independents and local party members. But an important and more recent development has been the emergence in the 1980s of the Liberal/SDP Alliance as a more significant 'third force' in local politics, and the associated increase in the number of 'hung' councils – those on which no single party holds an overall majority of seats. Both of these trends can be seen illustrated in Table 4.

There is an important distinction, however, to be drawn here between *effectively* and merely nominally hung authorities, since at first sight the figures in Tables 1 and 2 might suggest that, at least arithmetically, plenty of such councils existed even in the pre-reorganization era. The key difference in recent years has been the emergence of more hung authorities against a background of greatly extended and intensified party politicization.

Perhaps the best way of illustrating this change is by reference to the fivefold categorization of hung authorities devised by Leach and Stewart:

1 Low partisanship

These are authorities on which no one party has a majority of seats, but where the ethos of the council is such that party politics are fairly embryonic or low-key. Party groups are likely to be of limited significance, chairs and certainly vice-chairs may be shared amongst some or all the different political groupings, possibly on a territorial or seniority basis. The outcome is that the council tends to behave as a hung authority in much the same way as it would if one party did have a majority. Many, and perhaps even most, of the pre-reorganization hung authorities would have come into this category, and current (1987) examples would include Cornwall, Dyfed and Clwyd County Councils and South Somerset and South Lakeside DCs.

2   *The formal coalition*

Two or more parties agree to form a joint administration, on the basis of some form of working agreement. To the surprise of some overseas observers, formal coalitions are still comparatively rare in this country. Where they are formed, they often involve Conservative and Independents, although in the Grampians Region of Scotland it is the three smallest parties (Alliance, Independents and SNP) who form a minority coalition with the tacit support of the Labour group.

3   *The minority administration*

This is the most prevalent form of hung authority. It involves one party group being 'allowed' to form an administration, with the implicit or explicit 'support' of another party. It is distinguisable from the formal coalition in that whatever form this support takes, it stops short of an actual sharing of chairs.

4   *'Knife-edge' control*

In this particular type of minority control, although no party has a majority of council seats, one party does have precisely half of them. This party can therefore form an administration, provided it can secure the election of one of its members as council chairman (or mayor), who can then use a casting vote to give the party a majority.

5   *No administration*

Finally, there are a few authorities in which it is either difficult or inappropriate to identify any ongoing administration at all. No one party holds the chairs, nor are they shared out on any agreed basis. Though normally only a temporary situation, examples have arisen since 1985 of committee chairs being elected in Bedfordshire County Council on an *ad hoc* basis, meeting by meeting, and in Oxfordshire County Council on an agreed revolving pattern.   (Leach and Stewart, 1987, pp. 3ff.)

On the basis of a survey conducted in July 1986, supplemented by data from other sources, Leach and Stewart estimated the proportion of currently hung authorities which fell into each of their five categories, showing that just over a half operated with minority administrations (Table 6). These hung authorities, then, like the non-partisan councils described previously, differ both among themselves and from those that are controlled by a majority party administration. But these majority party administrations differ too, one from

another. There is no single uniform pattern of organization
and operation, as can be seen from Table 7.

	Conservative		Labour	
	Yes %	No %	Yes %	No %
Majority party takes all chairmanships of committees	95	5	99	1
Majority party takes all chairmanships of sub-committees	90	10	96	4
Majority party has 'always voted as a party' at council meetings over the past year	23	77	59	41
Absence of any 'cross-voting' by party members at council meetings over the past year	9	91	49	51
Majority party has 'always voted as a party' at committee meetings over the past year	5	95	15	85
Absence of any 'cross-voting' by party members at committee meetings over the past year	3	97	11	89
Base	175		139	

Source: Widdicombe Committee, Research Vol. I, 1986, Tables A.13, 15,
20, 21, 23 and 24 (pp. 259 70).

Table 7 *Variations in majority party control and voting discipline
(1985)*
(Conservative and Labour majority administrations only)

This table serves as a brief introduction to some of the
topics to which we shall be returning in later chapters.
Compiled from the postal questionnaire survey on the
political organization of local authorities for the Widdicombe
Committee, it shows some of the ways in which party control
and discipline may vary, even among majority administrations. In these days of intensified party politicization there

are still a few councils, for instance, on which the majority party does *not* automatically take for itself all positions of responsibility on council committees and sub-committees. Nor is voting solidarity anything like as universal a practice in local government as is sometimes supposed. Hardly surprisingly, most party groups do 'vote as a party' on most council and committee decisions. Equally unsurprisingly, if party members feel they are unable to support their own party on a particular issue, they will be more inclined to abstain than to 'cross-vote'. But as our figures show, there are plenty of at least occasional examples – even among the generally more highly disciplined Labour groups – of abstentions at full council meetings and cross-voting at committee.

There is, above all, variation – between majority administrations of the different parties, across types of authority, and even within the same authority as its party arithmetic changes. To return to our opening theme: the process of party politicization has undoubtedly advanced apace over the past fifteen years in particular. If, as a result, our local councils may seem on the surface, statistically and formally, more homogeneous, beneath that surface there is still a wealth of diversity to be discovered.

2
Councillors

Forty years ago the historian Eugene Hasluck produced the second edition of his introductory study of *Local Government in England*. His overall judgement of what he saw stopped well short of the eulogistic, but it was not uncharitable:

... it may be said, taking a broad view over the whole of local services, that the present system gives generally satisfactory results (Hasluck, 1948, p. 323)

There was, however, one part of the system with which, not to put too fine a point on it, he was less than impressed:

It is the elected element that makes the poorest show in a survey of our system of Local Government .... The elected Council in a great number of instances provides a veritable storehouse of 'awful examples' of inefficiency and incompetence – resembling in some extreme instances what the Americans call a 'dime museum' – a collection of mental freaks. ... even the comparative dignity and formality of a full-dress Council meeting often leave gaps through which stupidity and ignorance force their obtrusive way. Editors of local newspapers are often hard put to it to reduce the illiterate babblings of local worthies to something approaching intelligible English ... far too many Councils consist for the most part of administrators to whom the application of the term 'mediocrity' would be unctuous flattery.   (Hasluck, 1948, pp. 334, 337)

Just supposing, forty years on, Hasluck had found himself appointed to the Widdicombe Committee: would his judgement have changed at all? Or would he still have cause to emphasize the 'mediocrity, stupidity and ignorance' of councillors and liken some of them to 'a collection of mental freaks'? Obviously, we cannot know, but there is at least one reason to suppose his views might have softened somewhat. It is to be found in a qualification he made towards the end of the paragraph quoted above:

As always, there are conspicuous exceptions, particularly in those Councils where closely contested party strife lends a stimulus to each side to put its most capable and effective men into positions of prominence.   (Hasluck, 1948, p. 337)

Setting aside the sexism for a moment, the party politicization of local government represented for Hasluck an almost unqualifiedly positive development, overcoming many of what he saw as 'the weak points in the Independent systems' (p. 36). The presence of active political parties tended greatly to increase the 'fund of candidates . . . of the best type that the party organisation can manage to find'. It thereby greatly reduced the numbers of uncontested elections and reduced also 'the utter ignorance of the mass of the voters as to the problems to be dealt with on the local Council'. And finally, 'when the Council is elected and begins its work . . . it is better to have controversies and divisions based on some definite political principle represented by recognised national parties than on the petty intrigues and jealousies of the cliques which grow up so readily on Councils elected on the Independent system' (pp. 36–37).

In this chapter we examine, much more systematically and statistically than Hasluck was able to, some of the characteristics, activities and attitudes of today's generation of local councillors. To do so, we rely heavily on three of the surveys commissioned by the Widdicombe Committee:

1   The questionnaire survey of all local authorities in Great Britain concerning their political organization, backed up by the interview survey in over 100 authorities reported in Research Volume I.
2   The questionnaire survey of a 10 per cent sample of councillors – carried out by Jude England of SCPR and reported in Research Volume II.

3 The shorter questionnaire survey of all local authority treasurers on the payment of financial allowances and expenses to their members – carried out by Phillip Ramsdale and Stuart Capon of IPF and also reported in Research Volume II.

Contested elections

There are two basic, but none the less crucially important, attributes possessed by the great majority of councillors today that would have struck Hasluck and his contemporaries particularly forcefully. The first is that, as we saw in the previous chapter, almost 90 per cent of them were elected as representatives of nationally-based political parties.

Second, and directly and causally related to this first attribute, almost all of them actually *were* elected. They were not, in other words, returned unopposed, but had to fight electoral contests against at least one or two other candidates, usually themselves standing for other political parties. This may not sound very remarkable, but it is strikingly different from the situation of even a relatively few years ago.

Hasluck mentions in his book some of the county council elections of 1934. in Kent, for example, out of seventy-five seats, sixty were filled by unopposed returns; in Cornwall there were three contests in sixty-six constituencies; and Cumberland with forty constituencies had no contests at all – thirty-eight unopposed returns and two constituencies left unrepresented through a total absence of candidates (p. 47). Between the Second World War and the reorganization of local government in the early 1970s these figures for uncontested elections increased rather than decreased, as was recorded by Harrison and Norton in their research for the Maud Committee in the 1960s:

Of 40,859 seats for councillors above parish level which fell vacant in the three-year cycle 1962 to 1964, members were returned for 16,743 (41%) without having to contest elections.

In the county boroughs only 10% of seats were uncontested; in the non-county boroughs and urban districts 26%; in the counties 55% and in the rural districts 70%. . . . There were four county boroughs

(5% of the total) where half or more of the councillors were returned unopposed, while this happened in 34 counties (62%) . . . in 137 second-tier authorities *all* candidates were returned unopposed. . . . Thus, for example, 49 members of the Hexham Rural District Council were returned unopposed and so were all 42 members of the Rothbury Rural District Council. . . . A number of the county councillors interviewed had fought contests only at their first one or two elections and had subsequently been returned unopposed; in fact in some electoral areas it seems that once a candidate has won a seat, he is likely to retain it undisturbed for as long as he wishes. . . . It seems likely that about one in three of· county councillors and about one in two of rural district councillors have never had to fight an election. (Maud Committee, vol. 5, 1967, pp. 48–9)

Immediately upon reorganization, as we saw in the opening chapter, the proportion of 'partisan' authorities increased significantly. That increase was accompanied, equally immediately, by an even more marked rise in the proportion of contested seats at the first set of post-reorganization elections. The 55 per cent of unopposed county council returns noted by Harrison and Norton, for instance, fell in England by about three-quarters, a fall which has continued through to the present day, as can be seen in Table 8.

In the 1985 county council elections, out of 3005 divisions, there were 2944 contests involving 8745 candidates. For what must almost certainly have been the first time, there were no uncontested seats at all in over 60 per cent of the counties, and only in Cornwall, the one remaining England county council with a sizeable representation of Independents, did the number exceed 15 per cent. The proportion of the English electorate effectively disenfranchised at these elections had therefore been reduced to just 1.3 per cent – the kind of figure approached before reorganization only in London and the large county boroughs.

In the metropolitan districts and boroughs too unopposed returns have become rare occurrences indeed: just six in 1983 and thirteen in 1987 out of nearly 830 wards. It is in fact only in the remoter and more rural parts of the country, precisely those areas in which the national party organiza-

	County councils %	County boroughs %	Non-county boroughs/ UDCs %	RDCs %
1945/6	40.6	7.8	7.1	60.5
1955	56.3	18.1	29.9	73.4
1964	49.9	8.7	17.6	69.6
1970	49.7	5.1	21.1	70.1

REORGANIZATION

	County councils %	Metropolitan districts %	Shire districts %
1973	12.7	2.6	12.3
1976/7	11.9	1.5	16.3
1985/7	2.0	1.6	n/a

Sources: Bristow, 1978, p. 17; Karran and Bochel, 1986, p.iv; Byrne, 1986, pp. 102–3; Rallings and Thrasher, 1987.

Table 8 *Unopposed returns in local elections*
(English local authorities only, excluding London).

tions are weakest, that an incumbent councillor can expect nowadays to survive unchallenged for any length of time. In Wales, for instance, the comparable figures for those 1985 county council elections make distinctly less impressive reading: nearly 28 per cent of seats were uncontested, leaving some 20 per cent of the Welsh electorate effectively disenfranchised. The Scottish figures, to judge from the 1982 regional elections, fall in between those for England and Wales: 14 per cent of seats had unopposed returns, affecting 7 per cent of the potential electorate (Karran and Bochel, 1986).

Despite the invaluable work on local election results now carried out at Plymouth Polytechnic and the University of Dundee, it is still not as easy to get complete and up-to-date statistics for the English shire districts, not least because since

1980 the government's Office of Population, Censuses and Surveys (OPCS) has discontinued its previous useful practice of gathering and publishing such data. What evidence there is, though, suggests clearly that in these authorities as well there has been a substantial decline in the numbers of unopposed returns since the impetus to party politicization provided by reorganization. As a result, more and more voters are at least being offered the basic democratic opportunity to choose their local representatives from among competing candidates standing on competing policy platforms. Later on, in Chapter 7 we shall be looking in more detail at the way in which they choose to avail themselves of this opportunity: we shall examine, for instance, the extent to which they actually turn out to vote at local elections and the influence of local, as opposed to national, considerations in determining the direction of those votes. But for the moment we turn our attention to the end-product of the electoral process: the successful candidates, the councillors themselves. Who are they? What kinds of backgrounds do they come from? How typical are they of the voters who elect them?

Personal characteristics of councillors

It is interesting to compare the profile of present-day councillors that emerged from the Widdicombe Committee's SCPR survey with the findings from the Maud Committee's Government Social Survey back in 1964, which were summarized as follows:

It is clear . . . that members do not reflect the community in terms of age, sex, occupation or education. Members tend to be drawn from the older sections of the population . . . over half the men are over 55 . . . only about 12% of members are women . . . a fifth of all members are retired people . . . employers and managers, and farmers and professional workers, occupy a larger proportion of seats in the councils than their proportion in the general adult male population . . . the converse is true of skilled and unskilled manual workers . . . members of local authorities are, on the average, better qualified than electors, whether in terms of GCE passes, teachers' certificates, professional qualifications or degrees. (Maud Committee, Vol. 1, 1967, p. 135)

In brief, then, they were overwhelmingly male, middle-aged, middle-class – and, of course, white. It was a picture that had changed relatively little more than ten years later, by the time of the 1976 survey carried out for the Robinson Committee on the Remuneration of Councillors. But what happened in the years after Robinson? There was not, until Widdicombe, any comprehensive evidence, but there seemed good reason to suppose that councils were increasingly being run by groups of relatively younger members, from different kinds of social and occupational backgrounds from their predecessors, and among whom both women and blacks were considerably more strongly represented than previously.

Certainly, the local politicians most prominently in the news hardly seemed to fit Ken Livingstone's graphic depiction of local government in the 1960s as dominated by 'old white men. . . talking about rubbish collection' (Boddy and Fudge, 1984, p. 263). There was Livingstone himself, Leader of the Greater London Council (GLC) at 35; Valerie Wise, Chair of its controversial Women's Committee at 26; David Blunkett, Leader of Sheffield City Council; Derek Hatton, Deputy Leader of Liverpool, and Dominic Brady, Chair of that city's Education Committee at 24; Bernie Grant, Leader of Haringey, and Merle Amory, youngest-ever black woman councillor at 23 and later Leader of Brent. Were these members of what Livingstone terms 'the post-1968 generation in politics' typical of some major transformation that was taking place among the elected personnel in local government across the country? Or was part of their newsworthiness their very atypicality; were they more the high-profile exceptions that proved the previous rules?

Probably the fairest answer, confusing though it initially appears, is: Yes, they were both typical and atypical. To reduce the confusion a little, we need to examine a few figures. Table 9 compares some of the personal characteristics of SCPR's sample of councillors with the results from the Maud and Robinson studies, and also with figures for the overall population. It would seem to support the 'atypical' line of argument. For, as the table indicates, while there have been changes over the twenty-year period, those changes have for the most part been distinctly gradual and limited. As Jude England notes at the start of her report:

When the personal characteristics are compared across the three studies, perhaps the most remarkable aspect is the stability of the population (of councillors), particularly since the Robinson study . . . elected members as a group are still highly unrepresentative of the overall population. (Widdicombe Committee, Research Vol. II, 1986, p. 19)

The proportion of women councillors, for instance, is certainly higher today than it used to be. But more of that increase seems to have taken place before 1976, rather than since, and the figure remains far below the 51 per cent of women in the population as a whole. It is also, by way of comparison, well under half the percentage of (appointed) women magistrates (42 per cent in 1982, according to Cooke, 1984); though, at the same time, it is three times the proportion of women MPs, which, following the 1987 General Election, reached 6 per cent for the first time.

As far as the age profile of councillors is concerned, the most remarkable feature must be its almost complete *lack* of aggregate change since 1964, let alone since 1976. There was in the 1985 sample a slightly higher proportion of councillors in the 'younger' age groups (i.e. under 44) and slightly fewer in the oldest groups. But, contrary to what must have been some people's impressions, there were actually rather *fewer* councillors under 35 and fractionally *more* over 75 than had been recorded in 1976. The majority of members remained aged 45 or over, with none in the SCPR sample under 24, and the oldest 85.

Today, as in 1964, councillors are much more likely than their constituents to be owner occupiers, and correspondingly less likely to be living in accommodation rented from the local authority. And there is a similar, and possibly increasing disparity to be seen in respect of educational attainment: councillors are more than four times as likely to have degree-level qualifications as the general population, and are much less likely to have no formal qualifications at

	England and Wales only 1964 %	Great Britain 1976 %	1985 %	Population (mid-1980s) %
Gender				
Male	88	83	81	49
Female	12	17	19	51
Age				
Up to 34	5	9	7	29
35–44	16	17	19	17
45–54	26	24	25	14
55–64	31	30	27	15
65–74	18	19	19	13
75 and over	4	2	3	12
Housing tenure				
Owner occupier	66	76	85	57
Rented from local authority	16	16	10	32
Rented privately/rent free	18	8	4	11
Education – highest qualifications				
Degree or equivalent	8	–	22	5
Higher qualification below degree level	15	–	9	8
GCE A-level or equivalent	3	–	8	6
GCE O-level or equivalent	14	–	30	17
CSE (other than Grade 1)	n/a	–	1	14
Other	10	–	7	n/a
No formal qualifications	49	–	23	48
Base (excludes those not answering, so varies slightly from question to question)	3,445– 3,970	3,848– 4,731	1,479– 1,552	

Sources: Maud Committee, Vol. 2, 1967, ch. I; Robinson Committee, Vol. II, 1977, Section I; Widdicombe Committee, Research Vol. II, 1986, ch. 2.

Table 9 Personal characteristics of councillors (1964–85)

all. Granted that the mere possession of paper qualifications does not in itself dispel the stupidity and ignorance that Eugene Hasluck found so prevalent among his generation of councillors, this tendency is surely one that would have met with his approval.

Finally, we come to the ethnic background of councillors. Like the 1981 Census, the SCPR survey did not include any race or ethnic group question, so we do not have the comprehensive information that we have for other personal characteristics. But, even *after* the post-Widdicombe London Borough elections of May 1986 which certainly increased their numbers, the proportion of black councillors (i.e. both Afro-Caribbean and Asian) in the country as a whole is unlikely to exceed 1 per cent – i.e. roughly 250 out of nearly 25,000. Not surprisingly, the largest concentrations of black councillors are in Inner London and in those Outer London boroughs and provincial cities with particularly high ethnic minority populations (for example Brent, Ealing, Birmingham, Bradford, Leicester). And perhaps equally unsurprisingly, the great majority of them sit as Labour members (Anwar, 1986). Of black, as of women, councillors, then, it could be said that their numbers are increasing gradually, but they remain at present well below the overall population figures (4.2 per cent in the 1981 Census) and somewhat below the proportion of black magistrates (King and May, 1985), yet substantially above that of black MPs, even after their historic 'breakthrough' in the 1987 general election.

The national picture presented by Table 9, therefore, is one of only fairly slow change in the population of our councillors and of a continuing major mismatch – in terms of personal characteristics – between them and their electorates. When some of those aggregate figures in Table 9, though, are reclassified by 'type of authority' as in Table 10, a rather different view emerges. Councillors *are* getting younger, but only significantly so in the London boroughs and other metropolitan areas. In the English shires they are getting older. There *are* more women being elected, but much less noticeably in Wales or Scotland, for instance, than in the major English authorities. There are also similar variations across types of authority in members' educational

Type of Authority	Gender	Age			Education	
	Female	*Under 44*	*45–59*	*60 or over*	*Degree or equivalent*	*None*
	%	*%*	*%*	*%*	*%*	*%*
England						
Metropolitan counties	13	36	36	28	39	17
Shire counties	21	22	32	44	30	26
London boroughs	22	50	30	19	39	12
Metropolitan districts	23	36	37	25	23	26
Shire districts	19	22	39	37	16	23
Wales						
County councils	5	8	37	54	16	37
District councils	14	17	41	42	21	33
Scotland						
Regions and Islands	13	20	41	38	26	23
Districts	24	32	42	26	18	12
Total	19	26	38	36	22	23

Base = 1,479 – 1,552

Source: Widdicombe Committee, Research Vol. II, 1986, Tables 2.2, 2.3, 2.4, 2.9 (pp. 20–5).

Table 10 *Personal characteristics of councillors, by type of authority, 1985*

qualifications. As Ken Young puts it:

... the lesson that one takes is not that councillors are getting younger or that councillors are staying the same, but that councillors are getting more different from one another, and that's an amplification of that diversity that characterises local government. (Young, 1986c, p. 30)

Occupational characteristics of councillors

There has been plenty of speculation too in recent years

about the changing occupational characteristics of councillors. David Walker, for example, argued that:

In the local government of urban Britain there is an interest group of elected members bound together with an occupational stake in public sector jobs. A growing proportion of councillors depend for their livelihood on municipal employment in one form or another: they work as social workers, teachers or, a growing category, as 'professional councillors' living off the subsistence and attendance allowances paid.   (Walker, 1983, p. 94)

Walker's concern about this 'public service class' of councillors, 'with a latent interest in public and especially in municipal expenditures' (p. 96), was fuelled by a small-scale but nationwide survey of councillors conducted by Market and Opinion Research International (MORI) for *The Sunday Times* in August 1982. This MORI survey showed that, out of a sample of 176 councillors on six councils in England, 39 per cent of the total, and 48 per cent of Labour members, were employed in the public sector, mostly as civil servants, teachers or council officers. An additional 14 per cent of the total, and 18 per cent of Labour members, worked in the voluntary sector, primarily as full-time trade-union officials or with housing associations, leaving just 20 per cent, and only 12 per cent of Labour members, in the private sector (Lipsey, 1982).

Figures such as these, coupled with regular expressions of ministerial concern about 'soft jobs', 'jobs for the boys', and 'the new breed of Labour councillor', led to considerable press speculation about the possibility of future government legislation, outlawing, or at least severely restricting, the rights of local authority employees to become councillors. It was recognized that any legislation would have to be extremely carefully drafted. But an additional problem, as one journalist acknowledged, was the lack of accurate information:

There are no exact figures about how many council workers serve as councillors on another authority, but the number runs into hundreds.   (Grigsby, 1985)

Whatever its more general value, then, the SCPR data on

		1976 %	1985 %
Activity status	Working – full-time	65 }72	54 }60
	– part-time	7	6
	Unemployed	2	4
	Retired	16	25
	Looking after a home/ family	7	8
	Other	3	2
	Base	4,717	1,540

		% of councillors currently employed	% of all councillors
Employment sector	Public sector	36	21
	Private sector	61	39
	Not stated	3	
	Base	943	

		% of councillors employed in the public sector	% of all councillors
Type of public sector employment	Local government	45	10
	Central government	19	4
	Other public sector	33	7
	Base	340	

Source: Widdicombe Committee, Research Vol. II, 1986, Tables 3.1, 3.6, 3.8 (pp. 28–33).

Table 11 *Occupational characteristics of councillors (1976–85)*

councillors' occupational backgrounds have enabled us to attach some proper figures to this phenomenon of 'cross membership' or 'twin-tracking' – an officer or employee of one authority serving as a councillor in another. It amounted, as can be seen in Table 11, to 10 per cent of the SCPR sample, or 16 per cent of all currently employed councillors.

The SCPR figures showed first that there has been a significant fall in the past ten years in the proportion of councillors in paid employment – from 72 per cent to 60 per cent. That fall has been matched by what seems like a surprisingly small increase in the numbers who are unemployed and a much more substantial increase in the self-styled 'retired'. Commenting on these figures, though, England considers it likely that in this latter group were a number of members under 65 who had in fact taken early retirement or had been made redundant, say, between 55 and 64 and, having poor prospects of obtaining further employment, chose to describe themselves as retired, rather than unemployed (Widdicombe Committee, Research Vol. II, 1986, p. 28).

As was previously found in the Maud and Robinson surveys, councillors are drawn from a much narrower range of socio-economic backgrounds than are represented in the population as a whole. Only one-fifth of currently employed councillors were in manual jobs, compared with nearly half of their constituents. Conversely, three times as many (41 per cent compared with 14 per cent) were in professional or managerial employment. Turning to employment *sectors*, though, we find a different picture. Of all councillors employed at the time of the SCPR survey 36 per cent worked in the public sector, which, as England notes, 'compares exactly with the general population – one of the very few dimensions on which councillors actually mirror their electors' (p. 32). Again, however, there were significant differences by type of authority, with David Walker's 'public service class' rising to 47 per cent among London councillors and 55 per cent among members of the since abolished metropolitan county councils.

Of those in public sector employment, 45 per cent were

found to work in local government, which, as we saw above, amounts to one in ten of all councillors. Well over half of this group (58 per cent) were either teachers or lecturers at further education colleges; 14 per cent were local government administrators; 16 per cent in professional jobs (for example housing officers, planners, accountants, social workers), and the remaining 12 per cent in manual or other types of employment. There are in total some three million local authority employees (full-time and part-time), 14 per cent of the workforce, including roughly 500,000 teachers. Contrary to some people's impressions, therefore, these groups do not turn out to be greatly over-represented amongst councillors. If ever there were to be a complete disqualification of all these categories of local authority employees from sitting as elected members, some 2500 currently serving councillors would be forced either to resign their seats or change their jobs. In addition, as the Widdicombe Report argued, three million people would have their rights as individual citizens reduced, and council membership would become even less representative than it as at present.

The Widdicombe Committee did in fact reject quite forcefully the idea that there was any automatic conflict of interest involved in the practice of 'twin-tracking'. Referring to their own commissioned research, the Committee pointed out that if it had any validity

the argument . . . would apply more strongly to those who are councillors in more than one local authority; our survey of councillors shows that this is a more common phenomenon than twin-tracking, with 13% of all councillors being councillors of two (or more) authorities. We do not believe that the external loyalty created by being an employee of another authority is any more a cause for prima facie concern than many other external loyalties created by employment that are not the subject of disqualification.

(Widdicombe Committee, Report, 1986, p. 111)

The Committee did, however, take the view that a partial ban was justified. They argued that *senior* officers, defined, somewhat controversially, as anyone employed at the rank of principal officer or above, might have their political impartiality compromised by serving as councillors of another authority, and should therefore be statutorily prohibited from doing so and, indeed, from engaging in any other form of 'political activity'. In the words of the Committee, such a ban would confine the infringement of citizen rights to 'only' about 70,000 local authority employees or less than 3 per cent of the total (Report, 1986, p. 112).

Party differences

We have seen in the preceding sections that the background characteristics of councillors differ considerably from one type of local authority to another. It may be, though, that much of this variation can be better described in terms of the party affiliations of the members concerned. With Labour members, for instance, holding two-thirds of all metropolitan district council seats and yet barely a quarter of those on England shire district councils, what appears like a difference between the two classes of authority may actually be a difference between the major parties.

The extent to which this is the case can be seen in Table 12, which we have adapted from the summary table in Research Volume II of the Widdicombe Committee Report (p. 39). The very fact that this table was able to be produced is, in its own way, a reflection of the relatively recent spred of the party politicization of local government which we described in the previous chapter. For the SCPR questionnaire was the first of these government sponsored surveys actually to ask councillors a question about their party affiliation. Previously, such a question had presumably been considered either inappropriate or indelicate, and the Maud Committee survey, for example, exhaustive though it was, contented itself with a rather coy inquiry about membership of 'any organisations connected with politics'. As a result, we learn that two-thirds of all councillors were members of 'political organisations' and that just over one-third were 'asked to stand by a political body' (Maud Committee, Vol. 2, 1976, p. 196). But these enigmatic organizations and bodies are never identified, and so no cross-party analyses are possible for any of the Maud councillor data.

	All Councillors	Cons.	Lab.	Lib.	Indep.	(Population)
Gender						
Male	81	78	83	79	81	(49)
Female	19	21	17	21	19	(51)
Age						
18–44	26	19	33	49	11	(46)
45–59	37	42	33	30	36	(21)
60 and over	36	37	32	22	52	(33)
Activity status						
Employed (full- or part-time)	60	64	59	74	47	
Unemployed	4	2	8	3	1	
Retired	25	24	22	13	40	
Looking after a home/family	8	9	6	9	9	
Other	2	–	3	–	1	
Socio-economic group						
Professional	9	11	6	15	8	(3)
Employers/ Managers	32	42	20	28	37	(11)
Intermediate non-manual	18	14	22	23	11	(9)
Junior non-manual	10	8	11	15	6	(18)
(Total non-manual)	(69)	(75)	(59)	(81)	(62)	(41)
Skilled manual/ own account non-professional	16	10	25	8	14	(23)
Semi-skilled/ unskilled manual	5	1	10	4	6	(24)
(Total manual)	(21)	(11)	(35)	(12)	(20)	(47)
Armed forces/not available	11	12	8	8	16	(10)
Income						
Over £15,000	16	25	7	18	14	
£10,000–£14,999	22	22	23	29	17	
£6,000–£9,999	26	23	28	23	27	
Up to £5,999	28	22	38	23	29	
None	1	1	1	2	2	
Refused/ not available	7	8	4	3	10	
Base = 1,557						

Source: Widdicombe Committee, Research Vol. II, 1986, Table 4.5 (p. 39).
Note: Percentages may not total 100 due to non-responses and rounding.

Table 12 *Characteristics of councillors by party membership (1985) (%)*

The figures in Table 12, however, are of sufficient interest on their own, even without any comparisons with the past. They show, at a glance, that there are indeed some quite striking differences in the councillor profiles across the political party groups. Liberals, for instance, emerge as by far the most youthful of the groups: nearly half of them are under 45, compared with under one in five of the Conservatives and barely one in ten of the Independents, over half of the latter being over 60, and 40 per cent retired. Among Labour councillors, roughly one in twelve described themselves as unemployed, a far higher figure than for any other party group; and over one-third had manual working-class backgrounds, three times the proportion of Conservatives and Liberals. Income, of course, is closely related to occupation, and it is perhaps not surprising to find a quarter of all Conservative members earning over £15,000 a year. By comparison, two-thirds of Labour members earn less than £10,000, despite the party's numerically superior strength in London, the highest paid area in the country.

We have already seen how councillors as a whole differ considerably in their personal and occupational characteristics from the electors whose votes they seek. With only a few quite minor amendments, the quotation from the Maud Report with which we opened this discussion could be reprised here with equal applicability. What Table 12 shows, though, is something that could only be guessed at in 1964, namely, that some party groups are slightly more or less unrepresentative in this respect than others. And if there is any kind of merit in a party's politicians being *less* socially unrepresentative, then Labour, with its fractionally higher proportion of women members, its moderate youthful age profile, its more even balance of manual and non-manual workers, and its more modest income levels, can probably stake the fairest claim to it.

Councillor experience and turnover

Social representativeness is by no means the only attribute that voters might reasonably look for in their local politicians.

It is almost certainly not the main one, and would probably for many people rank well below acquired experience in the job. But if, as we have seen, more and more local elections are being contested, and at least some slightly younger members replacing older ones, the result must almost inevitably be an increase in the rate of councillor turnover and a consequential reduction in what might be termed 'collective member experience'. As is shown in Table 13, this has indeed been the case. There are today significantly fewer members with more than ten years' council service than there were at the time of the 1964 Maud Committee survey, while the number with more than twenty-one years' service has fallen by over two-thirds in the space of less than ten years.

Like the other statistics we have looked at, though, these aggregate figures can mask some enormous differences across different types of authority and from one authority to another. And in recent years this reduction in collective member experience is likely to have been especially strongly felt in those authorities on which the four-year terms of members all coincide: for example, the English and Welsh counties, the Scottish authorities, and the London boroughs, which are required to hold 'whole council' or 'all out' elections every four years, and the approximately 60 per cent of English and Welsh shire districts which choose to do so. If a set of 'all out' elections happens to come at a time of extreme national unpopularity for one or other of the major parties, there can be widespread repercussions at the local level, with sweeping changes in the political control of councils and massive influxes of new and mostly inexperienced members. The brief electoral history of the six metropolitan county councils, comprising as it did just three sets of all-out elections, provides a particularly vivid illustration of this tendency.

As can be seen in Table 14, nearly half of all metropolitan county council seats changed hands in 1977 and again in 1981, reflecting the prevailing unpopularity of, respectively, the national Labour and Conservative governments of the time. In the case of Greater Manchester and the West Midlands in particular, not only did their political control change in both years, but roughly half the councillors elected were completely new to their councils. Some similarly startling lurches in political control and in the elective composition of councils resulted from the shire county elections held in the same years. In 1977, for example, Labour lost over 55 per cent of the nearly 1100 seats it had previously held on the thirty-nine English county councils, leaving it in overall control of just one: Durham. But four years later the party won back all the lost seats and more, and it was the Conservatives' turn to lose its former overall control of eighteen of the thirty-nine councils.

	1964 %	1976 %	1985 %
0–3 years	26	28	25
4–9 years	31	35	40
10–20 years	39 ⎫ 48	26 ⎫ 36	32 ⎫ 35
21 years or more	9 ⎭	10 ⎭	3 ⎭
Base	3930	4691	1536

Source: Widdicombe Committee, Research Vol. II, 1986, p.35.

Table 13   *Councillors by length of service (1964–85)*

	1973			1977			1981		
	No. of seats	% of seats	% of votes	No. of seats	% of seats	% of votes	No. of seats	% of seats	% of votes
Conservatives	141	23	36	360	60	53	122	20	31
Labour	402	67	47	213	35	35	426	71	50
Liberals	49	8	13	19	3	8	50	8	17
Others	9	1	3	9	1	4	3	1	2
Con-Lab swing (%)				−34.5	−14.5		+38	+18.5	
Total seats	601			601			601		

Source: Bristow *et al.*, 1984, Ch. 8.

Table 14   *The metropolitan county council elections (1973–81)*

These dramatic pendulum swings of tranches of seats, far greater than the swings in votes which bring them about (see Table 14), and the discontinuities of membership which they cause are partly a product of our non-proportional, simple majority electoral system. They owe something also to the increasingly volatile political atmosphere of the past decade or so. The impact of these factors is magnified however by a regime of four-yearly all-out elections. On those authorities which hold elections 'by thirds', the metropolitan districts and about one-third of the English and Welsh shire districts, the actual turnover of councillors tends to take place rather more slowly, and newly elected members can be eased in more gently.

If one wished, therefore, to reduce these sudden and extreme electoral swings, to produce councils that are more continuously reflective of the normal political complexion of their localities, and at the same time to enhance members' consciousness of their political accountability, a more wide-spread system of elections by thirds, or even annual elections, would probably commend itself. At the same time, though, there are the counter-arguments to be considered. In an authority which is not overwhelmingly dominated by a single party and where the whole council comes up for re-election together, any party which wins an election, even by a narrow majority, knows that, barring disasters, it is in power for four years and can operate on a four-year planning cycle. In a similar authority where elections are by thirds, the time horizon and planning period shrink to one or, at the most, two years. Both members and officers in such authorities acknowledge that there can be something resembling a 'silly season' beginning in about December each year, as the parties and prospective candidates start to anticipate the forthcoming May elections and, perhaps more seriously, the electoral impact of the rate-setting process which closely precedes them. Difficult, and certainly potentially expensive, decisions can easily get deferred, for fear of the possible loss of votes that they may entail.

Both sets of arguments were examined at some length by the Widdicombe Committee (Report, 1986, pp. 167–70), who felt them to be very evenly balanced. But to some people's surprise, bearing in mind that one of the Committee's terms of reference had been to look for ways of 'strengthening the democratic process', the Committee came down in favour of abandoning elections by thirds altogether and switching to a country-side system of quadrennial, whole council elections (Recommendation 54(ii)). If such a recommendation were to be enacted, it might be expected to have at least a two fold bearing on our foregoing discussion of councillors. It could, in a rapidly changing political climate, lead to a higher and more staccato turnover of members – both at individual elections and also in the longer term, as some defeated councillors use their enforced four-year absence to invest their time and energy in other interests. It might also, however, have the effect of improving the selection chances of minority group, and particularly ethnic minority, representatives, as local parties have to find three times the number of candidates for any particular set of elections.

Working life of the councillor

Most of the preceding discussion focused on the involuntary turnover of councillors, as a consequence of electoral defeat. But at least as frequent a phenomenon nowadays is *voluntary turnover:* incumbent members choosing, for one reason or another, not to put themselves forward for re-election. The reasons can be several and varied, but they undoubtedly include the 'disillusion, age and frustration' that eye-catchingly headlined one of the very few systematic studies of councillor turnover, that conducted by Colin Rallings and Michael Thrasher (1981). The study was confined to retiring members of four south-west county councils, but it still produced some interesting insights.

Not unexpectedly, the commonest reason for standing down was old age or ill health. Other factors regularly mentioned though were the time-consuming nature of the job, its detrimental effects on one's family and social life and paid employment, and, just about as frequently, general disenchantment:

There are signs among our retiring respondents of more fundamental disenchantment, both with the system of local government and with the relationship between local authorities and Westminster. Indeed, 40% of councillors who had decided not to stand again in 1981 mentioned discontent of this kind. (Rallings and Thrasher, 1981, p. 1042)

In this section of the chapter we shall examine each of these facets of the councillor's working life in turn, referring as before to the relevant Widdicombe research. Unfortunately, the Widdicombe Committee was unable to replicate in any way the fascinating comparative study of councillors and ex-councillors that had been undertaken for the Maud Committee (Vol. 2, 1967, Ch. IX). We have no contemporary equivalent, therefore, of Maud's statistical summary of the reasons 'why councillors leave' (Vol. 2, 1967, p. 259; also Byrne, 1986, p. 124). We do, however, have access to two sizeable bodies of interview material: that gathered by the present authors in the course of their own contribution to the Widdicombe research; and also the extensive verbatim quotations included in a more recently published study by a research team from Bristol Polytechnic – appositely entitled *Married to the Council? The Private Costs of Public Service* (Barron *et al.*, 1987). There is also a wealth of statistical data from the SCPR study on councillors' workloads and patterns of remuneration which, in broad terms at least, can be compared with the Maud and Robinson councillor surveys.

Councillor workloads

In Table 15 we present a summary of the SCPR survey data on the time that councillors reported spending on a range of council duties. The average time spent on all council duties was estimated at 74 hours per 'typical month', or some 18½ hours per week, far higher than the figure in the Maud study, but slightly *lower* than that reported in 1976. This latter finding conflicts strongly with the impressions gained by other members of the Widdicombe research team (Research Vol. I, 1986, pp. 51–2, 62–5) and also with other recent measures of councillors' workloads (Martlew *et al.*, 1985; Barron *et al.*, 1987), and Jude England, in her report, suggests several reasons why it should be treated with some caution (Research Vol. II, 1986, pp. 41–2). The fact that the

	All Councillors		
	1964	*1976*	*1985*
Average number of hours spent in a typical month on:			
Attending meetings of the council, its committees or sub-committees	11	23	21
Preparing for such meetings (e.g. reading papers, meeting council officers)	18	18	18
Travelling to and from such meetings		8	7
Attending party meetings relating to council activities[a]	–	5	5
Dealing with electors' problems, surgeries and pressure groups	8	13	13
Meeting external organisations or bodies as a representative of the council	5	8	8
Public consultation meetings[b]	–	–	2
Other[c]	10	4	–
Total average no. of hours	52	79	74
Base	3,970	4,637	1,557

Source: Widdicombe Committee, Research Vol. II, 1986, Tables 5.1–5.12 (pp. 42–53).

Notes:
[a] 'Party meetings' not included in 1964 study.
[b] 'Public consultation meetings' not included in 1964 and 1976 studies.
[c] 'Other' not included in 1985 study.

Table 15   *Time spent by councillors on council duties (1964, 1976, 1985)*

1976 survey was undertaken shortly after the upheaval of local government reorganization, for instance, and that it was primarily concerned with the remuneration of councillors could easily have affected respondents' recall and reporting of 'time spent in a typical month', as could the slightly different sets of categories employed in the two questionnaires.

Certainly, the very definite message received by the authors of the Widdicombe interview survey on aspects of

Highest average	Type of authority (1985 figs)	Lowest average	Political party	
(Scottish regions and islands)	English shire counties	(English shire districts)	Conserv.	Labour
44	31	16	20	26
30	24	15	17	21
17	13	5	7	9
5	7	4	4	8
16	13	11	10	16
12	11	6	8	9
5	2	1	2	3
–	–	–	–	–
129	101	58	68	92
32	189	819	595	496

political organization was that the time required of, or actually being worked by, elected members had *increased* noticeably in recent years (Research Vol. I, 1986, p. 51). Few, if any, suggestions were made during these open-ended interviews with large numbers of both members and officers that council work today requires any *less* time spent on it than in the recent past. On the contrary, there were a great many proffered explanations as to why and in what ways the demands on councillors' time were increasing. Table 16,

Suggested causes of increased demands on councillors' time in recent years

Externally imposed on the local authority and its members

Self-generated by the members themselves

Structural changes
Larger authorities and larger wards since local government reorganization;
Larger wards/divisions following local boundary reorganizations

Electoral pressures
Increasing electoral volatility – necessitating greater contact with voters
More hung, or nearly hung, councils

Socio-demographic changes
Increasing numbers of old people, leading to more casework
Increasing prominence of ethnic minorities
Spread of owner-occupation, leading to planning becoming a more visible issue

Economic pressures
Scarcer resources – management of contraction is harder than management of growth
Unemployment – leading to concern with economic development, more casework, etc.

Central government pressures
More, and more complicated, legislation
More statutory duties
More central government intervention, especially in budgeting (targets, penalties, etc.)
Abolition of GLC and metropolitan counties
Pressures from government and Central Office to maintain closer political control over officers and the local government machine

Requirement from government to consult more widely with certain local organizations

Community Pressures
Local political parties, demanding greater accountability of members, more consultation
Local interest groups – now more numerous and better organized
Clients facing more serious social problems
Constituents – more assertive, and with inflated expectations of councillors' powers
More aggressive media interest

Councillors' own interests and inclinations
Political commitment to radical change – 'seeing the manifesto through'
Greater concern with the management of the council's resources, with the implementation of policy and service delivery
Distrust of senior officers, leading to reduced delegation of powers, more contact with middle managers and service providers
New issues and areas of concern (employment, equal opportunities, privatization, council house sales, etc.)
Wish to consult more widely with clients, interest groups, and the general public
Distrust of own party leaders and committee chairmen – leading to more decisions going to committee
More unemployed, early-retired, and effectively full-time members
Concern to maximize attendance allowances by longer and more frequent meetings

Source: Widdicombe Committee, Research Vol. I, 1986, p. 63.

Table 16 *Demands on councillors' time*

prepared originally for the Widdicombe Committee (Research Vol. I. 1986, p. 63), sets out an inventory of the explanations most commonly put forward, very broadly arrayed along a spectrum running from those reasons that are wholly 'externally imposed' upon the members of an authority to those which are partly or completely 'self-generated'.

Many of these suggested causes are almost entirely self-explanatory; and others, and particularly those reflecting the increased activism and assertiveness of members themselves, are commented on elsewhere in this book. One or two of the more externally imposed changes, however, may benefit from a little explanation. It is, for instance, sometimes overlooked that, while the external boundaries of local authorities remained basically fixed between the reorganizations of 1974–5 and the abolition of the GLC and the metropolitan county councils in 1986, their internal ward boundaries may have changed considerably, and the actual number of wards may have been reduced. If, as was true of some authorities during this period, there is suddenly a reduction of up to 20 per cent in the number of councillors, then those councillors remaining are inevitably required to take over responsibility both for new and possibly unfamiliar geographical areas and for new and almost certaily unfamiliar electors. More recently, of course, the abolition of the GLC and the metropolitan county councils has had a similar effect, but on a much wider scale, reducing by a total of 693 the number of councillors available to electors in these often problem-ridden areas. As at least some of the functions of the abolished authorities are taken over by borough and district councils, so the elected members of these councils have found themselves confronted by even heavier consti-tuency caseloads than previously.

The debate about abolition itself of course occupied a fair amount of members' time and energy but abolition has been only one of several time-increasing pressures emanating from the actions of central government. The massive prog-ramme of legislation impinging upon local councils, particu-larly upon their financial and budgetary processes, is widely felt to have increased councillors' workloads, and most especially those of leading members. It is generally accepted, almost as a truism, that the management of contraction and decline is a more difficult and demanding exercise than the management of growth – 'cutbacks take more work and are more time-consuming', as the leader of a Labour metropolitan district put it.

Mention of leaders and leading members brings us back to the figures in Table 15. It has constantly to be kept in mind that, unless otherwise indicated, these are figures for some hypothetical 'average' member of an 'average' council in a 'typical' month. There are, as indicated in the table, major variations by type of authority, by political party, and also by the personal characteristics of the individual councillor and position held on the council. Councillors in Wales and especially in Scotland, for instance, reported spending considerably more time on their council activities than those in England; councillors on upper-tier authorities more than those on lower-tier authorities, not least because of the greater travelling time to and from meetings; and those in the metropolitan areas of England more than those in the shire areas. At the extremes, members of regional and island councils in Scotland spend well over twice the time of the average English shire district councillor.

Labour councillors tend to spend considerably more time than those from other parties, with Independents (61 hours per month) recording the lightest workloads. Liberals, in keeping with their emphasis on 'community politics' spend the most time (17 hours per month) on dealing with electors' problems, and least in connection with formal council meetings. Not surprisingly, leaders and other office-holders give more of their time (93 and 80 hours per month respectively) than do backbenchers (64 hours) – the biggest difference here being in the much greater time spent preparing for meetings.

A criticism is often levelled at figures like those listed in Table 15, to the effect that, because they rely on councillors' perceptions and recall, they are likely to be both unreliable and systematically skewed. Surely, it is suggested, there will be a tendency for members to over-report the time they spend on their council and other public duties? It is a plausible suggestion, but it is one that, in the case of Widdicombe survey data, should almost certainly be rejected. Some recent evidence gathered in the innovative study by Jacqueline Barron and her colleagues suggests strongly that, if there is any systematic unconscious error in the data, it is likely to be in the direction of *under*-reporting, rather than the reverse.

In the course of a detailed exploration of the links between the demands of council work and councillors' private lives, Barron *et al.* used two different methods to measure as accurately as possible the hours of work put in by their sample of shire county councillors. First, there was the 'recall' method, similar to that employed in the SCPR questionnaire. Councillors were asked to go through their appointment diaries and to recall the meetings attended and their other relevant commitments over a period of two weeks. Second, there was a 'diary' method, in which councillors were asked to record for one wekk in a specially designed diary *all* incidents, activities, conversations and events that stemmed from their council membership. Comparison of the two methods, as in Table 17, shows that: 'in almost every case, the hours recorded in the diary weeks were considerably more than those reported for either of the two recall weeks, the common pattern being between one-and-a-half and two-and-a-half times as much' (Barron *et al.*, 1987, p. 44). From recall information the mean average hours reported by councillors were 20.7 per week, that is, slightly under the SCPR/ Widdicombe figure for county councillors in Table 8. But from the diaries this average rose to 34.2 hours per week, or well over 130 hours per month. On the basis of these comparisons, then, it seems fair to conclude at the very least that the figures in Table 15 do not present an exaggerated picture of the time commitment required of the modern-day councillor.

Interpretations of the councillor's role

The diary exercise in particular seems also to call into question the Widdicombe Committee's conclusion that 'the trend towards full-time councillors has probably been over-

| | **Hours per week** | |
	Recall	*Diary*
All councillors	20.7	34.2
Females	23.1	37.6
Males	18.6	30.8
Conservative	20.5	28.9
Labour	22.7	37.8
Liberal	15.5	34.8
Chairs	25.3	38.4
Backbenchers	15.9	29.4
Base	61	54

Source: Barron *et al.*, 1987, p.45.

Table 17 *Councillors' average hours of work, by recall and diary*

stated' (Report, 1986, p. 126). It obviously depends how 'full-time' is defined, but it seems certain that there are quite large numbers of councillors nowadays who, even though they may have outside occupations, are nevertheless spending the equivalent of a full working week on their various council-related activities. In terms of the useful typology suggested by Barron *et al.*, these effectively full-time members can be said to adopt a 'pro-active' stance towards their council work, seeing it either as a vocation or a job. They can be contrasted with those who take a more 'reactive' or 'minimalist' view and treat it as more akin to a hobby or part-time leisure interest (Barron *et al.*, 1987, cc. 5 and 12).

One considerable merit of even this limited differentiation of role interpretations is that it brings us back again to the 'externally imposed'/'self-generated' distinction in Table 9. Like the inventory of suggested new demands on councillors' time, existing demands too can be crudely divided into the externally imposed and the self-generated. If council activity is undertaken essentially as a *hobby*, for example, the workload need not be excessive. There are likely to be certain irreducible 'externally imposed' demands, such as council, committee, party group, and perhaps even occasional local branch meetings to attend, with possibly a certain amount of preparation required beforehand. Constituency casework, on the other hand, is much more discretionary. Cases and problems can be dealt with as they come up, but there is no obligation positively to go out looking for them. Membership of outside organizations can be kept to a minimum, as can any attendance at their meetings.

In their limited sample of county councillors Barron *et al.* found that those adopting this type of reactive role interpretation were in a minority, and were disproportionately Conservative males, but they certainly existed, as can be gathered from the following fragments of quotation:

. . . politics is like a hobby, and you've got to treat it as such. Once it becomes like the work, the job, it's when you have to start thinking seriously about what you're doing.   (Labour backbencher)

. . . it's a leisure activity, learning more about the county . . . just enjoying life, that's it.   (Conservative backbencher)

(Barron *et al.*, 1987, p. 95)

Many councillors, however, will either personally wish, or feel it incumbent upon them, to adopt a far more pro-active approach, and will not be satisfied merely to respond to external demands. Some may see being a councillor less as a vacation than as a *vocation:* as 'providing a service for the community' or for a specific section of the community. Attending council and committee meetings is seen as only a relatively minor part of the councillor's role, which also involves making oneself readily, if not constantly, available and keeping oneself as fully informed as possible about the problems and issues of one's area:

Well, it's my way of looking at it . . . from the community point of view. It's to get yourself involved in the community and . . . to be available at all times, really. You know, if you're going to do it half-heartedly, don't bother.   (Liberal backbencher)

I am a totally committed councillor. Twenty-four hours a day. And that is my password, and has been.   (Labour backbencher)

My job is not just to listen to the officers. My job is to actually go round to voluntary organisations that represent the elderly, like the borough councils, and get opinions from those. (Labour backbencher)

(Barron *et al.*, 1987, pp. 76–9)

Then there are those for whom council work is, or should be, a *job*: an important and responsible position, requiring a major commitment of time if it is to be performed properly – time that should be acknowledged and rewarded properly. 'Local government is big business', emphasized one such councillor during one of our Widdicombe research interviews, before going on to argue that its size, complexity and the various growing demands now being made upon councils made it more or less imperative that at least the leading members of a council be effectively full-time. This may not be a startlingly original view, but it was all the more interesting coming as it did from the Conservative leader of a shire district with an annual financial turnover of less than one-tenth of that of some of the authorities we visited. This leader's point was that, in order to understand and to begin politically to control 'even' an organization of this relatively modest size, the full-time involvement of at least some elected members is required.

The Widdicombe Committee, relying primarily on its SCPR recall data, averaged out as it was across the more than 500 upper- and lower-tier authorities in the country, took the view that there were still only a relatively few councillors who 'worked full-time, or practically so' on council business, and that this was as it should be:

We do not . . . think that it should be regarded as the norm that councillors, even leading councillors, should work full-time, nor that such practice should in any way be formalised or encouraged. (Report, 1986, pp. 126–7)

The diary and interview data provided by the sample of county councillors in the Bristol Polytechnic study, on the other hand, offers a rather different emphasis. No less than one-third of the sample, and a majority of the women members, *did see* their role as involving or requiring a full-time commitment (Barron *et al.*, 1987, p. 92). True, only for about half of them was this full-time commitment actually achieved in terms of their work hours, and this is where the issues of 'pressure' and 'stress' become relevant.

The pressures and conflicts of council work

When councillors talk of the pressure or stress of council work, or – in the phrase used by Rallings and Thrasher – of finding it frustrating or disillusioning, what they are likely to be describing is some kind of mismatch between their aspirations or expectations and their actual day-to-day experience; or, to put it another way, an inability fully and satisfactorily to interpret the councillor's role in the way they would ideally wish. It is a statement of the obvious, but the time involved in any job only manifests itself as a 'pressure' to a person who wants or finds they need to give *more* time to it. For those councillors, the minority in the Bristol Polytechnic study, who see council work as a hobby or leisure pursuit, time need not constitute any great pressure. They can limit their workloads in such a way as to minimize any interference with their family or social life or with their paid employment.

But for the majority of councillors, the increasing amount of time that council work appears to them to require does represent a pressure – at least on occasions. For an additional problematic aspect of the councillor's workload can be its irregularity and unpredictability – the unevenly spaced and awkwardly timed meetings, the erratic and sometimes intrusive nature of constituency casework, the particular frenzy and disruption of election campaigns, and the enormous, and almost always unanticipated, quantity of paperwork (Barron *et al.*, 1987, Ch. 3). The demands of council work, therefore, have to be balanced against the potentially conflicting demands of, in particular, family and social life and outside employment.

In the Bristol Polytechnic study both councillors and their partners described eloquently some of the principal points of friction in this balancing process: the disturbed home life; the increased domestic workload for other family members; the difficulties of organizing childcare, especially for female councillors with young children; the shortage of shared leisure time; the neglected friends; the postponed and interrupted holidays (Barron *et al.*, 1987, Chs 7–9). At the same time, it was also acknowledged that council work could have its positive and beneficial effects: the broadening of outlook and interests; the shared involvement of a supportive partner and children; the increased opportunities to meet a wide range of people and develop new friends.

There can occasionally be benefits too for the councillor who has to reconcile council work with a full-time job, for example the development and carry-over of relevant knowledge and skills from employment to council work, but they seem to be fairly few and far between. As Barron *et al.*, conclude:

The benefits to councillors arising from employment seem small in relation to the costs . . . a simple and straightforward conclusion is obvious: councillors in employment lose. These losses or 'costs' are both very specific and pervasive, e.g. loss of promotion, financial loss, loss of pension rights, workload problems, employer ambivalence. Furthermore, these losses are not only cited by those who have direct and personal experience themselves. Many non-employed and retired councillors remarked on the great difficulties faced by their employed colleagues on the council. (Barron *et al.*, 1987, p. 219)

These losses and difficulties would be confirmed also by members and officers throughout the country, to judge from the evidence of our own Widdicombe interviews. Among the respondents to the SCPR survey, there were relatively few (6 per cent) who claimed actually to have lost or resigned from their last jobs for reasons directly related to their council work. But for every individual who has either been sacked or forced to resign, there are many who have felt threatened or have felt their future promotion prospects likely to be damaged. Several such instances were cited to us and also to Barron and her colleagues, often in quite an offhand manner, as if the situation was only to be expected:

When firms are looking to cut back on staff, they tend to pick out the councillors . . . who then find it hard to get new jobs. (Labour leader, northern metropolitan district)

(Widdicombe Committee, Research Vol. I, 1986, p. 52)

Yes, I think it does affect your job and job prospects. There is limited promotion available, but you're very rarely considered for that. I was one of the senior members on my section, and when one of the more responsible jobs came up, for section leader, I was simply by-passed because of my council commitments. (Labour backbencher)

(Barron *et al.*, 1987, p. 204)

In fact, quite a few of my colleagues have had promotion during the last two years, and part of that promotion was that they had to give up council membership at the next election.   (Labour backbencher)

(Barron *et al.*, 1987, p. 204)

Despite the fact that all three of these brief quotes come from Labour members, there was no apparent suggestion that it would make much difference to the employer concerned with party the councillor represented: being a councillor was in itself enough to get oneself labelled as a bad risk. Indeed the signs are that it has been the Conservative party that has perhaps lost more sitting councillors and potential candidates through what might be termed 'career and occupational pressures' than the other parties. Certainly, at the time of our programme of interviews for the Widdicombe Committee, in the latter half of 1985, it was local Conservative parties that seemed most frequently to be finding problems recruiting candidates, or at least what they felt to be 'good calibre' candidates. And it is Conservative-run councils that seem increasingly forced to rely on retired, non-working or self-employed members to fill key leadership positions:

You've got to be self-employed to be a county councillor, because of the time element involved, because meetings are in the day. . . . You've got to be a housewife or a retired service chap, as most of them are in the county hall, or self-employed. These are really the only categories of people you can have, simply because you don't pay them enough to let them earn their keep. (Conservative chairman)

(Barron *et al.*, 1987, pp. 216–17)

The point about daytime meetings is a most relevant one. The IPF survey for the Widdicombe Committee found that 22 per cent of councils held most of their council and committee meetings in the morning, with a further 25 per cent starting theirs between midday and 4 p.m. Thus very nearly half of *all* councils, not simply county councils, meet almost entirely within 'normal' working hours, which makes it hardly surprising that councillors turn out to be so socially and occupationally unrepresentative of the population as a whole.

The pressures and stresses we have looked at so far have tended to focus on the boundary, or, rather, on the blurring of the boundary, between a councillor's public and private life. There is here a potential boundary conflict which, if not satisfactorily resolved, can lead eventually to the councillor's 'voluntary' resignation. Indeed, it is probably the most frequently cited reason for the recently increasing voluntary turnover of members which we noted. There are, however, other kinds of contributory reasons as well: the 'signs of more fundamental disenchantment, both with the system of local government and with the relationship between local authorities and Westminster' that were identified by Rallings and Thrasher.

There seem to be several distinct strands to this generalized 'disenchantment', of which the following are probably the most frequently mentioned. First, and particularly common amongst older Conservative members as well as surviving Independents, is an irritation with what is seen as the excessive party politicization of local government. It is argued that party organization constrains and polarizes debate and can thereby act as a barrier to good decision-making. A slightly different, if related, criticism can be that a party system tends to concentrate a council's policy leadership in the hands of a small group of councillors, from which other members are excluded. This frustration of exclusion or opposition can be felt as much by members of majority as of minority parties, as the second of our illustrative quotes reveals:

When one's in opposition it's a little different, because you know before you start that . . . nobody's going to take any notice of you, and it builds therefore a considerable element of frustration there, almost impotence to be able to achieve anything other than campaigning all the time to take power at the next election. (Labour Chair)

(Barron *et al.*, 1987, p. 105)

The county council has become too fossilised, with a large Conservative majority which is controlled in an inner and unobtrusive caucus.
What is desperately needed is a basic political shake-up which will
produce new personalities, fresh ideas, and revived energy, and will
shake out the deadweight. I am part of the deadweight, and it's time
for me to go.   (Conservative backbencher)

(Rallings and Thrasher, 1981, p. 1042)

A second type of councillor complaint relates not to the
dominance of particular groups of fellow members, but to
the perceived power of officers. The authors of the Bristol
Polytechnic study record that 'approximately half of the
comments we received on officers were negative in character,
and asserted or implied a view that officers had too much
influence' (Barron *et al.*, 1987, p. 90). This proportion, as it
happens, is almost exactly reflective of the sample of
councillors in the SCPR/Widdicombe survey. It was a view
held particularly strongly, as can be seen in Table 18, by non-
office holders, and also by the most recently elected group of
councillors. As Jude England comments:

This would appear to bear out the common impression that local
government officers are finding the new generation of councillors to
be more assertive than their predecessors.   (Widdicombe Committee, Research Vol. II, 1986, p. 67)

A third and unquestionably increasing source of frustration and disillusion for councillors is the combination of
central government financial restraint and general interference that has characterized local government in the 1980s.
The frustration is felt in different ways by members of the
different political parties, Labour members, for instance,
tending to focus especially on the immediate shortage of
resources:

I think the major frustration that I've experienced . . . is, of course,
the financial constraints in which councils are placed, that you are
not able to do those things that you should do and certainly would
like to do . . . we talk of these things and have visions of policies, but
can't implement them because of the difficulty of financing
them.   (Labour chair)

(Barron *et al.*, 1987, p. 105)

'Council officials have too much influence on council decision-making'

	Agree %	Neither %	Disagree %
All Councillors	47	20	33
Length of service:			
Under 4 years	49	24	26
4–9 years	48	20	33
10 years or more	45	15	39
Council office held:			
Leaders	30	18	53
Other office holders	45	19	34
No office held	51	19	28

Base = 1,557

Source: Widdicombe Committee, Research Vol. II, 1986, Tables 7.2, 7.3, 7.5, pp. 66–9.

Table 18 *Councillors' views on influence of council officials*

Labour members, however, hardly expect to find themselves in sympathy with a Conservative government, no matter what its policies towards local government might be. Conservative councillors, on the other hand, do; and it was our impression, from our Widdicombe research interviews, that it was within the Conservative party that this disillusion with central government intervention was having perhaps its more serious long-term impact. One Liberal councillor described, with apparently quite genuine regret, the difficulties the local Conservative party had had in finding a candidate to stand against him at the recent election:

I do believe that an awful lot has got to do with the independence of local government from central government. We lost some absolutely first-class Conservatives from this county council before the last election, because they were fed up to the back teeth with the way in which their activities were being constrained by central government.

The Conservative leader of another shire county council made much the same point and was able to support his case with some personal illustrations:

The greatest difficulty now in getting people to stand is the way in which local government is being bashed – particularly people who are involved in business and commerce at a high level . . . this county has always produced a lot of people from the City, bankers and so on, and these are definitely draining away. A director of one of our big construction companies was very keen a few years ago, but when I asked him at the end of last year if he'd be interested in standing, he said: 'Oh, I don't think I could. I think my colleagues would be terribly worried if I got caught up with rate-capping or anything like that.'

Without doubt, the constant criticism of local government over the last few years has had its effect on the propensity of people who are working, who are able to contribute, to put themselves forward. It's the people who are in the financial world, whose abilities are in finance, who find it the most difficult to understand the logic of the system of local government finance that's being imposed on us. They look at this council's record and say: 'You're paying off your debt fast, you've disposed of your unwanted property to create new assets, you don't borrow . . .' and they would look at our Annual Report and see that it would stand up to the way that, say, ICI runs its finances. And they simply cannot understand why there's almost a complete block on spending the proceeds on the unwanted assets the Government's telling us to sell. Or that the more we save, and the less we waste, the more we're penalised . . . the man in business cannot understand that.   (Widdicombe Committee, Research Vol. I, 1986, pp. 54-5)

The remuneration of councillors

We have in the preceding few pages endeavoured to identify some of the pressures and conflicts facing the modern-day councillor, some of the possible sources of frustration which can qualify the undoubted satisfaction and enjoyment that the role also offers. For some councillors that satisfaction and enjoyment is reward enough: the interest and challenge that the work presents, often greater than in their paid employment; the sense of achievement from holding a senior council position, from 'getting things done', or from dealing with the problems of their constituents and fellow citizens:

If I weren't doing this . . . I'd go stark raving mad. (Labour backbencher)

Council work is something I thoroughly enjoy doing and I'm happy doing, so that could be classed as part of my leisure. (Conservative backbencher)

(Barron *et al.*, 1987, p. 102)

As we have seen, though, most councillors nowadays either cannot afford or do not wish to treat their council work as a purely leisure activity, which brings us to the question of remuneration. We have deliberately left it until towards the end of the chapter not because of its lack of importance, and certainly not because of any dearth of expressed views about it, but because it helps to return us again to where we began, with the calibre and representativeness of councillors. The Robinson Committee which, unlike Widdicombe, was solely and directly concerned with the issue of remuneration, could hardly have articulated this linkage more forcefully:

We believe that it is absolutely fundamental to the effective working of democracy that there should be no unnecessary impediment to the freedom of anyone to put themselves forward for election . . . membership of local authorities should be truly open to all sectors of our society without fear that it will entail financial hardship. . . . In so far as it is possible to reduce or eliminate any distortions in the pattern of representation which may result from financial consider- ations, we believe it should be done. We note, for example, the continuing under-representation of manual workers on councils. It may well be that financial constraints are not the only factors standing in the way of an increase in the proportion of manual workers, but our survey reveals that they are in the group who are most likely to have their earnings reduced as a result of council membership. (Robinson Committee Report, Vol. I, 19877, p. 35)

Ten years on, however, the 'distortions' in the pattern of councillor representation have been very far from elimin- ated. The proportion of councillors in manual occupations, for example, has in fact declined from the 27 per cent recorded by both the Maud and Robinson studies to the 21 per cent in Table 12. And, as the Widdicombe surveys indicated, council membership for many would and *does* entail financial hardship. Many councillors, in other words, are being financially penalized for their public service, as the comments of members and officers alike affirm.

'Pathetic', was the summary view of the present allowance system expressed by the chief executive of a Midlands shire district, 'it comes nowhere near even covering members' genuine expenses.' 'Derisory', said the leader of another Midlands shire district, 'there are people on this council who are in really desperate financial situations.' 'An insult to anyone who is tolerably successful outside', complained the Conservative leader of a southern shire district; 'I'm appalled at the way the government treats its local councillors', said another leading Conservative member from a shire county.

The present allowance system

The regulations governing the existing system of remuneration for councillors derive from the Local Government Act 1972 and the Local Government (Scotland) Act 1973, subsequently modified by the Local Government, Planning and Land Act 1980. These regulations provide for a threefold system of allowances:

1 *Attendance allowance* – which may be claimed by council members whenever they undertake an 'approved duty', which includes attendance at council meetings, committee and sub-committee meetings, and can include other associated duties at the discretion of the individual local authority. The allowance is taxable, and is subject to a daily maximum prescribed by the Secretary of State. Within this maximum, which with effect from April 1988 is £18.25 per day, authorities may vary the amounts they pay, according to the time of day and the length of duty.

2 *Financial loss allowance* – which councillors may opt to receive *instead* of attendance allowance. The recipient must demonstrate the actual financial loss suffered. It too is

subject to a daily maximum – £29.70 in 1988–89 – but is not taxable.

3 *Special responsibility allowance (SRA)* – an additional allowance which local authorities *may* at their discretion pay to councillors with special responsibilities. The maximum which any authority may pay – both in total and to an individual councillor – is again laid down by the Secretary of State, and varies according to the type of authority and its population. The 1988–89 maxima for an individual councillor range from £525 up to £5,215 p.a.

In addition, members are entitled to claim travel and subsistence allowances, again up to maximum rates set by the Secretary of State.

The IPF survey for the Widdicombe Committee investigated how this system of allowances operates in practice. The survey's major findings are summarized in Table 19. The total expenditure in Great Britain on members' allowances and expenses in 1984–5 was estimated at £28.1 million, or less than 0.1 per cent of total local authority rate- and grant-borne expenditure. Roughly two-thirds of this total went on the attendance allowance payments claimed by 87 per cent of members, and a further quarter on travel and subsistance allowances. Financial loss allowance, by comparison, was claimed by only just over 1 per cent, leaving 12 per cent of councillors making no claim at all.

The average annual payment of attendance allowance across Great Britain was £852, though it was rather higher than this in Wales, and very much higher in Scotland, where authorities tend to adopt a rather less curmudgeonly approach to members' remuneration than prevails elsewhere in the country. One illustration of this different approach is the practice of almost all Scottish authorities, but only just over a quarter of English, to pay the maximum daily rate allowable, regardless of the length of attendance. They also make much more extensive use of SRAs and, as can be seen in Table 20, compiled from councillors' responses to the SCPR survey, they incline towards a more liberal definition of what qualify as 'approved duties'.

Returning to Table 19, only 43 per cent of authorities were

Type of authority	% claiming %	Attendance allowance	
		Av. annual payment to each member £	% of authorities paying max. daily rate, regardless of length of duty %
England			
Metrop. counties + GLC	89	1853	67
Shire counties	84	920	33
Inner London boroughs	83	574	0
Outer London boroughs	84	585	24
Metrop. districts	92	1306	53
Shire districts	86	513	24
England – all authorities	86	728	28
Wales			
Counties	89	1438	63
Districts	87	876	52
Wales – all authorities	88	1057	54
Scotland			
Regions and islands	96	2034	100
Districts	96	2150	90
Scotland – all authorities	96	2112	92
Total	87	852	38

Source: Widdicombe Committee, Research Vol. II, 1986, ch.3, pp.134–42.
Note: 0 = less than 0.5 per cent.

Table 19   *Allowances paid to councillors, by type of authority (1984–5)*

found to be taking advantage of the provision for special responsibility payments, with Labour authorities considerably more likely to do so that Conservative (62 per cent against 34 per cent). As one might expect, the posts most commonly benefiting are those of leader (in 49 per cent of

	Special responsibility allowance		All allowances (excl. travel and subsistence)					
			Distribution of members' receipts					
% of authorities making SRA payments %	*Av. number of members in receipt*	*Av. payment per person in receipt* £	*Nil* %	*Up to £999* %	*£1,000– £1,999* %	*£2,000– £2,999* %	*£3,000– £4,999* %	*£5,000+* %
100	18	1043	7	25	34	17	12	4
36	12	909	12	58	19	6	4	1
60	13	. 417	17	57	20	5	1	0
71	11	702	16	67	13	2	1	–
66	17	631	6	42	31	12	7	1
34	7	265	13	77	7	1	1	0
41	10	545	12	67	14	4	3	0
25	6	1271	9	39	24	16	11	0
13	6	189	12	55	27	5	0	–
16	6	540	11	50	26	9	4	0
100	13	715	1	16	27	23	27	6
76	8	258	2	31	23	19	25	2
80	9	417	2	26	24	20	25	3
43	9	518	12	63	15	5	4	1

councils paying SRA) and committee chairs (in 78 per cent). But, as Ramsdale and Capon note in their IPF report, it is also interesting that 34 per cent of all councils making SRA payments included a payment to the leader or leaders of opposition parties (Widdicombe Committee, Research Vol.

II, 1986, p. 139). Adding all these allowances together (including financial loss, but excluding travel and subsistence claims), it turned out that 75 per cent of all members received less than £1000 in 1984–5, and 90 per cent less than £2000 – for an average claimed workload, it will be remembered, of 74 hours per month, or nearly 900 hours per annum,

Those who address their criticisms to the operation of this existing system almost invariably cite first the failure of

	Average number of 1976	
Type of activity	Financial allowance received Hrs	No financial allowance Hrs
Attending meetings of the council, its committees, or sub-committees	17	5
Preparing for such meetings (e.g. reading papers, meeting council officers)	} 8 {	} 17 {
Travelling to and from such meetings		
Attending party meetings relating to council activities	1	4
Dealing with electors' problems, surgeries and pressure groups	2	11
Meeting external organizations or bodies as a representative of the council	3	5
Public consultation meetings[a]	–	–
Other[b]	1	3
Total average number of hours	33	46
% of total	42%	58%

Source: Widdicombe Committee, Research Vol. II, 1986, Calculations based on figures in Tables 6.1, 6.6, 6.7, 6.8 and 6.9 (pp.55–63).

Notes:
[a] 'Public consultation meetings' not included in 1976 studies.
[b] 'Other' not included in 1985 study.
0 = less than 0.5 per cent.

Table 20   *Councillors' reported receipt of financial allowances (1976 and 1985)*

allowances to keep pace with inflation. If the initial 1973 maximum figure of £10 per day had been uprated annually, it would today be around £40, that is, well over double the actual rate. Moreover, as can be seen from Table 20, the proportion of hours for which this relatively reduced rate of allowance was received had itself fallen, from 42 per cent of all hours in 1976 down to 34 per cent in 1985. Specifically, there had been a decrease in financial allowance receipt for

hours per 'typical' month 1985		% of councillors receiving allowance 1985		
Financial allowance received Hrs	No financial allowance Hrs	England %	Wales %	Scotland %
18	3	85	77	87
2	16	15	7	31
4	3	n/a	n/a	n/a
0	5	4	2	20
0	13	4	3	37
2	6	20	20	45
0	2	5	1	12
–	–	–	–	–
26	49			
34%	66%			

activities such as dealing with electors' problems and attending party meetings, aspects of the modern councillor's role which many members would rank as being at least as important as the attending of council and committee meeting.

The criticisms of the present system, though, extend some way beyond the actual rates of allowance and the arbitrariness of the definition of an 'approved duty'. Particular 'anomalies' mentioned frequently to us during our Widdicombe interviews included: the loss of entitlement to unemployment benefit, sickness, injury, and invalidity benefit, because receipt of an attendance allowance is taken to imply, respectively, unavailability for or capability for work; the loss of pension entitlement, through attendance allowance being regarded as earnings; and the loss of holiday rights.

Alternative proposals

When it investigated many of these tax and social security problems, the Robinson Committee readily acknowledged that the way in which the rules are applied 'can cause serious difficulties to individual councillors' (Robinson Committee Report, Vol. I, 1977, p. 29). And it went a great deal further. The Report was severely critical of the very principle of an attendance allowance system, which it saw as being inappropriate for councillors, many of whose duties do *not* entail attending formal meetings. Accordingly, it recommended that the present system be abolished, to be replaced by a three-element system comprising a basic flat-rate annual payment to all councillors, a financial loss allowance, and special responsibility allowances. The first of these elements was not accepted, but the financial loss and SRAs were introduced, as we have seen, albeit in a different form and at lower rates than Robinson had recommended.

The Widdicombe Committee adopted an essentially similar approach to that of Robinson, although its principal recommendations (Nos 25–8) were for a two-element system:

1   *basic flat-rate allowance* – to replace both the attendance and financial loss allowance, and to be paid to all councillors,

varying (unlike the Robinson proposal) according to the population size and type of council. The Committee's proposed rates of allowance ranged from £1,500 per member of a small English district council to maxima of £3,250 and £4,000 for the largest councils in England and Scotland respectively – the difference being intended to reflect the fact that Scottish councillors represent, on average, 50% more people than their English and Welsh counterparts.

2 *special responsibility allowance* – to continue to be available for leading councillors, but on a statutory basis: local authorities should not have the right, exercised by over half of them at present (see Table 19), to opt out of the arrangements. The Committee proposed that the then existing maximum rates be doubled, so that the maximum figures for individual councillors would range from £900 to £10,000 per annum.

The total cost of these new arrangements was estimated in the Committee's Report 'to amount to about £56 million, an increase of some £36.5 million' (p. 134). Explaining these figures, the Committee gave a clear indication of its sympathy with councillors' present financial situation:

The current levels of allowance are substantially below what they should be. They present a disincentive to standing for election and are an inadequate reflection of the responsibilities of, and time spent on, council duties. ... No recommendation involving an increse in public expenditure is welcome. Even, however, after the increase the total cost of allowances would represent under 0.2% of local authority rate- and grant-borne expenditure. We believe this is a remarkably low price for a system of democratic representatio. (Report, 1986, pp. 132–4).

More radical and outspoken critics, of course, would argue that it was still *too* low a price. Some would favour the introduction of salaries, for at least certain leading councillors, or for those wishing and able to give a full-time commitment to the job. Perhaps ironically, in view of the much greater time commitment given by councillors since local government reorganization, this proposal found less favour with the Robinson and Widdicombe Committees than with their 1969 predecessor, the (Wheatley) Royal Commission on Local Government in Scotland: 'There is a job to be done and the labourer is worthy of his hire . . . we believe that to pay a salary is the simplest, least invidious and generally most satisfactory way of dealing with a real problem'. (Report, pp. 214–5)

The Robinson and Widdicombe Committees, however, were much more concerned with the possible damage which they felt that full-time, let alone salaried, councillors might do to the relationship between members and officers, 'by tending to blur the well-established distinction that exists now between their respective roles' (Robinson Committee, Report, Vol. I, 1977, p. 38). As the Widdicombe Report put it:

There is a danger that it will alter the character of councillors, so that they become full-time administrators, rather than people who are representative of the local community which they serve. We do not believe this is desirable. Councillors, while retaining overall legal responsibility for the delivery of services, should seek to leave the day-to-day management of those services as far as possible to officers. (Report, 1986, p. 127)

This imperative lies at the heart of the Widdicombe analysis, and explains both the Committee's rejection of councillor salaries and also its proposal that there be a statutory upper limit of twenty-six paid days leave a year (i.e. one half day per week) for councillors who are public sector employees (Recommendation 32). The justification for this latter proposal, differentiating as it does between public and private sector councillors, is the need to safeguard public funds (Report, 1986, p. 136). It does, however, have the effect of reinforcing the notion that council work is to be seen more as a cost to the community than a benefit. This is perhaps inevitable if the 'problem' of remuneration is taken to be one of devising an appropriate system of compensation for councillors as individuals, rather than for *council work*.

If, on the other hand, to return to the point made at the start of this section, council membership is genuinely to become more representative, with members drawn from all sections of the community, then, as a former Labour metropolitan county councillor put it to us, the issue becomes one of 'how to protect *both* the individual councillor *and* the employer'. If at least some councillors are to be able to spend two or three days a week or more on their various council duties – which, as we have seen, is how many of them do interpret the requirements of the role – then what is required is something along the lines of an 'absolute right' to paid time off, backed by a full and automatic reimbursement of the member's employer at his or her wage rate.

Support services for councillors

This idea of employer reimbursement was but one of several such suggestions put to us during our programme of interviews for the Widdicombe Committee. Probably the majority of councillors to whom we spoke had their own spontaneous views and criticisms about the current remuneration system and suggestions as to how it should be reformed or, in some instances, revolutionized.

By comparison, relatively few were anything like as critical, or as thoughtfully constructive, about all the various non-financial aspects of their working lives as councillors, namely the services and facilities provided (or not provided) by their authorities to assist them in their work. Yet all the available evidence suggests that the job of the modern-day councillor is just as under-resourced and, by implication, under-valued in terms of administrative and organizational support as it is financially. Some of this evidence derives from the postal questionnaire survey of aspects of local authorities' political organization (Widdicombe Committee, Research Vol. I, 1986, pp. 75–81). But much the most comprehensive information is contained in two surveys of *Support Services for Councillors* carried out on behalf of the Association of Councillors: the first in 1980 by the School for Advanced Urban Studies (SAUS) at the University of Bristol, and published as the Thomas Report (1982); and the second in 1985, published in the form of a report by Peter Arnold and Ian Cole (1987).

It is a summary of the findings of this 1985 follow-up survey that are represented in Table 21. The survey focuses

Service	All authorities %	Shire districts %	Counties %	Metrop. Districts plus London %
Secretarial support services				
Secretarial services for *all* members	45	37	71	75
Secretarial services for *some* members	51	60	26	29
Photocopying service provided	82	79	89	93
Filing service provided	36	32	42	55
Provision of accommodation				
Office for leader	56	35	87	98
Office for leader of opposition	35	16	68	76
Office for committee chairmen	14	5	36	40
Lounge for all members	49	39	92	71
Interview room for all members	23	21	22	36
Surgery accommodation provided (1980 only)	39	28	37	79
Home- and self-support services				
Headed stationery	63	54	92	87
Pre-paid envelopes	30	20	61	58
Standard enquiry forms	24	21	14	47
File cabinet at home	7	4	8	24
Part/all telephone installation costs	37	29	44	71
Part/all telephone rental	43	35	53	78
Part/all telephone calls	26	24	25	38

Service	All authorities %	Shire districts %	Counties %	Metrop. Districts plus London %
Information services				
Summary of all committee decisions available (1980 only)	10	7	13	9
Press cutting service provided for all members	27	22	44	35
Research facility for members	18	15	22	33
Information on new legislation provided	61	59	61	69
Training and organization				
Members' training budget	53	49	67	58
Base	310	230	36	44
% of all contacted authorities	75%	77%	80%	64%

Source: Association of Councillors, 1985, pp.50-6.

Table 21 *Support services for councillors, by type of authority (1985)* (English authorities only)

on the principal areas of work in which the Thomas Committee felt elected members were most in need of systematic support, and about which it had made some twenty-two specific recommendations: administrative and secretarial services, accommodation, home-based provisions, and organizational arrangements. But despite these recommendations and despite the considerable publicity that the Committee had given to the whole issue of member support services, the 1985 survey found few signs of any substantial improvement in provision:

The evidence . . . suggests quite clearly that the recommendations made in 1982 have been implemented in a half-hearted manner by many responding authorities, and in many there is a definite need to return to basics.   (Association of Councillors, 1985, p. 14)

As for the 25 per cent of non-responding authorities, one can only presume that their record is likely to be, if anything, poorer still. There were, for example, 4 per cent of the surveyed authorities who reported making no secretarial provision of any kind for even their Mayor/Chairman and leading members, and also 4 per cent in which even members' official phone calls are not free of charge – figures that would most probably be increased, were the information available from the non-respondents.

As in the survey, secretarial services were confined mainly to correspondence (93 per cent) and photocopying (82 per cent); only just over a third of authorities offer a filing service and about the same proportion an answerphone service. As with just about all these survey figures, provision tends to be relatively more extensive in the large, urban (and predomi-nantly Labour-controlled) authorities, and lower in the shire districts. The shire counties and, on the evidence of the Widdicombe data, the Scottish regions tend, although not invariably, to fall between the two extremes. Office accom-modation, where any is provided, seems to be limited almost entirely to members holding formal positions, and there is still a majority of all authorities on which there is not even a lounge to which members can retire, let alone a dining room in which they can eat. In neither of the Association of Councillors' surveys, unfortunately, were any questions inclu-ded about the existence, for example, of childcare facilities, or arrangements for the disabled, but the impression we formed from our Widdicombe interviews in over 100 author-ities was that in very few indeed have such issues, in the context of member support, even been considered.

Home support services, which were given particular emph-asis in the Thomas Report, appear to have improved slightly over the past five years, but less than two-thirds of author-ities, for instance, issued headed stationery and less than one-third pre-paid envelopes for the use of their councillors. This absence of provision can obviously have financial implications for the members concerned, as can the still widespread lack of assistance with what Arnold and Cole term 'the elected member's chief aid, the telephone', in the form of installation and rental costs. It is a fact that often passes unrecognized even by officers who come into daily contact with members, but, as the authors of the 1985 survey note:

In 1982 the Thomas Committee remarked that 'most councillors bear both the *workload* and the *majority of costs* of dealing with enquiries, correspondence and other work'. This appears to have altered little in 1985. (Association of Councillors, 1987, p. 53 – emphasis in original)

The similarly low overall level of information and research provision can also have at least an indirect cost effect, members having to spend more time or to work less efficiently or productively than they otherwise would have.

With this relatively low level of provision of even quite tangible support services, it is perhaps not surprising to learn that barely a half of the surveyed authorities had an identifiable members' training budget, and less than one in five a Members' Service Unit. The Association of Councillors sees this latter facility as constituting the key to any significant extension of members' support services in the future, and have recommended that:

Every local authority should establish a properly staffed and adequately financed Members' Services Unit to provide and co-ordinate support services for elected members. The Unit should be made responsible in line management terms to the chief executive officer, or other nominated officer. (Association of Councillors, 1987, pp. 14–15)

'Hear! Hear! And not before time!', one can almost imagine Eugene Hasluck concurring. There must be some doubt as to whether his intemperate observations about councillors with which we opened this chapter were fully justified even at the time he was writing. The evidence that we have summarized in this chapter suggests that, by comparison with their predecessors of half a century ago, today's councillors are better trained and educated, more committed, immensely harder working and more demanding, and, above all, more electorally accountable. They are, on the other hand, much less socially and occupationally representative than they might be, and, on the whole, poorly compensated and poorly resourced for the work they do. If any councils today bear passing resemblance to a 'dime museum', to use Hasluck's graphic phrase, it is *not* in the sense that he had in mind; it would derive purely from the comparative seniority of some of the membership and from their low level of financial remuneration.

3

The changing role of officers

The primary concern of the Widdicombe Committee was the role of *party* politics in local government, and the impact which increasing politicization (in this sense) was having on the conduct of local authority business. The content of the research programme commissioned by the Committee reflected this emphasis. However, no discussion of the politics of local government in the *wider* sense (i.e. in relation to the distribution of power and influence in decision-making amongst key actors – whether or not they are elected councillors) would be plausible without a detailed consideration of the changing role of professional (and non-professional) local government officers in the decision-making process. Of all the influences on 'the council', potentially the most powerful is the group of chief and senior officers which advises the council, or crucial elements within it, for example the majority party, the leadership elite, individual committee chairmen. In public authorities the 'inner circle' of key influentials typically comprises both politicians and permanent officials (see Allison, 1976, pp. 162ff). Indeed, as Newton (1976, p.145ff) pointed out, although the 'dictatorship of the official' was not as overwhelming (in Birmingham at least) as many had previously argued there is a range of resources which officers possess to a greater degree than members in influencing decisions – not least of which are sheer numerical strength and time availability! The potential dominance of the professional officer is well illustrated by a quote from Young (Leach,

1986, p.65):

I can remember listening to a very distinguished director of housing not ten years ago, who began his address with the claim that he had never in his time as housing director in several authorities failed to get his committee to do exactly what he wanted them to do.

Significantly Young goes on to add '. . . now that is not a claim that many directors of housing would make today'.

The strength of the influence of the professional officer is further illustrated by a number of area-specific case studies of decision-making in a range of different local services such as land-use planning (Dennis, 1970; 1972) housing improvement (Davies, 1972) slum clearance (Muchnick, 1970) and high-rise flats (Dunleavy, 1981). All these studies however were carried out in the 1960s and 1970s, and as Young's comment implies, by the time of the Widdicombe research things had changed significantly. As Newton shows (1976, p.187) pressures from the wider public (including pressure groups) are often mediated through the officer structure, although this is also less prevalent now than it was in the 1970s (see Chapter 7). None the less an analysis of 'bureaucratic politics' – the influence of professional officers on the exercise of political power – is as essential to an understanding of the changing role of party politics in local government now, as it was then.

Because the Widdicombe research programme was not concerned with professional officers *per se*, research evidence on their changing role was gathered indirectly rather than directly, for example in the course of interviews about the impact of politicization on member-officer relations (see Chapter 4). None the less, during the course of our Widdicombe Committee research nearly 250 officers were interviewed who, in the course of answering such questions, provided a range of insights into the changing role and self-image of the professional officer. These insights form the basis of this chapter, together with evidence from other sources, notably Young (1987), Laffin and Young (1985), Stewart (1986) and Alexander (1982).

A strong impression formed during our research interviews and elsewhere (see for example Laffin and Young,

1985; Young, 1987) is that in the town and county halls of Britain there is a feeling of increasing *beleagueredness* amongst chief and senior officers. Laffin and Young (1985, p.40) write that 'officers at both junior and senior levels are finding it increasingly difficult to gain the professional satisfactions for which they originally entered local government'. Our research interviews conveyed a similar impression, particularly in the urban areas.

The sources of the challenge to professionalism

There are a number of different factors which lie behind this sense of beleagueredness and loss of job satisfaction. At the time of publication of the Widdicombe Report in June 1986 over ten years had elapsed since Tony Crosland's famous dictum that 'the party is over', and seven years had elapsed since the election of a Conservative government committed to 'rolling back the frontiers of the state'. In that decade there have been few chief officers who have not experienced pressure from some or all of the following sources:

1 *Public scepticism about professionalism*
A growing challenge to the omnipotence of professional expertise and to the credibility of professional advice, from central and local government politicians and the wider public.

2 *Erosion of professional domains*
An erosion (or threatened erosion) of their domain of responsibility for the direct provision of public services.

3 *Reduced professional problem-solving capacity*
A growing gap between the societal problems which they are expected to deal with, and their perceived capacity (including – but not compromising – financial resources) for dealing with them. This element is linked to and often a cause of 'public scepticism' (see above).

4 *Politicization of professional roles*
A growing predisposition amongst local politicians of all parties to challenge the customary division of responsibilities between members and officers (i.e. a blurring of the professional/managerial and political roles in local govern-

ment). This challenge can take a variety of forms.

5   Staff management and motivation problems
The increasing difficulty of managing and motivating staff
in a period when promotion opportunities have become
significantly reduced, and there has been an increasing
predisposition amongst junior staff to become more politicized and trade unionized.

All these pressures are likely to be subject to further
intensification following the 1987 general election result.
Collectively they have already contributed to the erosion of
the self-confidence and motivation of many chief and senior
officers.

The pressures have not however impinged uniformly upon
the different professional groups. As we shall see there are
some professional skills, for example public sector accountancy and entrepreneurial approaches to economic development, which have been seen as central to new political
priorities and have typically become highly valued. It is
particularly in the welfare-oriented profession and quasi-
professions – social work, educational administration and
housing management – together with land-use planning,
that the pressures have been most strongly felt. It is not the
fact of change as such that has been destabilizing and
demoralizing. Good officers thrive (up to a point) on the
challenge of changing problems and opportunities. It is
rather that, in these fields, many of the legislative changes
involved have been seen as irrational (i.e. not related to a real
understanding of the problem) and piecemeal. Most importantly, they are seen as impositions from a central government which has little basic sympathy with the concept of a
local authority as a relatively autonomous multi-purpose
service-providing agency *per se,* and which is looking with
increasing commitment towards alternative institutional
arrangements. In such circumstances, it is hardly surprising
if crisis management becomes the norm, long-term planning
appears futile, and sheer survival, or at best 'holding on to
what we have' replaces a commitment to service development
and innovation.

It is also hardly surprising in these circumstances that

there is a strong temptation on the part of chief officers to look back to a golden age when professional expertise was respected, professional advice (predominantly) accepted, new committee chairmen could be educated into the predominant (professional) value system of the department, growth in resources was the norm, and central-local relationships were consensual. This temptation is of course strongest for those chief officers who were in senior positions in the pre-1976 era; those who have moved into the upper echelons of the hierarchy within the past seven or so years tend to be much more sanguine about the challenge of operating in the current financial and political climate.

Although this picture of the 'golden age' and its comparison with current reality is something of a pastiche, it does in fact represent the essence of a set of substantive changes which have transformed the role of the professional officer in local government. Ten years ago, as Laffin and Young (1985, p.42) point out,

the basically collaborative and harmonious relationship between officers and members which obtained under conditions of growth was based on . . . the principle of *mutuality* . . . this relationship was one of partnership reflecting a broad consensus between members and officers as to goals (emphasis in original).

The change in the climate of central-local relations has been well-documented (see Rhodes, 1986) as has the impact of financial constraint on budgetary processes (see for example Greenwood, 1983), in which

chief officers who have become accustomed to the considerable autonomy made possible by growth have found it difficult to adjust to making trade-offs in service expenditure. (Laffin and Young, 1985, p.42)

The scope for career advancement amongst junior (and indeed senior) staff has become more limited since the bonanza of reorganization and the three or four years following it. The loss of public confidence in the capacity of the local welfare state to deliver the goods is widely acknowledged (see Deakin, 1987). Hence although the impact of these changes has varied (there are still many officer dominated councils and committee chairmen; rural areas where the increasing imperviousness of social problems to public action is less apparent; shire districts where the proceeds from council house sales have provided leeway for growth in other services) their reality in overall national terms is indisputable. Chief officers may have had a relatively easy time in the 1960s and early 1970s; they are in the main having an inordinately difficult and demanding time in the 1980s to redress the balance.

In the remainder of this chapter, we consider first the nature of the major pressures on the role of the (professional) chief officer, in more detail (although discussion of the politicization of professional roles is mainly dealt with in the next chapter). The effects of these changes on the concept of professionalism, the nature of management (emphasizing the role of the chief executive and the management team), the interdepartmental balance of power, and the departmental structure of local authorities are then discussed and some likely changes in the Thatcher government's third term are identified.

The decline in public acceptance of professional solutions

In the twenty-five years which followed the Second World War, when party politics nationally were much less polarized than they have become since 1980, and there was a bipartisan commitment to the concept of the welfare state, and to the spread of certain types of public good (public housing; educational opportunity; personal mobility), the position of the professional officer in local government can be seen in retrospect as relatively unproblematical. Nationally there was a political consensus about the urgent tasks for local government, particularly in the wake of the war. The legacy of unfit housing built before 1880 had to be cleared and replaced; a large-scale public (and private) housing programme was necessary to cope with war damage, household formation and slum clearance; the pressures of increasing car ownership had to be catered for through road improvements and (in due course) the provision of urban motorways; educational opportunity should be made available to all social classes, initially through the tripartite system (grammar school/technical school/secondary modern) and later through the comprehensive school system. In all these cases, the task concerned was seen as urgent (at least for some time during this period), the solution in principle as largely unproblematical, and the role of the professional advice as central and largely unquestioned. Until the later 1960s, it was a brave councillor who would express concern about the social effects of redevelopment policies, or would question the effectiveness of high-rise flats or the appropriateness of urban motorways. The conviction with which the professionals concerned – the engineer, the architect, the planner, the environmental health officer, the housing manager – advocated their solutions, the apparent technical rationality of what they proposed, and the usually unqualified support from central government generated an impetus and subsequently a momentum which it was difficult to challenge. The role of the leading councillors, of whatever party, seemed to consist largely of legitimizing the recommendations of their professional advisors, making public pronouncements which extolled the virtues of what was being proposed, and taking the credit for the physical artifacts which in due course appeared. Much of the policy impetus in local authorities came from interdepartmental power battles (Stoker and Wilson, 1986).

In the late 1960s and early 1970s a series of performance failures and expressions of public protest began to challenge the 'unproblematic' nature of the professional solutions. The collapse of Ronan Point was one of the early and all too tangible symbols of a breakdown in public confidence. The expression of adverse public reaction to high-rise flats grew quickly in the 1970s (Dunleavy, 1981). Protests about the displacement and amenity-loss effects of urban (and inter-urban) motorways spread and became increasingly effective at about the same time (Tyme, 1971). More recently, the dilution of public confidence has spread, in certain areas at least, to standards of educational provision; social services (especially in relation to child abuse and standards in old peoples' homes); housing maintenance and the operation of housing benefits.

It could be argued with justification that many of these

examples of the breakdown of a professional service are isolated exceptions, or have been caused by resource constraints, and that they mask the vast body of professional-provided activities which are being provided competently and unproblematically.

None the less the cumulative effect of such well-publicized 'failures' coupled with the apparent inability of professional officers to make much impression on the seemingly intractable problems of multiple deprivation, inner-city decline and 'problem' housing estates has led to a marked change in the climate in which the local government professions now operate. The days in which their advice was uncritically accepted – by politicians, central government or the public – have for the moment gone. The mystique of the 'professional solution' – the city centre redevelopment scheme, the inner-city ring road; the educational reorganization – is no longer impervious to political or public challenge.

Such challenges to professional expertise have of course only been taken so far. The actual design of a road scheme is still unlikely to be disputed (although its necessity almost certainly would be). Nor, except in times of crisis, are social wokers' case diagnoses. However, what is clear is that in many local authorities, chief officers can rarely now rely on professional advice as the clinching argument. It has to be justified in other terms, particularly in relation to the political priorities of the majority party, and it can be expected to be subjected to considerable probing and questioning, not least from councillors who are themselves professionaly qualified in the field in which advice is being given and who may indeed work for other local authorities or who have access to independent sources of advice.

The decline of professional self-confidence has been further fuelled by the increasing predisposition of central government to override professional advice or pressure (for example in the case of the abolition of the GLC and the metropolitan county councils (MCCs), when the majority of the professional groups concerned were highly critical of the effects of the proposals), and by the growing likelihood of success of well-briefed and orchestrated public campaigns against 'unpopular' professional proposals, which in many authorities are now much more likely to be taken seriously by the party in power than used to be the case (see Chapter 7).

The erosion of professional domains

Whatever the problems caused to the operation and self-image of local government professionalism by the resource constraints and growing party politicization of the second half of the 1970s, there was, until 1979, no challenge to the dominance of its role in tackling local problems. Central government departments then still regulated, exhorted, promoted and provided finance as they had long done. There was no question that within the constraints of the law, local service delivery was the prerogative of the local authority, and, in effect, of the local authority professions. The introduction in 1977 of the Labour government's policy initiative on the inner cities, for example, relied heavily on local expertise for both diagnosis of problems and developments of appropriate solutions.

Local authorities are the natural agencies to tackle inner area problems. They have wide powers and substantial resources. They are democratically accountable bodies; they have long experience of running local services, most of which no other body could provide as effectively or as sensitively to local needs; and they have working links with other bodies concerned. Their local judgement of needs and solutions will be essential, and in large measure it is their resources which will need to be called upon. (*Policy for the Inner Cities*, 1977, p.9)

There is almost an 'of course' flavour about the above statement. Who else would central government look to? Since 1979 however, and in particular since Nicholas Ridley's appointment as Secretary of State for the Environment in 1986, this assumption has become less tenable. The increasing tendency for central government to require activities traditionally carried out directly by local authority departments to be contracted out is well-documented (see for example Stoker, 1988). The range of services to be considered for contracting out and the intensity of pressures on local authorities to do so, have both been extended in a major way in the 1988 Local Government Act. But equally important has been the growing tendency for central government to legislate on the detail of service provision, thus constraining the scope of local professional solutions (for example the legislation on council house sales; the tightening of rules regarding Transport Policies and Programmes and Housing Investment Programmes; the proposed imposition of a national curriculum in education). In addition, it is clear from the 1987 Conservative manifesto that a new dimension in the erosion of local professional domains is emerging. The proposals that individual schools should be enabled to 'opt out' of local authority control and that housing estates should have a choice of landlord (for example be able to opt for a housing association rather than a local authority) are the first manifestations of this switch in Conservative policy. Others may be expected to follow.

The impact of these changes, and in particular the most recent set of government proposals, has been to intensify the sense of threat which many local authority professionals already felt. At the same time as their professional judgement is increasingly being called into question by local politicians, so their scope of action and (potentially) the nature of their task is being transformed by central government politicians. The implication of the government's actions over the past few years has been initially to cut the size of the chief officer's establishment (as services are switched to the private sector) and ultimately to turn his or her department's primary role from that of service provision to regulation. This change would have important effects on the role of the chief officer, diluting perhaps his professional service role, whilst increasing his managerial role. At present certain chief officers (housing, education) appear to be under more threat (in this sense) than others.

Reduction in perceived problem-solving capacity

In retrospect, the twenty-year period after the Second World War appears as a time of great optimism in relation to public policy. Full employment could be (and soon was) achieved. The implementation of the Beveridge proposals would eliminate poverty and provide 'cradle to grave' protection. The slums could be cleared and replaced with decent housing for all. Greater inter-class equality in educational achievement would be achieved. Cities would be adapted to cope with the growth in car ownership. The spectacular growth of the town planning profession in the 1960s and early 1970s (and the expectations placed upon it) was perhaps the single most significant manifestation of this optimism. In the design and implementation of the state programmes to deal with these problems, the committed professionally-based local authority department was seen as having a major role to play.

The prevailing ethos is now a very different one. Many of the major problems which were tackled with such confidence in the 1950s and 1960s now seem insurmountable, and their intractability endemic. Whatever claims the government make about their intention to transform the inner cities, there is little confidence amongst the professions involved that anything more than a damage limitation exercise can be achieved. Concern within and outside the professions involved, over rising crime rates, long-term unemployment, educational standards, the state of the nation's health, or the quality of life of the poor is no longer matched by any conviction that such problems can be solved, or even substantially reduced (see for example Deakin, 1987). The whole climate within which the public service professions operate has changed radically since the late 1960s and early 1970s. Less is expected of the social workers, the town planners and the educational administrators than was then the case, and the status of such professions is perceived, both internally and externally, to have fallen.

The new problems of staff management

The intensification of the various *external* pressures on the chief officers' role has already been discussed. (The effect of increasing politicization is discussed in Chapter 4). The final pressure which has changed the role of the chief officer, and particularly his or her *capacity to manage* stems from the changing attitudes of departmental staff. As Laffin and Young point out (1985, p. 43) staff have become more difficult to handle, as the new generations of officers joining local government have become progressively better educated and more assertive. The educational level of younger officers is now much higher than it was, following the steadily increasing graduate entry into local government in the 1970s and 1980s. Such officers are much more likely to challenge the conventional wisdom of established senior staff, who will often be academically less well-qualified, and whose professional qualification will typically have been acquired two or three decades ago.

Such inter-generational and intra-professional tensions can be more easily handled in periods of budgetary and departmental growth. Hence in the period leading up to the 1974 reorganization and for two or three years thereafter the spectacular growth of job opportunities, especially in departments such as planning, social services and recreation, diluted these tensions by providing rapid promotion and career development opportunities for new graduates. Since 1977, 'the financial squeeze has significantly increased the problems of motivating staff and maintaining morale, as career opportunities have narrowed and job pressures have increased' (Laffin and Young, 1985, p. 43). In such circumstances tolerance of 'out of date' professional perspectives and traditional non-participative management styles are likely to diminish.

This blocking of promotion opportunities has in turn led to an intensification of union activity amongst staff. The rise in assertive trade union activity amongst groups of local authority officers who previously showed little inclination to deploy it has been a striking feature of local government over the past ten years. Thus it has not just been the local authority manual workers such as the National Union of Public Employees (NUPE) and the Transport Workers (TGWU) who have turned to such actions, as in the celebrated 'winter of discontent' in 1977. It is also the teachers, the residential social workers, and *in extremis* the professional and technical members of the National and Local Government Officers Association (NALGO) generally who have become involved in strikes, working to rule and demonstrations. This change has had the consequence of making the management task of chief and senior officers much more difficult, in ways which would hardly have been conceived of before 1974.

Our interview research uncovered a further problematical dimension of staff management which directly reflected the process of politicization. There is a widespread awarness amongst chief officers that their staff have become 'more politically active'. Becoming 'more politically active' can of course mean a number of different things. It can mean, at one extreme, merely the movement away from the view that an officer's political views should not intrude into his or her work life, nor indeed should they even be indentifiable in this milieux. The cumulative strength of the central government attack on local government has probably done as much to break down this tradition as any exogenous increase in political activity amongst local government officers.

Second, as we have seen, one-tenth of all councillors are currently employed by local authorities, in one capacity or another. Given the lack of comparative information over time, it is not clear how much of an increase this represents over earlier situations (for example before 1974). But the 1974 reorganization, through its introduction of an across-the-board two-tier system, certainly increased the opportunities for 'twin-tracking'. In particular those teachers who, prior to 1974, had worked and lived in county boroughs and were thus precluded from becoming councillors, were, after reorganization, able to stand as councillors for 'the other tier' – i.e. the district in shire county areas, and the county in metropolitan areas. The fact that two-thirds of all twin-track councillors are teachers, and that there has been a growth of political activity amongst the teaching profession since 1974, certainly suggests a significant increase in this category.

Third, and most commonly, 'more politically active' can mean 'active membership' of a political party. Politically active teachers, because of their physical and organizational distance from council decision-making processes, pose fewer potential problems for directors of education than do politically active social workers, planners, housing administrators or economic development officers for their respective directors. The major potential problem stems from the fact that if one or more junior officers of a department are tied into party political networks, there arises a channel for the transfer of information which the chief officer would regard as premature, or confidential, or simply as part of his or her own responsibility to pass on. This potential problem is greatest where the officer or officers concerned are from the controlling political party, or if the authority is hung, though even links with minority parties can be problematical. Our interview research showed however that although increased political activity amongst officers does present a potential problem, it is not common for that potential to materialise. This issue is discussed further in Chapter 4 in the context of councillor-officer relationships.

A further management problem that can be created for chief officers stem from the close informal links which have development in some authorities – usually Labour-controlled – between trade unions and the administration. At a departmental level such links can undermine the capacity of a director to manage satisfactorily, particularly in relation to matters such as disciplinary actions and reorganizations of structure or work pattern. Again, in practice, although this problem was certainly apparent in a limited number of authorities, it is by no means as prevalent as the much-publicized experience of a few authorities might suggest.

These various changes have transformed the environment in which chief officers seek to manage their departments, and professionals regard and apply their professionalism. The transformation has been greatest in the highly-politicized urban authorities but ripples of it are being felt, certainly in the shire counties, and even in the backwaters of the more rural shire districts.

The changing nature of professionalism

Many of the officers we interviewed in the Widdicombe research were well aware of the changing attitude to professionalism both within and outside their authorities. In a recent seminar, on the changing nature of professionalism, a re-examination of the essential elements of the concept took place.

In the past

'professionalism' was a convenient concept for marking out the role of the officer and stabilising relationships with members. But in many authorities it can no longer service this purpose. (Young, 1987, p. 2)

An important distinction was drawn between the *'traditional'* style of professionalism and the *'new'* style. Traditional, old-style Professionalism (with a large P) stressed qualities of restrictiveness (with a cautionary and formal role emphasis) and distance. The new-style professionalism (with a small p) emphasized 'enabling skills' and engagement. There was no consensus that the new-style model was to be preferred; but there was a general acceptance that the pressures, particularly in the more politicized and urban authorities do point unequivocally in that direction.

Some of the self-doubts which are beginning to emerge and change the self-conception of the professional officer in local government are well illustrated by two of the statements made at the above seminar (Young, 1987, p. 8):

professionalism is just a fancy word. What you owe to members is simple integrity . . .

the important thing about the public service professional is not a special corpus of knowledge or set of obligations. It's rather the ability to manage in a political context. True professionalism is therefore a creative business . . .

Neither of these perceptions would have been likely to be heard at a seminar on professionalism in the mid-1970s. But the days when chief officers could confront members head on and pit their own professional authority against that of councillors have gone. There remains however the notion of a 'bottom line' – a point at which a sense of (professional) obligation is invoked against a course of action. (Young, 1987, p. 9). Some instances of the invoking of this 'bottom line' were encountered during the research and are discussed in Chapter 4.

The changing nature of local authority management

In the pre-1974 era of increasing resources, self-confident

and largely unchallenged professionalism, bi-partisan politics and relatively acquiescent trade unions and unproblematical staff relations, the management task of both the chief executive and the directors of service departments was much more straightforward, in principle at least, than it is today. The new problems of staff management have already been discussed (pp. 105–8) and may be characterized as a switch from service management to 'political management'.

The new circumstances have also however put considerable pressure on the management task of the central officer in the local authority – the chief executive – and the management team, and also brought in their wake a number of internal changes of status and structure. It is to these repercussions that we now turn.

The changing role of the chief executive

One of the major effects of the changing politics of local government on the officer structure has been to change, and potentially to strengthen, the role of the chief executive. Increasing politicization, whether in the form of a more politically assertive majority group or of a hung council, has given the relationship between the chief executive and the political leadership an even greater significance than it had ten years ago. Indeed, his or her function of acting as the main link between the councillors and the officer hierarchy, which was given relatively little emphasis in the Bains report, has in many authorities overtaken in importance some of the roles which Bains did stress, such as his suggested responsibilities for 'effective and equitable' manpower policies, and the organization and administration of the local authority.

It is significant, for example, that almost all of the 103 authorities involved in our survey had a designated chief executive (sometimes combined with other titles such as clerk or treasurer). This finding equates with that of a survey by Greenwood and Warner (1985) which showed that 97 per cent of a sample of 216 local authorities had such a post. Contrary to some predictions that were being made in the first few years after the 1974 reorganization (for example in the light of the celebrated Birmingham decision to dispense with a chief executive (see Haynes, 1978) the position of chief executive has become well-established in local government. Indeed the handful of authorities which we visited which did not have such a post were in various ways experiencing problems associated with its absence. In such cases there was always a 'designated chief officer' – typically a treasurer or clerk/secretary. But his or her lack of status (*vis-à-vis* other chief officers) and associated difficulty in acting as 'effective head of the council's paid service' in each case created problems both for the incumbent and for the authority. In particular one hung authority visited in the survey was clearly having great difficulty in coping with the hung situation. The political vacuum at the centre was matched by the vacuum in the officer structure.

The existence of a chief executive does not in itself mean that the person concerned has adjusted successfully to the new role demands of the mid-1980s. Such demands reflect not only the impact of increased politicization, but also financial constraint and cutback, which push the chief executive towards a deeper concern with the budgetary process, and the problems of declining local economies and increasing unemployment, which are resulting in pressures on chief executives to develop entrepreneurial responses – for example in relation to the attraction of new industry in the local authority.

Some chief executives whom we interviewed clearly felt uneasy in the face of some or all of these pressures. Increasing politicization, which in numerical terms is just as likely to mean the development of a party system in a shire district accustomed to an 'Independent' or 'low partisan' style of operation, as it is the growing intensity of political activity in an urban authority where parties have long dominated, is seen by some chief executives as an intrusion into the traditional and more predictable pattern of local authority administration. If this stance is maintained then there develops a growing mismatch between the nature of the political demands (explicit and implicit) on the system and the traditional management style of the authority. Several such authorities were visited, where the mutual frustration of chief executive and leading members was apparent. Other chief executives have little wish to get involved in the intricacies of the budget and remain content to leave such matters to the treasurer, which is likely to do the latter's internal status position no harm at all. Equally the legal and administrative skills of a traditional town or county clerk may not be compatible either with the recognition of the case for an authority to act in entrepreneurial style, or the capacity to facilitate it.

Thus the self-perceived and actual role of chief executives still varies considerably from the familiar *primus inter pares* (and sometimes hardly even that) to the 'policy maker and director' (see Greenwood *et al.*, 1976, p. 104). What has become apparent is that some chief executives are becoming highly skilled in securing, within organizational constraints, the implementation of political priorities. Indeed in hung authorities, the chief executive's role can go beyond this, to facilitating the political process itself. In one hung county visited, the chief executive had played a skilful networking role immediately after the 1985 election, bringing the party leaders together in such a way that the formation of an administration was speeded up. In other hung authorities the lack of such skills can result in a lengthy period of hiatus. Hung authorities provide perhaps the best illustration of the kind of skills which are currently often required of a chief executive: the ability to maintain close contact with all groups, to develop settings and processes to assist the political process, and to enable consistent policies to be achieved. Such skills are also at a premium in the rather different settings of majority-controlled authorities.

In coping with his or her enhanced political role, it is not surprising that the chief executive has come to feel the need for some form of departmental support. As Greenwood and Warner (1985) show, whereas in 1974 about two-thirds of chief executives had no department, by 1984 the reverse was true, with two-thirds having departmental responsibilities. The departments involved do not necessarily correspond, however, to the former 'clerks' departments'. The chief executive's department is more likely to be built around some combination of research and intelligence, management services, personnel, corporate planning, economic development, public relations and project co-ordination (Stewart, 1986). The staff numbers involved will not necessarily be large. But the existence of such a department does give the chief executive an independent set of levers and information services which a free-standing position could not provide. This theme of the increasing importance of the chief executive role at a time of (*inter alia*) increasing politicization is taken up and considerably developed in the Widdicombe Report itself. Several of the report's recommendations involve placing responsibilities onto the chief executive which currently he or she does not possess. All local authorities would be required to appoint such a post (Recommendation 35), and the chief executive, it is recommended, should be given a statutory responsibility for all staff appointments below principal officer level (Recommendation 38), for the detailed application of the principle of proportional representation on committees (Recommendation 37(i)), for deciding on the right of councillors to examine certain kinds of document (Recommendation 37(ii)), for deciding who should attend a party group meeting (Recommendation 44) together with several other duties of a similar type. It would not be possible to dismiss him or her except by a two-thirds majority vote in council (Recommendation 49), and outside assessors would be required to be present at his or her appointment (Recommendation 47). It is widely recognized that these and other recommendations add up to a considerable strengthening of the chief executive's role in formal terms, but as several writers have pointed out (see for example Loughlin, 1987, p. 82) more as a set of safeguards against increasing politicization than as a facilitation of the political process.

The reaction of the Society of Local Authority Chief Executives (SOLACE) to the Widdicombe Report is interesting in its firm rejection of this strengthened role (SOLACE, 1986). It is certainly true that, were the Report's recommendations to be implemented, they would standardize the role of the chief executive in a way which is incompatible with the wide variety of role interpretations which currently exist. They would also formalize many of the processes which chief executives currently operate informally. The SOLACE reaction makes it clear that the scope for facilitation and networking provided by the current relative absence of formal duties and responsibilities governing the member-officer interface is beneficial, and that the formalization of the role would not help chief executives in responding to the 'new politics'. Whatever materializes, the heightened significance of the chief executive's role is apparent both from our own research (see also Stewart, 1986) and the analysis of the Widdicombe Committee itself.

The changing role of the management team

It is still the norm for the chief executive, in connection with his responsibility for 'the efficient and effective implementation of the Council's programmes and policies' (Bains, 1972, p. 165), to work with or through a management team. The Widdicombe questionnaire survey showed that 95 per cent of all authorities in Britain have a management team. This reflects a marginal retreat from the position immediately after the 1974 reorganization, when management teams were adopted almost universally (see Hinings and Greenwood, 1975, p. 17).

The management team has never really established itself firmly as a key structural element in local authority management. Confusion over its role, and reservations about its effectiveness were widely reported in the late 1970s (see Greenwood *et al.* 1976, Ch. 3; Hinings *et al.*, 1980; Alexander, 1982, pp. 80–7). In the increasingly turbulent climate of local authority operations in the 1980s, with party politicization, financial uncertainty and environmental change seemingly endemic, it is clear that its role has changed. How it has changed is however more open to question.

One argument is that in the kind of management climate described above, the management team would be likely to take on a new significance, at the very least as a mechanism for providing group security and a 'common front' against external and internal challenges. This is the position taken by Laffin and Young (1985, p. 56).

In so far as officers have different aims and allegiances and face different political conditions, it is difficult for them to form a united front on issues of administrative responsibility. However chief officers are becoming more aware of this weakness and of the potential benefits of more group solidarity. One of the main outcomes of this awareness is the greater stress that many are placing on the chief officer's management team. The emergence of a more cohesive management team appears to be a response to the unpredictability and inconsistency experienced by chief officers working in authorities characterised by idealogical polarity and political instability . . .

On the other hand Stewart (1986, p.6), in a discussion of the changing role of the chief executive (see pp. 110–14), identifies a retreat from the management team.

The management team has survived in most local authorities, but in few does it probably retain the importance attached to it in the Bains Report. Whereas the report saw the management team as the main instrument through which the chief executive established his role, that would rarely be accepted today.

There are, Stewart argues, two main reasons for this. The first is the key importance of the political process in establishing and defining the role of the chief executive. Whereas in 1974 most chief executives, asked to define their role, would have mentioned first the management team, today most would emphasize the link with the political leadership. The second reason lies in the inherent ambiguity in the concept of the management team as an expression of the corporate approach. As Hinings *et al.* (1980) and Alexander (1982) demonstrate, management teams have rarely operated as the main source of corporate initiative nor the main instrument for the achievement of corporate objectives. Given the inevitable tension between the chief officer's role as head of and advocate for his or her service *and* as a member of the corporate team, these findings are hardly surprising.

The lack of emphasis on the management team was largely borne out in the Widdicombe interview survey. In discussions with chief executives and other chief officers about the key elements of decision-making machinery, it was rare for the management team to be mentioned at all. Other channels such as member-officer groups of various kinds, officer attendance at 'inner circle' meetings of the ruling group, and more selective and *ad hoc* contacts between chief officers over specific issues were given much more emphasis. On the other hand, in some of the authorities visited, the management team was clearly seen as moving towards the kind of 'mutual support' role identified by Laffin and Young. This development was most prevalent in some (but not all) of the examples of hung authorities visited, and in some (but not all) of the political administrations viewed by officers as particularly unpredictable, polarized or 'extreme'.

Whilst internal (or external) uncertainty or threat clearly offers an *inducement* to the use of the management team as a source of both mutual support and 'consistency of officer tone', the reality is that even in such circumstances individual chief officers may see their prospects for advancement (or in extreme cases survival) better served by other means. Strong links with the political leadership may be more attractive to some chief executives than 'common fronts' in management teams. Similarly for individual chief officers, a reliance on a close relationship with a committee chairman may be preferred. It only takes one or two management team members who are not prepared to support a management team group ethos, for it to be almost impossible for the team to operate in the kinds of terms portrayed by Laffin and Young. In addition, some chief executives may lack the necessary personal skills to facilitate the operation of the team in this kind of collectively supportive way. The costs of a divided or ineffective management team can however be considerable, in conditions of political uncertainty or instability associated with either majority party or hung administrations. Some of the most difficult management problems and morale-sapping management uncertainties were identified (in the Widdicombe interview research) in authorities of this type, where for one reason or another the management team was ineffective and/or the chief officers divided.

Two other features of significance about management teams emerged from the research. First, meetings of management teams remain predominantly 'officer-only' occasions. In only 5 per cent of British local authorities does the leader of the council attend management team meetings frequently, and of these, four-fifths are in shire or Scottish districts. In 78 per cent of all authorities, councillors never attend. In 17 per cent of authorities (including about a quarter of shire counties, metropolitan districts and London boroughs) 'rare' attendance of council leaders takes palce. These findings reflect little change from the situation reported by Greenwood *et al.* (1976) and Alexander (1982). What does seem to have changed is the *attitude* of members to the management team. Greenwood *et al.* refer to 'the suspicion on the part of many members towards the management team' (1976, p.205). Alexander reports that in 18 per cent of the authorities he visited, there had been 'a degree of member suspicion and antagonism towards the establishment and functions of the management team' (1982, p.96). In our 1985 survey, little evidence of this suspicion or antagonism was found. In so far as it was apparent, it tended to be found in smaller shire districts rather than the larger or more politicized authorities. This change can be explained in two ways. First, there is the growing political self-confidence which has been a feature of the political climate of many authorities in the 1980s. Second, it has become apparent to some astute politicians that many management teams are not particularly effective and that there is little to be suspicious of! Committee recommendations attributed to a management team *per se* are still extremely rare, but even were they to occur, most political groups in the more politicized authorities would see themselves as capable of challenging such recommendations, and having the legitimacy to do so. There is no discernible pressure for council leaders to become more involved in management team activities; if anything, the reverse is true. There are other more appropriate channels and arenas in existence through which local politicians can provide the kind of policy and management direction they increasingly wish to provide.

One of the main factors militating against the effective operation of management teams was identified by both Greenwood *et al.* (1976) and Alexander (1982) as size. Large management teams, particularly those premised on a search for consensus, were and often are little more than talking shops. Smaller management teams were potentially more effective both as co-ordinators and corporate devices, but in authorities where such teams can only operate by excluding a number of chief officers, feelings of status-diminishment and resentment are likely to result. The few authorities encountered in our research where the management team was widely seen as an important and (relatively) effective part of the council's machinery were those in which there were few chief officers anyway (shire districts), or where a 'directorate' system of combined departments operated.

Change in the inter-departmental status hierarchy

Changes in the relative status of the different local authority chief officers (together with their related professional specialisms and the departments they head) have reflected both the strength of exogenous forces impinging on local government and changes in the political priorities of controlling parties. Thus whilst all categories of local government profession have been subjected to increasing role pressure and uncertainty, epitomized by the five trends discussed on pp. 97–8 above, the impact of such changes have been uneven.

The enhanced role of the chief executive has already been discussed. In an era of financial restraint, grant penalties and rate capping, skills of financial management are also at a premium. Especially (but not exclusively) in the more radical socialist authorities, the political pressures for the identification and application of 'creative accountancy' devices to mitigate the apparent incompatibility between desire to spend and the costs (in terms of great penalties and rate rises) of so doing have made considerable demands on the financial skills of treasurers. Where they have been perceived to be successful in meeting these demands, their status has been enhanced accordingly. As Blunkett (1986, p.12) writes:

Of all the groups employed by local authorities in the past few years, it is ironically that of the conservative and often dubbed the most reactionary of all – the Treasurer or Finance Officer – which has shown the greatest ingenuity and initiative of all. . . . It has in fact been the imagination and ability of politicians together with the professional initiative of [such] officers . . . which has most protected the delivery of services . . .

Many treasurers have clearly made themselves indispensable. However in an increasing number of authorities, the importance of budgetary and financial management processes is now so critical that these processes are no longer seen as issues which can remain in the domain of treasurers. Chief executives, who are increasingly likely anyway to be treasurers by professional background (Alexander, 1984), are typically insisting on a much more central role in such processes. The structural tension between chief executive and treasurer (especially where the former qualified in public sector accountancy) is potentially increased in such circumstances. In fact, several authorities have linked these posts into the single role of 'chief executive and treasurer.'

In a similar way, the central government pressures on local government man-power levels (epitomized by the Manpower Watch system), and the increasing complexity of local government salary scales and conditions of service has strengthened the position of the personnel officer, and resulted in the centralization of the personnel role in most local authorities, although there are now some signs of a switch to decentralization in this area (see Fowler, 1986).

However because of the central government induced reduction in capital expenditure programmes, the workload and status of the local authority architect has suffered, as, from this perspective, has the position of the engineer (in relation to road construction) and the chief housing officer (public sector housebuilding programme). At county level, the switch of responsibility for development control to the districts (introduced in the 1980 Local Government, Planning and Land Act) reduced the role and status of county planning departments and chief officers (but correspondingly increased those of district planning officers). This process was further extended in 1986 in metropolitan areas by the abolition of the metropolitan counties. Indeed, abolition gave a much-welcomed boost in metropolitan areas to the status of the district engineers (who gained sole responsibility for highway construction and maintenance, and, in some cases, waste disposal) and district environmental health officers (who gained responsibility for trading standards and, in some cases, waste disposal).

It can be argued that in a turbulent and fast-changing environment, the role of the central integrative functions of a local authority (for example chief executive, treasurer, personnel officer) are in principle enhanced. As we have seen, it is the service-providing local government departments – notably education, housing and social services – which have had the more problematic and often destabilizing experience in recent years. It is they who have borne the brunt of the periodic 'performance failures' relating to service delivery (for example in the case of housing departments, council house sales and the responsibility for housing benefits). From the evidence of the 1987 Conservative election manifesto it is clear that this latter process will intensify over the next five years, certainly in relation to housing (where it is proposed that council house tenants be given the opportunity to choose 'alternative' landlords) and education (loss of control over teachers salaries; national curriculum; the provision for schools to opt out of LEA control in certain circumstances). Social service departments are faced with the possible threat of a switch of at least some of their functions to health authorities. In addition all of these departments have been faced, and will continued to be faced with pressure to contract out ancillary (and, in a few cases, main-line) services.

In some authorities where the diagnosis of the problems of local government by the Thatcher government are rejected, the council will often be supportive of the uphill struggles of the Directors of Housing, Education and Social Services, and attempt, within the constraints of central government financial restrictions, to facilitate both financially and in other ways the capacity of these departments to respond to the pressures on them. In other authorities, however, the problems of central government 'interference' and increasing complexity of task are compounded by a critical stance from councillors who are committed to extending their influence on the implementation of policy and the management of departments (see Chapter 4). It is in such authorities, which may be Conservative- or Labour-controlled, where pressures on officers are greatest.

Other chief officer roles have however changed in significance because of the priorities of the councils themselves. Prevalent amongst these changes has been the enhancement of the 'Economic Development Officer' role, particularly in those authorities committed to an 'interventionist' approach to local economic problems. As the problem of endemic unemployment continues, the role of leisure and recreation officers may in some Labour authorities also develop a much higher profile.

Conclusion

This chapter has discussed how the impact of a series of major changes in the environment of local government – including politicization – has set in motion major changes in professional self-image and management style. Following the 1987 election result, it is likely that further changes will take place during the next four or five years. In particular, the impact of the legislation which requires local authorities to put out to competitive tender a specified range of services (which is likely to be increased in the future) is likely to switch the emphasis of the management role of some chief officers from one of managing the direct provision of a service towards that of contract management, i.e. setting the parameters for and monitoring its provision of services by external organizations. Similarly in so far as the government's proposals enabling schools and groups of council house tenants to opt out of local authority control are implemented, so the local authority manager's role will necessitate larger elements of external relations, and the co-ordination of the activities of an increasing number of external agencies. Both these skills – contract management and network co-ordination – although not wholly unfamiliar to some chief officers, have not typically been stressed in the professional or post-professional management courses undertaken by chief officers. They would be well advised to brace (and prepare) themselves for this further externally-imposed redefinition of their role!

4
Councillor-officer relations

In the previous chapter, a number of different ways in which the concept and practice of professionalism have been subjected to an increasing degree of challenge within local government were discussed. One of the most important sources of this challenge has been the growth in political assertiveness, which has been a major feature of the wider process of party politicization (discussed in Chapter 1) experienced over the past decade. Political assertiveness has impinged upon the operations of British local authorities in various ways, of which two are singled out as of particular significance here. First, it has put a considerable strain upon the formal machinery used to process local authority business, rendering some arenas and processes largely obsolete, transforming the role of others, and in yet other cases, setting in motion the search for newer more politically sensitive mechanisms. These issues are dealt with in Chapter 6. Second, it has profoundly affected the climate of member-officer relations. The ways in which it has done so form the substance of this chapter.

What has happened is that, over the past decade, local politicians of all the major parties have wanted to become 'more involved in running the authority', which can mean a number of different things. In particular, it can mean a greater involvement in policy implementation; in the management of an authority; or in the procedural mechanisms through which the business of an authority is transacted. Or it can involve attempts to draw officers more directly into political arenas and processes. In any particular authority, it may involve any combination of these four elements, including *in extremis*, all four.

Such attempts at greater involvement have not, of course, proceeded without controversy. The countervailing forces of political assertiveness and professional or departmental resistance (to what is often viewed as unwarranted political pressure for changes in existing practices governing member-officer relations) has led to uncertainty and tension on the part of many senior officers in many authorities: frictions between officers and members in several: and overt conflict in a few. As Young (1987, p.1) has written:

At the heart of the British system of local government lies a delicate and subtle relationship: between the lay elected councillor and the full-time professional adviser/manager. That relationship works well in times of stability and mutual understanding, when the boundaries of the respective roles are accepted. At times of rapid change and political polarisation, it comes under strain, and its inherent ambiguities and tensions come to the fore. We live today in such times.

In this chapter we use evidence from the Widdicombe political organization research and other sources to identify the major aspects of member-officer interaction though which these ambiguities and tensions are experienced, the different assumptions and expectations underlying them, and the principles upon which a new set of understandings might be constructed. The fourfold distinction identified above between management, implementation and procedural issues, and officer involvement in political processes provides a useful starting point.

To illustrate, however, the magnitude of the changes involved, it may be useful to provide a brief 'ideal type' portrait of the ways in which member-officer relations operated in the early 1970s in Milltown, a totally fictitious county borough in the North of England. Athough Milltown was in many ways typical of such county boroughs, there were even then several important exceptions to its pattern of operation, and the inevitable oversimplifications involved in the portrait presented mean that it should be interpreted as an illustration only. However, its usefulness as a benchmark against which the current situation can usefully be contrasted was apparent from the frequency with which the different elements within it were referred to – spontaneously if selectively – by those officer (and councillor) respondents in our survey, whose careers stretched back to that period. As a composite picture of the way things used to be it was widely recognized. It was also not infrequently upheld nostalgically by such respondents as a representation of the way things *ought* to be.

The political organization of Milltown in 1972

In Milltown, by 1972, party politics dominated the council, in that almost all councillors were overtly affiliated to a political party. Political control swung periodically from Labour to Conservative, with the former predominating. However, in Milltown the worlds of party politics and professional/ bureaucratic expertise were kept separate to a large extent, coming together only in carefully-controlled ways, such as the formal meetings of committee and council, the pre-committee briefings of the chairman and vice-chairman, and the formal responses to requests for information from individual councillors (which would routinely be copied to the relevant chairman). In addition there was an informal weekly meeting between the council leader (i.e. the leader of the majority party) and the town clerk, and occasionally, if a crisis of sufficient magnitude presented itself, a meeting between the 'inner circle' of majority party politicians, and the town clerk and other leading officials (management teams were – in Milltown and elsewhere – thin on the ground in 1972).

Apart from the formal meetings of the authority, and pre-arranged visits by leading members to consult with the town clerk or other chief officer, little was seen of members around the town hall. Indeed, we are told in 1985 in one metropolitan district: 'until recently, members were not encouraged to come into the town hall, except for formal meetings, or by appointment'. Attendance by officers at either majority or minority party group meetings was never requested, and would have been strongly contested by the town clerk if it had. In so doing, he would have used the protection of the 'purple book' (The *Scheme of Conditions of Service for Administrative, Professional and Technical Staff:* para. 70(c)), which included (and still includes) a clause to the effect that officers should not be expected to attend party group meetings. Nor would officers have taken kindly to the idea of providing help in drafting manifestos, although they had on occasions been prepared to remind members of the party currently in control of some of their more tangible achievements since the last election (for example numbers of council houses built; major redevelopment schemes completed; increase in number of home helps, etc.)

Officers of Milltown at senior levels were expected to adopt a position of strict political neutrality, in the sense that they should be able to demonstrate the ability to serve either major party (the Liberals were not, at the time, a significant force in Milltown). Officers at all levels should preferably not, it was felt, be active members of a political party; if they were, it was of less concern if they were politically active *outside* the authority in which they worked. In the limited number of cases where officers were politically active locally, they accepted that it was vital that they kept their working life and political life scrupulously separate. On no account would the unauthorized divulgence by politically active officers of 'draft' departmental policy documents or schemes, or detailed information held within a department have been tolerated, outside the formal channels or arenas. As one shire district chief executive responded when asked about political activity of junior officers in his authority 'Not if I catch 'em, they aren't.'

In Milltown, there existed detailed, long-standing and largely unquestioned procedures for the transaction of council business, embodied in a set of standing orders which, although capable of modification or suspension, gave the impression of permanency and unchallengeability. Within these standing orders, provisions for the delegation of specified types of decision from council to committee, and from committee to chief officer were set out. In any dispute about members' rights to operate in new ways, the standing orders would be solemnly invoked by the town clerk, and it was a brave member who would persist with his challenge. The standing orders did not contain details of the procedures whereby committee agendas were drawn up, and committee reports produced. It was not felt in Milltown that this was necessary. Such matters were governed by tradition and sustained by general acceptance. It was an acknowledged right of chief officers to draw up the agendas for the committees. There was however a mechanism whereby a chairman (or vice chairman) coud request that certain items be included on an agenda, and such requests were normally acceded to. The responsibility for drafting committee reports, and for the nature of the recommendations contained therein, also rested solely with the relevant officer (although experienced officers would bear in mind – in tone and language – the political views of the party in power, when drafting reports and framing recommendations).

In Milltown, there was an accepted procedure whereby chief officers provided a briefing for their committee chairman and vice-chairman, a few days prior to the committee meeting. At this brief meeting, the chief officer guided the chairman and vice-chairman through the agenda, advising them on how best to deal with each item, including warnings of possible difficult questions (and how best to handle them). The chairman then went through the agenda at the party group meeting of his committee colleagues immediately before the formal committee, using his or her authority (backed up) occasionally with the threat of disciplinary procedures to persuade recalcitrant colleagues of the right course of action.

At the committee meeting itself, officers almost always presented the reports and answered questions on them. The chairman chaired the discussions and encouraged the committee to take decisions in line with the officer recommendations. Usually they did so, and on the rare occasions when they did not, the officer would have had prior warning of this from the chairman before the committee meeting.

Standing orders of Milltown council contained a clause to regulate the way in which requests for information from members were dealt with. It was established that members (of both parties) should channel their information requests through the chief officer, or, by agreement with him or her, directly to specified deputies, for specified types of information. Members had no rights of access to junior officers, nor did they ever meet them, except, sometimes, at committee.

There was a clear understanding in Milltown that members had the responsibility for making policy whilst officers had the responsibility for implementing it. Although the interests of members in matters of detail affecting their ward constituents was accepted as legitimate, it was accepted also that such interests should be expressed through statements of support, or 'special pleading' to the department concerned. Officers would respond 'sympathetically' but within the constraints of rules associated with a policy (for example a housing waiting-list points system). Councillors did not have, and did not expect, in Milltown the right to allocate council houses themselves, nor did they expect to have any impact on the way in which a service was delivered. The local authority/ public interface was the concern of the professional officer and of the (often non-professional) counter or visiting staff. There was however an understanding that implementation details which had important political repercussions should be brought to the attention of the party in power, and discussed before a final decision was recommended.

In reality, in Milltown as in many other boroughs, many of the policy initiatives came from the officers themselves. The members' main contribution was typically to modify slightly and then approve (or occasionally reject) policies which were put forward by officers, in the light of their own perceptions of political priorities and the limits of political acceptability. Even though professionally-based ideas in good currency were a much more influential source of policy than party manifestos, members typically took the major share of credit for such policy initiatives. This was accepted as one of the 'rules of the game.'

There was an equally clear 'distinction in principle' in Milltown between 'policy' and 'management'. Just as a 'policy' was distinguished from 'implementation' as a basis for the division of responsibility between members and officers, so also was 'management' distingushed from 'policy'. Management was the responsibility of chief (and senior) officers. Members were not expected to probe into the way in which a chief officer managed his or her department, unless blatant evidence of mismanagement was uncovered (which it never was in Milltown). Efficient use of resources by departments was assumed, and in a time of annual growth in resource availability, budgeting processes concentrated on distributing the growth increment amongst the different departments, in a process which tended to hinge upon the political priorities of the 'inner circle' and the bargaining skills of the chief officers, with the relative strength of the chairman/chief officer relationships an important feature. The major constraint was the level of the rate increase that was felt by the major party to be acceptable (a figure which was always lower when the Conservatives held power in Milltown).

What Milltown politicians did exercise from time to time was the right to carry out structural reorganizations of the whole authority, usually at the suggestion or with the approval of the town clerk. But as far as other management issues were concerned – for example the appointment of staff – councillors, in so far as they were involved at all (in Milltown, they were involved at principal officer level and above, which was fairly typical), relied heavily on the views of chief officers (for a deputy or below), the town clerk (for a chief officer), and the outgoing town clerk for his successor. Political appointments in any sense were unheard of. Professional and (to a lesser extent) managerial ability were emphasized, as demonstrated by previous career patterns. If there was a bias in relation to appointments in Milltown, it was towards known (internal) staff at the expense of 'outsiders'. It was extremely rare for a chief officer to be obliged to take on within his or her department an appointee whom he did not at the very least find acceptable.

It is clear, from the above description, that in Milltown, member-officer relations were unproblematical. They reflected, in Laffin and Young's terms (1985, p.42), 'the principle of mutuality'. Even in 1972, however, there were many exceptions to the Milltown syndrome of member-officer relations, although the latter was certainly predominant. One or two authorities already operated with units or posts which specifically acknowledged a need for 'independent' advice tailored to political needs, which would not easily be provided by the traditional system. There were a much greater number of authorities in which councillors were directly involved in processes of implementation (for example the letting of council houses) or management (for example the appointment of staff down to relatively junior levels) or the detailed negotiation and awarding of contracts. In a few celebrated cases, notably in the North East, and South Wales, such involvement was subsequently found to be linked to corruption (see Doig, 1983).

Since the mid-1970s, the Milltown assumptions and ways of operating have become widely challenged, in Milltown as elsehere. The challenge has not been a uniform challenge, impacting in the same way throughout Britain. It has taken place unevenly, at different speeds and in different ways. As we wrote in Research Volume I of the Widdicombe Committee report (1986, p.204):

Despite the powerful trends represented by politicisation and intensification of political debate, elements of continuity remain, and traditional practices survive. The overall picture is one of an underlying diversity, which is mediating and channelling in different ways the impact of increased party politicisation.

Hence although local authorities in which political challenges to all or almost all of the traditional features of the Milltown syndrome were encountered in the Widdicombe research, such authorities were in 1985 relatively few in number. It was far more common for political challenges to have developed in connection with a limited selection of these. Indeed there are many shire districts and a few shire counties where the Milltown syndrome has survived with only limited or marginal challenge. Furthermore, there are still metropolitan districts and London boroughs where this pattern of organization, and its underlying set of assumptions, is still discernible in modified form. But in most of the metropolitan districts and London boroughs, many shire counties and Scottish regions, and in the more urbanized shires and Scottish districts, it has become a thing of the past.

The increasing involvement of officers in political processes

In Milltown, political direction and professional advice were brought together in a carefully regulated way. In a decade when there is a new determination on the part of councillors to take control of their authorities, many of the traditional formulae for the demarcation of boundaries lose their utility (Young, 1987, p.1). Professional advice is now required in a more systematic, and at the same time more varied and subtle way, than the traditional channels and arenas can normally provide. Sometimes this requirement has drawn officers more directly into political arenas and processes than many of them regard as legitimate. Three examples of this process are discussed below: the attendance of officers at party group meetings; the involvement of officers in the preparation of party manifestos; and the more active involvement of officers in party politics locally.

Attendance of officers at party group meetings

It is now common for officers – particularly chief executives – to attend party group meetings (see Table 24 in Chapter 6). Yet the evidence from our interview survey suggests that the significance of officer attendance at such meetings has been overestimated. Details of the nature of such meetings are discussed in Chapter 6. They are rarely perceived by the officers concerned to constitute a problem. We encountered no example of an officer who was obliged against his or her better judgement to attend a party group meeting. There were those who expressed to us an antipathy in principle to doing so. Our impression in these cases was that their antipathy was usually common knowledge within the authority, and that they would be unlikely to be asked to attend for that very reason! The one circumstance where unease was expressed was in relation to attendance at party groups where local authority employees (from the chief officer's own authority) were present as observers or party delegates. It was however more likely for chief executives (in particular) to welcome opportunities to attend group meetings, on occasions when important and difficult decisions were being discussed. As one chief executive told us: 'I'd much rather be in there, influencing things, than have them come along later and tell me they'd made some really stupid decisions.'

The role of officers in the drawing up of local party manifestos varies. In many authorities, particularly the smaller and less urbanized example, the issue does not arise because manifestos, if they exist at all, are still little more than the statement of a few general principles or slogans. Manifestoism, like the attendance of officers at group meetings, is still confined to a limited number of highly politicized authorities.

In authorities where one or more of the parties does take the production of a manifesto seriously, the most common situation is for officers to play no part at all in the process, and for politicians to see little need for them to do so. As in Milltown in 1972, some majority party groups ask for details of what they have achieved during the previous year, or four years. This is rarely seen as stepping outside the bounds of the acceptable (from the officers' perspective). Nor is the way in which some majority party groups select elements of officer-prepared policy documents such as corporate plans, for inclusion in a manifesto, particularly if it is done independently of any consultation with officers.

Involvement of officers in manifesto preparation

What is potentially more threatening to some officers is a process of more detailed member-officer consultation over the preparation of a manifesto, in the form, for example, of subject-specific manifesto 'working groups'. Even in the few instances identified in the research where this form of consultation took place, officer reactions were not necessarily hostile. One chief executive interviewed, from a metropolitan district of undoubted political moderation, claimed to have been personally largely responsible for the drafting of recent examples of both Conservative and Labour manifestos in his authority, and had clearly relished the opportunity involved. On the other hand, considerable unease was expressed in another metropolitan district about officer presence at manifesto working parties. The expectation by the majority party that leading officers would play such a role, coupled with the lack of the provision of similar facilities for the minority parties, were felt to place officers in an invidious position of being too closely involved with a 'political' activity (in circumstances where inter-party disagreement existed about the legitimacy of their so doing).

However, the problems created for officers by non-involvement in the drawing-up of manifestos are also significant. First, the opportunity to inject a sense of realism into the process has considerable advantage. If a local party is made aware of the cost of what it is proposing, of the doubtful legality of a particular innovatory measure, or the likely unintended consequences of a new policy, it may be persuaded to modify what it proposes before it becomes publicly committed to it. The second point is a corollary of the first. If a party produces an ambitious manifesto, without any consultation with officers, and then finds (when elected) that officers argue that the implementation of a manifesto presents problems, the party group concerned may be inclined to perceive this response as officer resistance which is preventing or limiting the achievement of legitimate political goals. This may be true; but it may also be unjust. Proposals developed without the benefit of assessment of cost or feasibility may present genuine problems even for officers predisposed to co-operate with a new radical administration of the right or of the left.

There is thus a strong case for officers seeking the opportunity to provide advice during the course of the manifesto preparation processes of *all* local parties. Such advice would be *reactive* advice, i.e. advice not about what the different parties ought to be doing, but advice about the likely costs, legality, feasibility and side-effects of the embryo policies and proposals which are emerging from the political process. If this facility is offered to all parties, it would certainly have the effect of smoothing the transition from one administration to another, whilst retaining both the professional integrity and political relevance of the officer cadre. Whether or not this relationship proves possible, there is much to be said for senior officers taking manifestos seriously in circumstances where they are *intended* to be taken seriously. Then, at the very least, the incoming party administration can be presented with the same kind of manifesto implementation briefing paper that ministers of a newly-elected *national* government are presented with. As a handful of chief executives have discovered to their cost, political groups are beginning to adopt manifesto documents as council policy at the first council meeting after they have been returned to power (see Chapter 5). Unless the document is in a suitable form (which usually implies some kind of prior officer scrutiny) this can prove to have frustrating repercussions for members and officers alike.

Politically active officers

It is the third aspect of officer involvement in political processes – the political neutrality (or otherwise) of officers themselves – which elicited the most widespread concern in the interview survey. As we saw in Chapter 3, officers have become much more politically active over the past decade. At the same time, the unions to which they are affiliated (for example NALGO, NUPE, TGWU) have played a much more high profile role both in industrial relation terms *and* within the Labour party (although NALGO remains a non-affiliated union, whose members become involved in local Labour parties in a *personal* capacity only).

Four aspects of this greater involvement merit attention: the degree of overtness of the political affiliation involved (including the increase in 'twin-tracking' – see Chapter 2); the effect of politically active officers' involvement in local political networks on chief officers' ability to manage; the heightened impact of trade union activity on political processes in local government; and the involvement of officers on an 'out of hours' basis in the preparation of manifestos.

The increase in political activity (on an 'out-of-office' basis) amongst local authority white-collar (and to a lesser extent, blue-collar) staff was noted in Chapter 3. It should be noted that politically active officers are by no means confined to the ranks of the Labour party, although our impression was that they are most commonly to be found there. This 'retreat' from the expectation of political neutrality is most apparent when the officer concerned is a councillor, of known political persuasion in some other local authority.

However, almost as likely to have their political affiliations widely recognized are officers who, although not councillors elsewhere, are known to be local party activists. This is particularly true where, for example, they are frequently seen in the company of local authority leaders of the same political persuasion (or as district party delegates at party group meetings).

The *fact* of widely known political affiliation is not in itself problematical. Indeed, we found that many politically-active officers, including some with quite senior posts, do seem able to compartmentalize their lives in ways satisfactory to both their authorities. Thus one chief officer interviewewed described one of his senior staff in the following terms.

He keeps his political role scrupulously separate from his role as a professional officer here ... his known political activities and affiliation don't cause any problem as far as I'm concerned.

The same is often true of officers who were actually councillors elsewhere and who were viewed as operating in this way with no apparent detriment to their performance within their employing authorities. For example, the Conservative leader of a shire district council on the fringes of a metropolitan county was employed as a third-tier social services officer in a large metropolitan district within that county, which was controlled at the time of our survey by the Labour party. In neither authority was any concern expressed, nor problems identified, in relation to his dual role.

Problems can occur in two ways. First, however impeccable the behaviour of the 'politically active' officers, if they are mistrusted by one or other of the parties to which they are not affiliated, in the employing authority, then their ability to carry out the job effectively is likely to be impaired, especially in circumstances where they are obliged as part of their duties to have regular contact with members of a majority party who do not share their political affiliation. A change in control, in their employing authority from 'supported' to 'not supported' party may cause particular problems of trust.

Second, problems may occur if the officer concerned is prepared to by-pass the normal channels of information provision in their employing authority, through their privileged access to the party group or local party to which they are sympathetic. This can happen in various ways. It can involve 'leakage' or premature disclosure of information by officers to councillors with whom they share party membership; it can involve pressure being put upon councillors through ward organizations in which officers are active; it can involve officers preferring to deal directly with councillors they know in a party context – and vice versa – rather than to employ the normal channels; or it can involve a similar process operating through union membership and machinery. All are potentially disruptive and problematical processes because they involve privileged use of political networks to cut across normal officer-member information flows. Because of that, they can cause considerable management problems for the head of department involved.

For example, a county director of social services interviewed was (understandably) uneasy about the fact that one of his staff was known to be a regular attender at the informal meetings of key Labour councillors and party members held at a local working men's club every Sunday lunchtime. The director had no doubt that 'confidential' departmental information was being passed on.

These kinds of problems can occur whether the process involves officers choosing to provide members with leaked information, or members trying to by-pass traditional rules or expectations about member access to officers in the authority. They are potentially greatest where the officer or officers concerned are from the controlling political party, or if the authority is hung. However, even links with minority parties can be problematical.

The heightened impact of trade union activity on local political processes has already been discussed in Chapter 4. The emphasis here is on its effect on member-officer relations. The most difficult situation for chief officers has certainly been in those few channels where the majority Labour party has adopted a 'workerist' philosophy, which involves giving more weight to the views of the unionized manual employees of the authority, over a range of policy issues, than to the normal bureaucratic channels of advice. Liverpool, during the days of its Militant-dominated administration provided one such example (Parkinson, 1985). Southwark has recently provided another (*Guardian*, 1 September 1987). Otherwise, although there were found to be echoes of this philosophy in small groups, within the majority party of some of the other Labour-controlled authorities visited, no additional examples of 'workerist' councils were found in our Widdicombe research.

In such situations, the main problem for the formal officer hierarchy is that it is faced with an alternative channel of advice to politicians, based on a clear 'interest' position, to which it has no access, but upon which it has reason to suppose that the ruling group will place more emphasis. If that alternative channel is influential over issues such as budgetary strategy (rate-setting and rate-capping), service policy changes with manpower implications (for example decentralization) and major disciplinary issues (for example the Nye Bevan Old Person's Home issue in Southwark), it places the formal officer hierarchy in an indivious position. *In extremis*, it can also interfere with the democratic procedures through which councils reach decisions. The vociferous and indeed intimidating lobby by Southwark manual workers of local Labour councillors at the time of the debate over the setting of the budget and the rate in February 1985 was a case in point. The relationship between a district party (or in London local government committee) and a party group presents a number of role confusions and dilemmas, if local authority employees are strongly represented on the district party.

When there is a major threat to organizational survival such as that faced by the metropolitan counties and the GLC in the three-year period preceding abolition, relationships between majority party groups and trade unions may also be incompatible with the ability of chief officers to provide judicious advice at key decision points. The decision to hold a one-day strike in Merseyside, which disrupted the local public transport system, and proved damaging to the level of public support for the Merseyside anti-abolition campaign, was taken at a councillor/union meeting without the benefit of chief officer advice. It is certainly difficult for chief officers to do their job properly if they are excluded from inner circles where key decisions are being taken. Similarly, it is difficult for them to carry out meaningful negotiations with trade unions, if they know that those with whom they are negotiating have privileged access to members.

Problems created by the formal involvement of officers in the preparation of manifestos were discussed on pp. 132–4. In connection with the political activity of officers, the informal participation of junior officers in manifesto preparation within a district or county party only causes problems if he or she makes use of confidential departmental information in the proces.

The increased tendency for officers to be drawn into political processes and arenas has resulted in a high degree of role confusion for some authorities. In the case of officer involvement in party groups and manifesto preparation, it is in certain circumstances clearly helpful for officers to be involved, and it is possible, in principle, to devise rules which safeguard officers' 'detachment' yet enable them to play a supportive role to politicians. In the case of officer involvement in local political parties – either individually as party members, or collectively as trade unions – although role conflict and management problems do not *necessarily* result, there is an increasing tendency for them to do so, and a view that this area of concern needs new regulative measures.

Political challenge to traditional procedures

Five procedures which operated unproblematically in Milltown but which have subsequently come under challenge in increasing numbers of authorities are discussed here: agenda setting, drafting of committee reports, pre-committee briefings, the nature of committee meetings, and the problem of member access to officers. It is in such apparently mundane areas of activity that some of the most difficult member-officer issues have in fact arisen.

Agenda setting

There is a sense in which the refusal of politicians to accept arguments from officers which rely on 'the way things have always been done here' can be viewed as intrinsically healthy. For example, the power to set the agenda is recognized as a major influence on decision processes (see Bachrach and Baratz, 1970). Newton (1976, pp. 154ff) shows how both agendas and reports can be manipulated by officers to enhance the probability of a decision being made which is in line with officer preference. The 'mystification' of issues and real choices by the presentation of long technical reports provides one example, and the positioning of key items at the end of a long agenda is another. It is hardly surprising that the more politically-committed and assertive party groups are now demanding more say in agenda-setting processes: nor in principle is it to be deprecated.

In the more political authorities, it is now commonplace for a chairman to wish to be consulted about the contents of the agenda of his or her committee. Such consultation may result in requests by him or her to add items (reflecting personal choice or party group pressure) or to change the order of items. There is normally little contention over such requests, although it may be argued to the chairman that there is inadequate time to prepare an officer's report on the item he or she wishes to include.

More problematical are those situations in which a chairman wishes to postpone or delete an item included by the chief officer. Much depends on the reasons for the request, and the urgency with which the officer views the item. If there are no legal or moral issues raised by delay, the request is typically acceded to. If, on the other hand, the argument for delay reflects or can be interpreted as reflecting motives of political gain (for example the avoidance of 'bad news' before a council election), or the item is one which the officer concerned feels he or she has a legal or moral duty to report at the earliest possible occasion, then the chief officer is in a difficult position. He or she may do well to refer the matter upward to the chief executive (and by implication to the political leadership). But in authorities where power still largely rests with committee chairman, this may not be easy or politically advisable.

One of the examples encountered in our Widdicombe research illustrates the difficulties well. In one large Labour-controlled shire district, the director of housing became aware two months before the date of the annual local elections that the level of the recently-issued allocation of money from central government for housing improvement grants over the next financial year meant that any individual recently or subsequently applying for such a grant would have absolutely no chance of obtaining one during the forthcoming year. He wished to report the details of the situation to the next committee meeting, to ensure that this became public knowledge and that current and future applicants should not have their expectations unjustifiably raised (on the basis of current departmental literature). The chairman of housing demanded that the issue should not be reported to the committee until *after* the local elections. Against his own better judgement, the chief officer concerned deferred to the political pressure.

It is unusual for a dispute over an agenda item to reach this kind of crisis point. However, the extreme case often casts light on the underlying principle, and what is needed, it can be argued, to protect an officer placed under this kind of pressure is some kind of internal 'safety-net' procedure which takes an issue of principle such as this out of the purview of an informal chairman-chief officer relationship into a more formalized and detached arena where the effect of personal pressures and relationships could be overriden.

Drafting of committee reports

There is a parallel issue to the 'control of the agenda' – namely the 'ownership of committee reports'. In the majority of authorities, it is still normal practice for reports to be written by officers and presented to committee members (including the chairman) without any oppportunity for members to comment on or suggest amendments beforehand. In the more politicized authorities this would no longer be politically aceptable. It is becoming increasingly common in such authorities for chairmen to expect to see at least the key reports in draft before they are submitted to committee, either at the agenda briefing meeting, or at informal meetings with the chief officer concerned.

Instances of chairmen – or indeed any other members – writing their own reports and presenting them to a committee are extremely rare, though not unknown. Where this happens, if it is made clear to the committee that the report stems from a member and not an officer, and if the officer concerned is permitted to express – either verbally or in writing – his or her professional views on the content of the member's report, then this phenomenon is not viewed as a particularly worrying one, so long as it operates on a one-off basis. It is not seen to threaten the distinction between members and officers' roles.

Of more concern in principle to officers are the situations in which a chairman tries to have the content of a report modified. For a long time in the major urban authorities, reports have been written with an awareness of the political complexion and political values of the party in power. Officers would still make it clear what they felt to be an appropriate course of action; but they would write reports in such a way as to acknowledge the political goals of the majority party. Clearly this requires skills of political sensitivity and of drafting. Almost all chief officers we spoke to in the more politicized authorities recognized that it was a reasonable expectation that they should write reports in this way. Many of them claimed to have become very skilled at it. It is clearly in their interests to be so, both to keep on good terms with their chairman, and also to sustain an officer-member climate in which their own policy suggestions will be sympathetically listened to.

Hence if a chairman's request for changes in a committee report amounts to little more than a few changes of wording which affect the *presentation* rather than the *content* of the report, the changes are likely to be made without dissension. If however the chairman wishes the officer to omit from the draft certain factual details or arguments which the officer sees as central to the decision concerned, or if he or she wishes the officer to change his considered recommendations then there is a major issue of officer-member role conflict. The officer's view is typically to accept the right of individual members, or the committee as a whole, to disagree with a report, and indeed to reject the recommendation and decide to do something different. However officers would stress their right to have their own professional or technical viewpoint known, recorded and not (significantly) amended by members in its published form. In many politicized authorities this point of view is accepted by members, despite the problems it may cause for them. In a handful of authorities visited major issues of this kind were reported. The examples included member-officer clashes over report content in both Conservative- and Labour-controlled authorities.

One instructive example occurred in a Conservative-controlled metropolitan district where there was in the late 1970s a major issue over the right of the senior officers in the education department to present a report which reflected their considered views of the legal, administrative and educational implications of a proposal by the majority party to halt the programme of the previous administration for the introduction of comprehensive schools. The leading Conservative figures involved held the view that the wording of the report did not reflect adequately an expected degree of officer commitment to the proposal. The officers argued that they were merely making clear their best professional judgement as to the consequences of the proposal. In the event the officers concerned managed to present reports which made their own positions clear, albeit at considerable threat to their personal positions.

Although the problems exemplified above have been confined to particular stages of the history of relatively small numbers of authorities, they are seen as raising important issues of principle. Even more problematical was the situation reported in one or two (Conservative-controlled) authorities where 'constant battles' between chairmen and chief officers over what the officers may or may not be allowed to say in reports were taking place together with a growing trend towards the vetting of reports.

Pre-committee briefings

The dynamics of pre-committee briefings have, in the more politicized authorities, changed considerably over the past decade, in ways which reflect both the increased confidence and assertiveness of committee chairmen and (in the Labour and Alliance parties at least) the increased predisposition of the groups to challenge a chairman's view. Thus the dialogue in the pre-committee briefing is now typically a much more equal one than it used to be. The chairman will be more likely to probe the basis for the professional recommendation, and to challenge it if it does not seem congruent with party policy. And even if he or she does not, the group meeting prior to the committee is likely to do so. Hence a second feature of the chief officer-chairman dialogue is the more limited extent to which a chairman can guarantee to deliver a vote over a controversial issue. It is no longer enough for the chief officer to convince the chairman. Even if he or she can do so, if the chairman cannot convince the group, then the recommendation will not necessarily go through. It was our strong impression that the problems of convincing group members were less prevalent for Conservative chairmen. The tradition of respect for the authority of the leader (or chairman) is still strong in local Conservative groups, who are anyway less likely to meet as a group before a committee meeting than their Labour counterparts. The changing nature of these pre-committee briefings does not as such pose any significant dilemmas for officers. It may be annoying for an officer if he or she fails to get through recommendations viewed not only as professionally sound but also compatible with the priorities of the party in power. However, so long as ample opportunity has been afforded to the officer to make their case both in the report and in the pre-committee briefing, there can be little ground for complaint.

One of the innovations which has developed in several hung authorities is a system whereby each of the parties represented has a right to a confidential pre-committee briefing from the chief officer either on specific agenda items or on the agenda as a whole. In hung authorities, uncertainty about the fate of recommendations in reports is endemic anyway, and formal recommendations may not even be made in reports. The quality of committee debate has been widely perceived to have increased in such authorities, and in principle there is no reason why similarly beneficial results could not be achieved in authorities under majority control, if briefing facilities were opened up to minority parties.

The nature of committee meetings

Similar changes have taken place in the conduct of committees, where typically chief officers now play a much less dominant role. Again this raises no issues of principle so long as officers are permitted by the chairman to feed in relevant information, and comment on councillors' contributions, where they feel it is important to do so. There were a handful of authorities (in both Labour and Conservative control) encountered in our research, where some difficulties had been experienced by officers in this respect.

Officer advice and the law

In essence the central issue involved in agenda-setting, report-writing, pre-committee briefing and committee conduct is the same. What officers want is the opportunity to make clear what their views on a particular policy proposal are, and to ensure that all relevant information is considered before a decision is taken. If these criteria are met, it is rare to find an officer who does not acknowledge the right of a committee to turn down a recommendation, or decide to do something different from what the officer feels ought to be done, so long as the consequences of so doing are made clear, and are on public record. This last requirement is not merely a reflection of professional pride. It can relate to a much more tangible problem: the possibility of officers being held legally responsible for a council decision which is not within the law. In an age of rate-capping, creative accounting and radical policy initiatives, this is by no means as unlikely an outcome as it would have been ten years ago. The considerable increase in the extent to which authorities have sought counsel's opinion about the legality of particular proposals or activities (see Loughlin, 1986a, pp. 193ff) is a clear indication of this change.

On the face of it, such a requirement from officers does not seem unreasonable, nor does it appear to pose problems in principle for the controlling party. In practice, just as national governments do not always welcome assessments of the consequences of their policies being made publicly avaiable, nor the publication of professional advice which raises questions about such policies, so controlling parties of local authorities may experience similar qualms. A report, or public statement by an officer which contains such evaluative material is likely to make it more difficult for a controlling party to get a controversial policy through, or at least to justify it in public. Such reports are seen as providing ammunition for the opposition and the press, and (sometimes) as demonstrating insufficient commitment to serving the party in power (as in the comprehensive school example discussed on p. 142). In particular, in metropolitan (and some shire) districts, where local elections take place three years in four, the electoral implications of proposals which results in a moral victory for the opposition or a bad press are a matter of great concern. An officer's report or statement which is seen as a potential contribution to such an outcome is hardly likely to be welcomed.

This issue came to a head in a number of authorities who were facing rate-capping in 1985, when there was a real question mark about the legality of some of the political options being considered. In one rate-capped Labour-controlled metropolitan district visited in the course of the Widdicombe research, the authority had recently been considering various policy options in response to the situation including refusing to set a legal rate by the time this was legally required. At the policy and resources committee meetings at which such options were discussed, the three central chief officers of the authority insisted that they should be permitted in each report presented on the subject to spell out the full legal, financial and other implications of the proposed options, so that all committee members would be aware of the effects of what they were committing themselves to. After some hesitation on the part of the leading majority party members, this was accepted.

This example illustrates a more general issue concerning the relationship between members and officers in situations where the legality of the ruling party's preferred course of action is in question. In most authorities it is still the case that, on the rare occasions when an issue of potential illegality is raised, members would quickly draw back on the receipt of officer advice that a proposed course of action might be illegal. In the more highly politicized authorities, however, the role of legal advice from officers operates rather differently. In such authorities, of both Labour and Conservative majority control, the chief officers concerned are often expected to 'push the law to its limits' in trying to find ways of enabling majority groups to achieve political priorities. In most cases, officers are prepared to act in this kind of way: indeed they would find themselves in an uncomfortable position if they did not. What they would expect in return, and usually receive, is an acceptance from the majority party that if after a serious search for 'legal' ways of implementing a policy, none can be found by the officers, that advice will be accepted and followed. In a few cases the majority group has not been prepared to follow such advice. In this case the fall-back position for officers is to make it clear, in documented form, to full council the nature of their advice, and their assessment of the legal risks of the majority group's intended action. There is also an increasing tendency in such circumstances to seek counsel's advice. As Carvel (1985, p. 126) shows, GLC officers sought Tory counsel under a Labour administration, and vice versa just to be on the safe side!

Member access to officers

The final procedural issue which has experienced significant change is the pattern of member access to officers. The way in which member access was channelled uncontroversially through the chief officer in Milltown (and elsewhere) has already been noted. The access of members to officers in most authorities still operates in accordance with established precedents which involves the member channelling any requests for information through certain specified departmental officers. Although in many cases such patterns are informal and traditional, in about one-third of all authorities access is governed by more formal rules or conventions. (Indeed, it is surprising that in metropolitan districts and counties and London boroughs, the proportion rises to 58 per cent.) However, this pattern has begun to change. It is becoming increasingly common for members to expect free access to whomsoever they wish to talk to in a department, rather than to feel obliged to operate through a chief officer. Pressures of this kind are hard to resist, unless the chief officer concerned knows that a member is contravening his own group's informal rules on such matters. In Scotland the usual pattern remains one of 'free and equal access to any officer of all members'.

Although there is an impression that chief officers experiencing this change would in most cases prefer the more traditional arrangements, most of them argued that the new practice did not really pose serious problems. If relations between the chief officer and committee members – in particular the chairman – are co-operative anyway, and if the department has a cohesive culture which ensures consistency in the information which was passed on to (or withheld from) councillors, then there is no reason why member access should not be broadened in this way. Problems occur only if either or both of these conditions do not apply. If the relationship between a chief officer and, for example, his chairman is a difficult one, and the latter feels he is not getting the co-operation or information he can reasonably expect from the former then he may well wish to tap other sources of information within a department. This would clearly be threatening to the chief officer whose own position in relation to the chairman would be undermined by his own lack of ability to control information flows to the chairman.

Second, if the departmental culture is a divided one, with conflicts existing between different sections within it which are known to the leading committee members, there may again be a temptation to by-pass the chief officer to tap 'alternative sources' of information or advice further down the departmental hierarchy (particularly if such sources are known to be political activists, or sympathizers with the policies of the party in power).

In this situation there are possible remedies open to the chief officer. He can appeal via the chief executive/council leader channel in an attempt to have the member(s) in question informally restrained or disciplined. This would only be successful if the practice of the member was out-of-line with informal majority group norms. Alternatively, he could try to reconstruct the relationship with the chairman so that the latter felt less need to obtain information through alternative channels.

The context of pressures for procedural change

Political pressures to re-assess and change established procedures concerned with agendas, reports, briefings and committees can be seen on the one hand as a legitimate attempt to 'clawback' power from the officer bureaucracy. As Young (in Leach, 1986, p.65) has put it:

Looking at the history of local government over the last hundred and fifty years, there have been periods of tension and crisis in member-officer relationships and then periods when conventions have been established which were then followed for a long time. There is a sense in which we went through a relatively cosy period in the years of post-war growth, but the stresses have begun to show again recently. There is at present an element of 'clawing back power' on the part of the elected member . . .

There is no doubt that the domination by officers of the kind of procedures discussed in this section were out of line with the spirit of local democracy. In some cases this was because members were content to go along with an officer-dominated culture; in others however we heard evidence from councillors of obstructiveness, with officers subtly resisting attempts by local politicians to redefine and extend (within legitimate boundaries) their political role. It is important to acknowledge that member-officer friction is by no means always attributable to unreasonable member demands.

On the other hand, there was also clear evidence of the new political assertiveness raising genuine dilemmas for officers, who in a limited number of cases felt (understandably in our view) that their 'bottom-line' (see Young, 1987h, p.9) was being threatened by political demands which were incompatible with the integrity of their positions. The examples quoted earlier in relation to housing improvement grants, the switch away from comprehensive school policy, and the delay in setting a rate all in different ways represented such dilemmas. Some were resolved satisfactorily. Others were not. The worry for officers is that a concession, over a point of principle, such as the right to include relevant information in a report, may set a precedent which it is difficut to reverse.

The rejection of an old set of rules or understandings as outdated does not mean that *some* pattern of rules or misunderstandings is not essential, if councils are to operate in a way in which legitimate political discretion on the part of members *and* officer integrity can both be accommodated. The challenge lies in identifying the nature and form of what is required.

The councillor's role in management and policy implementation

There is an important sense in which the formal division of responsibility between members and officers does not equate with the concepts of 'policy' and 'management' (or 'administration') respectively. If all that committees were really concerned with was policy, why should so many committee agendas still be cluttered with minor items, involving matters such as junior staff appointments, expenditures of small amounts of money and the applications of policies in ways which could on the face of it be easily dealt with by officers or managers?

One of the reasons for this is of course that in principle and in law councillors are accountable – and can be held responsible – for every decision made in the name of the council, however 'large' or 'small'. Thus unless specific arrangements for delegation have been made it is 'the council' which decides to allocate an individual council house, to turn down an application for a house extension, or to send a particular child to one children's home rather than another. In reality, of course, this formal responsibility would be impossible to discharge without a heavy reliance upon paid officials. Thus the provision to delegate a great deal of detailed decision-making to specified officers (for example council house allocation, certain types of development control decision) is widely used. In addition there is in most councils a *de facto* division of labour, in which even where formal delegation provisions do not exist detailed 'management' decisions, although referred to committee for formal approval, are expected to be, and invariably are, decided in line with officer advice.

Indeed the detailed administration of council business by officers would be extremely difficult *without* this kind of understanding. There has certainly been a widespread assumption in local government that 'management' in terms of 'the way a chief officer runs his or her department' is the prerogative of the chief officer. But because 'textbook' distinctions between 'policy' and 'administration' and between 'policy' and 'management' are a matter of tradition and convenience, rather than law, recent attempts by some councils and councillors to reassess the division of responsibility involved have a legitimacy in principle which is not always acknowledged. Indeed the isolated example of relationships in which local councillors are involved where their legal responsibility *is* confined to policy (for example the relationship between Passenger Transport Authority (PTA) and Passenger Transport Executive (PTE), or between Police Committee and Chief Constable) indicates the potential scope for more detailed involvement in the majority of their relationships which are not so prescribed. It is noteworthy that the Audit Commission, in their evidence to the Widdicombe Committee, advocated a PTA/PTE type of relationship in all areas of council activity. Until and unless such a change is made, what councillors choose to allow officers to decide – formally through delegation, or informally through tradition – is a matter of choice or administrative convenience, rather than a legal requirement. Like cabinet ministers, but unlike boards of directors in private companies, councillors can be held responsible for everything that happens in the council's name. It is therefore hardly surprising if they sometimes take their responsibility seriously.

The councillor's role in management

There are various ways in which councillors have recently attempted to become more involved in departmental (or authority-wide) management issues, in a more pro-active sense than that of formally authorizing officer recommendations about (for example) detailed expenditure items. Some stem from the political priorities of the right; others from those of the left. For example, particularly, but not wholly, in Conservative-controlled authorities there has developed over the past decade a strong commitment to a philosophy of 'value for money' or 'efficiency in service provision'. In operationalizing this philosophy, Conservative-controlled councils have become increasingly liable to initiate detailed investigations into the internal management processes of an authority or department. In the former case, external management consultants would normally be used: in the latter, the task may be carried out internally (i.e. by some unit within the authority) or by consultants.

In principle, it is difficult to argue against the right or reasonableness of members to initiatiate such investigations, particularly if they have evidence of inefficiency or ineffectiveness, in a department or authority's performance. Nor in principle can objections to the use of management consultants easily be sustained, particularly if there is not the internal capability within the authority concerned to carry out the task. Such investigations certainly make chief officers uneasy. Chief officers will invariably claim that resources are utilized efficiently and effectively in their departments (and indeed that more resources are needed for the job to be done properly) and will resist any implication that this is not the case. But 'management' investigations of this kind can hardly be regarded as undue interference. The major objections to this practice, other than an overall distaste for it reported in our Widdicombe research were of two types. Either officers felt that the basis of the investigation was not founded on objective evidence, but was rather the result of assumption, whim or personal vendetta, or they felt that the terms of reference provided for the consultants by the majority party did not enable a fair and dispassionate investigation to take place. It was impossible for us in the research to substantiate either type of claim. But the practice involved did not in itself appear to raise major role conflicts. After all it is not the members themselves who are assessing the management capabilities of their chief officers. They are merely setting such assessments in motion.

Indeed far more justifiable in our view was the concern of a small number of officers in the survey who were experiencing the problem of the full-time committee chairman who could not himself or herself distinguish between legitimate political issues and management issues. Such councillors were few in number; could be from any or no political party; and were just as likely to be encountered in small rural authorities as in large urban councils. They were typically retired, or unemployed, and either had their own office adjacent to that of the chief officer, or spent considerable amounts of time in or around the office of the latter. In a few cases, the tendency on the part of the chairman to take over or duplicate the executive role of the chief officer produced considerable problems of role conflict for the latter. There is a sense in which the manager's job does become almost impossible if he or she is not allowed to manage the department on a day-to-day basis. In particular the *ad hoc* nature of some chairmen's interventions was understandably resented. Such instances, although limited in number, do illustrate the need for *some* kind of agreed division of labour between chief officer and chairman, even if it is different from the one that has traditionally operated.

There is a third sense in which members have identified what they regard as a legitimate concern with management issues. All major parties have become increasingly likely to adopt in their local manifestos policies concerned with the way the authority is run, as opposed to the more familiar substantive policies. Thus a commitment to equal opportunities in an authority's own recruitment policies, or 'responsiveness to the customer's needs' or 'encouraging and rewarding initiative or entrepreneurship' all imply the involvement of councillors in the authority's management process, if only to ensure that such commitments are being effectively carried through.

	Shire and Scottish districts (except ex-county boroughs) %	All other authorities %	All authorities %
Chief officer	6	2	5
Deputy chief officer	26	28	27
Below deputy chief officer	62	66	63
All appointments	5	4	4

Source: Widdicombe Committee, Research Vol. I, 1986, p.132.

Table 22 *Lowest level of officer appointments in which members are routinely involved*

Member involvement in officer appointments.

Indeed, a concern with the 'equal opportunities' aspects of recruitment policies is but one example of the more general issue of councillors' involvement in staff recruitment. The questionnaire survey revealed a definite pattern of involvement, as shown in Table 22. The range of members' involvement revealed is considerable. Whilst in 5 per cent of all authorities, members were responsible only for chief officer appointments, in 4 per cent members were responsible for *all* staff appointments. In the vast majority of authorities, however, responsibility ceases at the deputy, third-tier or principal-officer level. Member involvement in officer appointments is increasing, although not in as spectacular a way as some had anticipated. In only 21 per cent of all authorities was an increase in member involvement 'in recent years' reported. However, what has become apparent is the development of an increasing 'flexibility at the margins'. In almost half of all authorities, members had been involved *below* the routine point for appointments seen as particularly politically sensitive, or relevant to the majority party's priorities. There was little difference between Labour and Conservative-controlled authorities in this respect.

At the time of our research, the most controversial aspect of the involvement of members in officers' appointments was the extent to which 'political' appointments were being made. It has remained so since. Before this issue can usefully be discussed it is necessary to make a number of important distinctions between the different dimensions of 'political appointments'.

First a distinction has to be drawn between appointments which are *explicitly* party political – for example personal assistants to the leader; policy analysts serving the majority party – and those which are not so designated. Of the latter, a distinction can usefully be drawn between appointments in 'new' policy areas specifically introduced by a majority party, and appointments within the more traditional local authority service areas and departments. Finally a distinction can be drawn between senior (in large urban authorities, third tier and above) and junior appointments.

Appointments which are *explicitly* party political are still relatively uncommon. Despite the long-term use of such positions in a few authorities (for example Nottinghamshire and the GLC) in 1985 only forty of the authorities responding to our questionnaire had made any such appointments, and several of these were of a secretarial nature. The number of authorities with political appointees has probably increased modestly since. Such appointments are least controversial when they are designated in relation to both (or all three) major parties represented on a council, or are explicitly treated in a different way from 'mainstream' staff appointments. For example, if it is accepted that the post concerned is 'temporary' in that, if party control changes, the post (or at least its occupant) may legitimately be dispensed with, it is more likely to be accepted by the opposition, albeit grudgingly. Frictions are more likely to arise if posts which are explicitly or in practice 'political advisory' posts are subsumed within the formal officer structure. Evidence was found of this situation in a small number of cases. As one chief executive told us, with reference to a new 'policy unit' attached to his department: 'In theory they're supposed to report through me: in fact they invariably go direct to the members'. But explicitly political appointments need not always be controversial. The Widdicombe Committee accepted the usefulness of such appointments and recommended that with certain safeguards they should be explicitly permitted. After all there is a 'political adviser' tradition in Whitehall which now stretches back twenty years. The following example shows what one authority has achieved in this respect.

In a metropolitan district in the North of England a system of policy advisers has been devised, which is acceptable to both the major party groups. These advisers are drawn from existing council staff, and provide a varied range of services (research, progress-chasing, independent briefing on reports) for both parties. They are selected by the two party leaders (with some input from the chief executive) and operate in this capacity for one year only, to avoid too close an identification in their subsequent career with a particular political party. The majority party has five such advisers; the opposition two.

There is a certain type of appointment which although not explicitly political in the way it is framed and advertised may have a strong element of self-selection about it. Newly-established units dealing with women's or ethnic minority issues, local economic planning, police monitoring or community development are likely to attract applications from people with previous records of activism in these (and related) fields and with known political affiliations or sympathies. It would for example be strange if a post of 'nuclear free zone officer' did not appeal particularly to active CND members. Hence, particular appointments which look as though they are 'political' may in fact have been the result of a process of self-selection. There were authorities where we were told, almost apologetically, 'I know he's the District Party Secretary . . . but he really was the best person for the job.' In most cases there was no apparent reason for disbelief! Such units and appointments have tended to be associated with Labour party priorities and administrations.

There is no reason in principle, however, why the same 'problem' should not be encountered with 'privatization' or 'asset-disposal' appointments.

The greatest controversy has arisen over the allegedly 'political nature' in some local authorities of appointments of chief (or deputy) officers of major service departments. The issues here are complex and merit extended discussion.

There is little evidence that in making such appointments, members of any party use specifically party political criteria in choosing between applicants. There *is* an increasing tendency in highly politicized authorities of all political persuasions to require, in addition to the normal expectations of professional and managerial competence, evidence that applicants can demonstrate that they *understand* the administration's policies, that they are in *sympathy* with them (preferable though not usually essential) and most importantly, that they can demonstrate a *capability to implement* them. These new expectations were illustrated most vividly in one Labour-controlled authority by the inclusion, in chief officer selection procedures, of the practice of setting short essays in which candidates were asked to set out how they would implement a specified council policy.

Thus some Labour authorities do now specify in job advertisements that they welcome or prefer applications from people who are in sympathy with the policies of the council. Conservative-controlled councils are not normally so explicit, but at the interview stage it is increasingly common for attempts to be made to establish that potential staff will fit in with the prevailing style and ethos of the council.

In a small number of Conservative-controlled councils, it was reported to us that contact had taken place between leading Conservative councillors and Conservative Central Office over the shortlist of candidates for senior staff, most typcially to ascertain whether anything was known about the political background of candidates which implied that they should be *excluded*. Councillors of all parties have of course long been accustomed to 'taking soundings' from their opposite numbers on other councils about the suitability of candidates for senior posts.

Examples were reported to us of the undue influence in

appointments procedures of not only party political considerations, but also of personal and freemasonry links. But such
examples were conspicuous by their rarity. Party leaders do
not welcome – or so they told us – explicit party identification
on application forms, and many even in highly politicized
authorities claim that this practice predisposes a selection
panel against a candidate. Although candidates are increasingly attempting to 'slant' this presentation of themselves in a
particular political direction, it does not necessarily help and
may indeed hinder them.

One of the reasons for the increasing concern by councillors to incorporate considerations of understanding, sympathy and capacity to implement in selection procedures, is
the frustration they have felt, when gaining power in an
authority, at what is perceived to be officer resistance. This in
turn often stems from the fact that the policies on which they
were elected had been *externally* generated without the
benefit of comment or advice from local authority officers. In
these circumstances, the involvement of officers in the
development of manifesto proposals (referred to on pp. 132–4)
could actually help to overcome this mutual lack of understanding.

'Political' considerations may also be brought to bear on
relatively junior appointments, which are technically the
responsibility of the chief officer. One officer interviewed was
experiencing great difficulties with his chairman and vice-
chairman, who regularly put pressure on him to appoint
people to junior posts whom they knew and felt to be
particularly suitable.

One of the management problems which can arise from
this practice, and indeed from any selection procedure where
members override the advice of a chief officer in appointing
one of his or her subordinates, is the subsequent difficulty
experienced by the chief officer in working with members of
staff who are recognized in one way or another as 'unsuitable' or at the very least sub-optimal. It should be added,
however, that it is rare for candidates whom a chief officer
regards as totally unsuitable to be appointed, and that
sometimes (as far as we could judge) some unreasonableness
could be attributed to the chief officer, especially in circumst-

ances in which a preferred internal candidate had been passed over.

Policy and implementation

Earlier in this chapter, problems in the division of responsibilities between members and officers over 'policy' and 'management' respectively were discussed. There are similar issues in relation to policy-making and policy-implementation. In some authorities the traditional distinction (i.e. members make policy and officers implement it) has never operated anyway. In many authorities, the distinction is now seen as an over-simplified one and a barrier to helpful discussion and redefinition. As David Blunkett (1980) has written (see Baddeley and James, 1987 p.37):

It is very difficult to have any clearcut idea that here are two separate groups, the politicians who get on with the formulation and direction of policy and officers who are aloof from this who have nothing to do with the political arena and actually get on with implementation. And both officers and members know that isn't true; that officers are inherently involved in the formulation of policy because of the nature of information giving that they are very deeply involved in and that members are involved in carrying these policies out. And they've got to be because changing policies is about knowing whether they're working and being able to monitor and evaluate the success of what's taking place.

Councillors who challenge the officers' claim to be responsible for the implementation of a policy typically argue along the following lines. Councillors clearly have a legitimate responsibility for *policy-making* (even though there are still authorities where they do not effectively exercise it). But policies are designed to achieve certain politically desired *effects* (such as increasing access to benefits of various kinds). What counts is not only 'policy as it appears on paper', but policy as it impinges in real life: policy as it is *experienced* by electors, clients or customers. Indeed in some theoretical perspectives (see for example Barrett and Fudge, 1981, p. 12), it is argued that in many policy sectors, 'the implementation is the policy'. Indeed, the chief executive of one London borough told us 'the execution is the policy here'! Policy, it is argued, is better represented by the pattern of detailed decisions made about planning applications, council house allocations, grant distributions, etc., than by an idealized or rationalized 'policy statement'.

If this argument is accepted, even partially, then councillors do have a legitimate political interest in implementation. After all policies as implemented are (in principle at least) the basis on which party performance will be assessed at the next election. And there is no doubt that councillors are often the recipients of praise or blame for individual implementation decisions made in the name of the council, whether or not responsibility for such decisions has been formally delegated to officers. There is a strong *constituency* impulse towards a councillor concern with implementation. Yet to argue for the total dismantling of the conventional distinction can lead to all sorts of problems, because it is inappropriate – or so the vast majority of our respondents argued – that councillors should actually implement policies themselves. There were authorities where this is what in effect was happening. To combine their most questionable qualities into a representative but manufactured example, small rural district councils still exist in which councillors appoint all staff, with personal linkages and nepotism amongst the considerations used in staff appointment: allocate all council houses, and frequently ignore waiting-list criteria in so doing, with similar considerations operating to those involved in staff appointments: allocate improvement grants on a similar basis; and award planning permissions in ways which are sometimes totally out-of-line with approved planning policy statements. The problems posed for chief personnel, housing and planning officers in such circumstances can well be imagined!

This 'extreme' case suggests the need for some kind of rules or conventions or understandings which preclude or at least make more difficult the operation of this kind of councillor 'involvement in implementation' and which allow professionally-qualified officers to apply agreed criteria with some reasonable degree of consistency. However, such conventions should also recognize the legitimate interest of councillors in implementation, and in particular embrace the capacity to identify the decision amongst a mass of apparently routine decisions which is a *critical* one. As Stewart (1988, p. 4) has put it:

The routine event can become a political issue. An apparently routine letting of council premises can cause a storm of controversy if the letting turns out to be an extremist organisation.

What is needed, perhaps, is a system in which councillors are enabled to examine the implementation of policy at first hand (for example through sitting-in at council/public interfaces) and also to review (and reverse) detailed implementation decisions, if they seem to raise an issue of principle. If they do so, however, there is an implicit requirement to review also the policy which gave rise to the decision, and to re-examine the criteria which the policy embodied.

In relation to this issue, and to much else discussed in this chapter, the growing irrelevance of the traditional rules or understandings about the division of responsibilities should not be taken to imply that there is no need for some kind of rules or conventions. The challenge is to shape them to reflect the new political realities, but also to acknowledge the need for delegation to officers (in practical terms, if nothing else) and the problems that can be created for officers if they are not able to apply agreed policy rules consistently. The appropriate status of such conventions or understandings is discussed in Chapter 8.

5
Party politics

As we saw in Chapter 1 the fact that the great majority of councillors are elected bearing a party label need not automatically imply that the machinery of party organization will appear within local authorities. In principle at least, it would be possible for councillors to regard party allegiance as being significant only at election time: between elections they might ignore the fact of party and function in effect as non-partisan councillors. In the majority of cases, however, this does not occur. Councillors of common political allegiance are more likely to form themselves into party groups in order, at the very least, to share information and pool ideas and, more ambitiously, to use their numbers to the maximum advantage in the decision making process.

The creation of such groups implies a certain view of the role of party in local government. This view sees parties as more than just mechanisms for securing the election of politicians. It sees them as institutions which represent certain social interests and which promote particular policies based on distinctive political principles. In order to carry out these functions of interest representation and policy promotion it is seen as essential that the party's representatives work in a reasonably concerted fashion, which in turn implies that they are themselves organized effectively both for deciding on issues of strategy and tactics and for delivering the maximum possible vote when decisions are to be taken. It may also be argued that the traditional structure of local authorities, with their separate service committees, tended to create something of a vacuum at the centre, which the full council meeting could not adequately fill. The need for some form of 'central' committee capable of taking an overview of a council's work was urged, on managerial grounds, in the 1960s and 1970s in both the Maud Report and the Bains Report. It is arguable that the party group structure has also represented an attempt to fill a vacuum at the centre, to create a political focus of decision-making which might allow resolution of the competing claims of a council's committees and departments.

From the point of view of the party outside the council, the need for some form of effective party structure within the council is nowadays quite clear. Party activists do not expend their time and resources securing the election of councillors only to lose interest thereafter in their performance on the council. Particularly at a time of heightened ideological politics and of multi-party and hung councils, local parties expect their councillors to defend and promote the party cause with vigour and determination. Fulfilling this expectation requires an effective party group organization on the council. It also raises the question of what ought to be the proper relations between the party group on the council and the party organization outside the council.

The group and the party

The Conservative, Labour and Liberal parties all have clear notions of what ought to be the relations between council groups and local party organizations and these are laid down in sets of rules published by the respective party headquarters. However, in the case of Conservative and Liberal parties, these rules are essentially guides to good practice which may or may not be adopted, in whole or in part, by local groups. The Labour party has, by contrast, a rather more formal arrangement with its Model Standing Orders for Labour groups forming part of the party's rulebook by which members are expected to abide.

The model standing orders made available to Liberal groups suggest that the local Liberal Association should send one representative to the Liberal group, which may itself co-opt additional members of the association: none of these are entitled to vote at group meetings. The role of the local association is seen as that of an 'independent check' on the group 'pushing them into adopting a definite Liberal approach' and ensuring that the group, if in power, does not just 'drift into being a standard administration concerned with the day to day problems the Council faces' (Association of Liberal Councillors, n.d., pp. 2 and 4).

The Conservative party places little emphasis on formal links between council groups and local Conservative constituency associations. Council policy issues are seen as the clear prerogative of the group although they may be discussed in a constituency association's Local Government Advisory Committee. These latter committees are encouraged by Conservative Central Office though they are by no means universal. Their composition is a matter for the local associations: they may include representatives of the council Conservative group. As their name implies, they are essentially advisory committees, mainly concerned with exchanging information, briefing candidates and publicizing local Conservative policies. They have no rights over the formulation of local election policies or manifestos, an area which tends to be the preserve of the councillors, particularly those in the leadership of the group. There is no provision, as there is in the Labour party, for the local association to have the automatic right to send representatives to Conservative group meetings. However, some 51 per cent of Conservative majority groups surveyed allowed non-council members to attend their meetings, usually as observers, rarely with any right to vote. It is most common for constituency chairmen and/or agents to fill these positions of observers: in some cases an agent may also act as secretary to the group, recording its decisions and undertaking any necessary correspondence. In one rare instance ex-councillors, prospective councillors, the local MP, and the constituency association publicity officer were all entitled to attend Conservative group meetings though this generous practice has now ceased.

Such arrangements within the Conservative party are less formalized than those which apply within the Labour party.

One reason for this is that, unlike the Conservatives, the Labour party possesses, in addition to a parlimanentary constituency-based organization, a separate set of structures based on districts, counties, London boroughs and Scottish regions. These bodies were designed quite specifically to strengthen the party's performance in local government and their relations with the corresponding council groups are set out in some detail in the party's rulebook. Such arrangements can also be seen as a reflection of Labour's traditional desire to ensure that its elected responsibilities on public bodies are in some way accountable to the party as well as to the voters and to do so through formal constitutional mechanisms. The Conservative party on the other hand has tended to rely less on formal machinery for such purposes and more on elements such as 'an underlying social unity, a common sense of hierarchy', an 'intense diplomacy . . . of feints and manoeuvres' and a 'traditional form of conversation' which stresses leadership, loyalty and mutual accommodation between leaders and led (Blondel, 1963, pp. 144–5; Pinto-Duchinsky, 1972, pp. 12–13; Behrens, 1980, p. 4).

The explanatory mechanism which accompanies Labour's model standing orders for council groups makes it plain that 'group members are part of the local party and not separate from it' and that 'party policy laid out in the local manifesto, or as directed by party conference and the National Executive Committee (NEC) should be adhered to'. The local party is responsible for election policy, including the formulation of any manifesto, and for the selection of candidates. The local party is entitled to send representatives to group meetings, who may speak but not vote, provided that their number is not greater than one-third of the membership of the group and it may also suggest names for consideration for election to positions in the group or the council. It is the prerogative of the group to take the decisions on all matters which come before the council both on policy matters and on elections to civic offices: it is the group which may decide both on the strategy of implementing election policies and on how to react to any issues not covered by those policies. Where senior and experienced members of the group are also key figures in the local party it is possible that they will effectively dominate party discussions on council matters, thus leaving the balance of influence with the group rather than the party.

In order to ensure that there is regular liaison between group and local party, joint meetings at least four times a year are called for to discuss policy implementation and new developments between elections. A new standing order approved at Labour's 1984 annual conference makes it clear that such arrangements are the minimum required and that more elaborate forms of consultation and co-operation may be instituted locally, subject to the final approval of the National Executive.

The introduction of this new standing order in 1984 was a response to left-wing proposals in the early 1980s to grant voting rights for the local party in group decisions: in particular it was suggested that the power to elect the group leader and council committee chairmen from amongst the Labour councillors should be conferred on the local party rather than the group. Such proposals met with opposition from the majority of Labour groups and were not eventually adopted. However, the philosophy behind them remains influential in some quarters and reflects a desire not only to secure the implementation of party policy but also a wish 'to prevent councillors being swamped and becoming "bureaucrats" or being "sucked" into the council' (Wainwright, 1987, pp. 122–3). In a few local authorities Labour party-group relations are consequently conducted in such a way as to allow the local party more power than it is formally entitled to.

Our survey shows, for example, that some eighteen Labour majority groups permit party representatives to vote at group meetings although this is contrary to the model standing orders. Also in contravention are the small number of cases where local party (general committee) members and council group members have in effect combined to form an electoral college and policy conference to select group and council office-holders and to vote on major issues of policy such as rate levels or spending cuts. Such 'decisions' however, may require to be ratified by a subsequent meeting of the Labour group alone in order to keep to the letter, if not the spirit, of the party's rules. Departures from the rules such as those indicated above are required to be notified to party headquarters for approval: in practice however such notification rarely happens and the local party thus secures more power than the model standing orders permit.

Where the local party does secure a position of some dominance over the group this may occur as a result of one or both of two situations. It may be that Labour councillors, or a majority of them, see the group and the local party as interlocking components with the group as the executive arm of the local party on council matters. If councillors so define their role than they may well concede a dominant role to the local party at least up to the point when they find that it is they alone, and not their party colleague, who may face legal and financial penalties if certain party policites are pursued. However it may also be the case that councillors have initially been selected as council candidates by the party on the basis of their readiness to concede it such a leading role once elected. The most overt example of the latter practice was that employed in Liverpool during the years of Militant ascendency. In compiling the panel of council candidates, from whom ward branches would later choose their own individual candidates, the district party employed what Parkinson (1986, p. 76) has called the 'candidacy test'. If would-be candidates did not agree that the district party rather than the group made municipal policy then they were not admitted to the panel. The result was described by the report of the Labour party's inquiry into the Liverpool district Labour party in 1986: 'the District Labour Party in Liverpool has gradually taken itself powers which ... according to the rules of the Party should rest ... with the Labour Group in the City Council.'

The nature of the selection process can thus be crucial in determinining the role accorded to the local party. A rule change in 1984 which guaranteed sitting councillors admission to candidate panels may have strengthened their position in this context, though it did not of course guarantee eventual re-selection at ward level: in Liverpool in any event the rule was circumvented by placing those sitting councillors who failed the candidacy test on a disregarded 'Supplementary Panel'.

Situations such as this are rare if not unknown in the Conservative or Liberal parties where somewhat looser ties between group and local party are regarded as normal. Liberals are encouraged to submit prospective council candidates to vetting by a constituency (or district or county) Approval Panel before the ward-based selection takes place and Conservative candidates selected by ward branches require approval by the constituency association executive. In both cases however the approval process focuses on the personal qualities of the would-be candidates rather than on issues of party-group relations. This does not mean that no disputes occur or that all sitting councillors are automatically re-selected. In individual cases de-selection can and does occur, through dissatisfaction over past performance or as a result of shifts of opinion amongst party workers or through the activities of influential individuals promoting or opposing particular candidates: such events however are not normally part of a strategy to secure greater party control over the workings of the group.

Party manifestos

There appears to be a recognizable trend towards the production of more detailed local election manifestos whose clear purpose is to guide council policy-making once power has been won at the ballot box. It is possible that such documents had their origins as political counterparts to the more management-oriented corporate plans and strategies which many authorities began to produce in the early 1970s: they also seem to have become more common during and after the elections to the newly reorganized local authorities in 1973 and 1974. They may thus have begun as political responses to the various managerial and structural changes which local government experienced in the first half of the 1970s: however the intensification of local politics during the subsequent decade provided further incentive for local parties and council groups to clarify their policy aims in some detail.

It should, however, be said that the longest and most

detailed manifestos are most likely to be found in the largest and most powerful authorities, and even here they are by no means universal. A survey of manifestos produced for the 1987 metropolitan district elections found that some 37 per cent could be regarded as 'substantial', running to between fifteen and forty pages of A4 paper, whereas 51 per cent were brief documents covering one or two pages (Leach, 1987). The size of a manifesto may not in itself of course indicate the scale of its political ambitions: a very brief one thousand word Conservative manifesto for Birmingham in 1982 committed the party to some very far-reaching propo- sals for the contracting out of services, the sale of council property, the retention of grammar and single-sex schools and the promotion of a national referendum on the reintro- duction of capital punishment. The preparation of a detailed manifesto for a large authority can be a very time-, and resource-, consuming activity. The 1981 Labour manifesto for the GLC elections, for example, was a 157-page docu- ment which drew on the efforts of some 200 people convened in five working parties meeting over a two-year period. The scale of such an effort was arguably commensurate with the size and political significance of the authority concerned but it is clearly beyond the reach of those operating at a more modest level of local politics. Small, rural districts are thus likely to inspire brief, rather generalized statements of intent. This is partly because of the lower tempo of local politics in such areas, partly because of their restricted range of functions, and partly because of the limited resources likely to be available to local parties in such cases.

As the previous paragraph implies, the mechanisms of drawing up a manifesto can vary greatly. The variations are likely to reflect not only the type or size of authority but also the differing practices of the political parties. On the Conservative side the preparation of an election manifesto is likely to be largely the responsibility of senior Conservative councillors, with the leader of the Conservative group taking a prominent part. There may be some consultation with the local Conservative association, perhaps through the latter's Local Government Advisory Committee, but the onus and the power in this matter rest with the group rather than with the local party organization. Much thus seems to depend on the view which the leading Conservative councillors take as to the significance of any possible manifesto document. In a safe Conservative authority a Conservative manifesto may amount to little more than a review of past achievements and a promise to keep working along familiar lines. Thus, for exampe, the 1985 Conservative manifesto for Kent referred to 'a successful formula' which had produced 'better, cheaper but more effective ways of providing the Council's services' in past years and which still constituted 'the only sensible way forward'.

Alternatively, where the political context is keener, senior Conservatives may manage to produce a comprehensive and detailed document capable of being used as a clear guide to policy-making after the election. Perhaps the most remarkable instance of this type was the 278-page manifesto produced for the Conservatives in Derbyshire in 1977, very largely due to the single-handed labours of their group leader, G. N. Wilson. The latter document is, however, something of an exception: as a general rule Conservative manifestos tend towards shortness and generalization, at least when compared with those of their Labour opponents.

The Labour party rules grant the power of election policy formulation to the local party organization, the district, county or Scottish regional party, or, in London, the borough local government committee of the party. By virtue of such party involvement in the preparation of the manifesto the latter becomes not merely a set of policy proposals but also a potential mechanism 'for holding the party group and leadership to account in the future' (Game and Skelcher, 1983, p. 32). A fairly typical procedure in cases where Labour manifesto preparation is taken seriously would be for the local party to set up a series of working groups, including both councillors and ordinary party members, to prepare proposals for the various aspects of the council's work – housing, planning, etc. These working groups would report to a meeting of the local party which would draw up a draft manifesto for consultation with the subordinate units of the party such as the ward branches. The draft manifesto, together with any comments it had generated in the course of consultation, would then be considered at a special policy conference of the local party – perhaps an all-day event – before a definitive version was produced for ratification at a final meeting of the local party.

The example of the 1981 manifesto for the GLC previously quoted has shown that this type of exercise can be undertaken on quite a large scale. Rather more common is the example of the Labour manifesto produced through similar procedures in 1987 for the small town and rural district of Braintree, which was effectively the work of approximately two dozen people, half of them councillors, meeting over a period of about six months and which took the final form of an eighteen-page A4 doucment. Whether ambitious or modest in scope, local Labour manifestos are thus likely to be the product of a more structured process of party-group interaction than is the case with the Conservative party: Labour is also more generally inclined to the idea of a programmatic politics. For both these reasons, Labour gives the impression of taking the business of local manifesto preparation more seriously than the Conservative party, though this is not universally true.

The Alliance parties have tended to stress the importance of securing a very wide basis of consultation amongst party members and supporters in the process of manifesto preparation, with one-day conferences forming a typical vehicle for this. Given the necessary degree of commitment they can, like the Labour and Conservative parties, produce quite detailed documents by way of manifestos. In Hackney, for example, the Liberals produced a 137-page 'discussion document' for the elections of 1986.

The preparation of party manifestos, where it occurs, it part and parcel of the process of fighting an election. The work of preparation itself may be educative and enjoyable for councillors, candidates and party activists; the contents of the manifesto may provide the raw material for individual election addresses, for correspondence in the local press, for items on local radio and for council speeches in the run-up to polling day. A major question, however, is that of the fate of the manifesto after the election: to what extent do councillors feel bound by its commitments? The SCPR survey for the

Widdicombe Committee found that some 52 per cent of councillors agreed with the proposition that manifesto implementation was the 'first concern' of the elected member. This view was more common among Labour than Conservative and Liberal councillors, the respective levels of agreement being 79 per cent, 49 per cent, and 33 per cent. It was only in English and Welsh non-metropolitan districts that support for the proposition fell to below 50 per cent: in all other cases it met with majority agreement, with as much as 76 per cent support in London boroughs (Research Vol. II, 1986, pp. 76–8). To those who attach importance to the manifesto, there is an implicit, or indeed in some cases explicit, adherence to the notion of the mandate conferred by the voters on the victors of an election. The mandate confers both a right and a duty to implement the contents of the manifesto. In the words of the 1977 Conservative manifesto for Derbyshire 'a Party Group should not be criticised for applying the politics on which it was elected'.

Implementation of a manifesto does not happen automatically, however much councillors may feel committed to its contents. There are clearly still authorities where manifestos are little more than electoral window dressing, most notably perhaps where an established Conservative majority group regards an election as a licence to carry on as before. In one such authority, the Conservative leader found it necessary to ask his secretary to find us a copy of the most recent manifesto: a copy was eventually dusted off from a pile in a corner cupboard. In another similar instance, the leader rummaged vainly through drawers and cupboards before giving up the search and commenting that its non-availability probably reflected its importance. It should be said at this point that such a cavalier attitude to the manifesto did not in either case imply any lack of political strategy. Both leaders knew the direction in which they and their party wished their councils to proceed, namely a continuation of fairly tight financial management: manifestos may have articulated such strategies but were not seen as intrinsic to their implementation.

This would not be the case where an incoming majority group were proposing a clear break with previous council policy, either as a result of electoral victory or as a consequence of a shift of power between factions within a re-elected majority group. Such circumstances have occurred, notably on the Labour side, but also for example in the case of the Liberal-led Alliance victory in Tower Hamlets in 1986. Under these conditions the manifesto becomes a serious statement of intent, with a majority group committed to securing its fullest implementation. In a few such authorities, mainly Labour controlled, the contents of the manifesto have been formally adopted as explicit council policy at council and/or committee meetings in the wake of the election. Chief officers have been instructed to address themselves specifically to the details of implementation and the majority group, sometimes jointly with their local party, have created mechanisms such as 'manifesto checklists' or 'manifesto monitoring groups' to gauge progress in that respect. Such procedures may be seen as representing the most full-hearted form of commitment to 'manifestoism'. Few authorities have yet to take matters that far, and at the opposite pole are those small, mainly rural districts, where party conflict is low key or non-existent and where manifestos are rudimentary or even unknown. The overall trend, however, seems to be clearly in the direction of according a greater significance to manifestos of greater substance than used to be the case.

Party groups in operation

It is the practice of actually meeting regularly as a group which, potentially at least, converts a collection of individual councillors elected under a common party label, into an effective political force. It is thus hardly surprising that 96 per cent of the respondents to our Widdicombe questionnaire survey of majority, or largest single party, groups met regularly before each full council meeting. What this might mean in terms of calendar frequency would clearly depend on the number of council meetings a year: some groups may also choose to meet more than just once in each council cycle. In fact, 42 per cent met at six-weekly intervals and 27 per cent at monthly intervals. Labour groups were more likely to meet at monthly intervals, or even more frequently, than were Conservative groups (Research Vol. I, 1986, p. 26).

Group meetings may be a necessary condition for exercising effective political control but they are not sufficient: the essential requirement for that purpose is to secure unity within the group. This cannot always be guaranteed, at least not without effort, since groups may contain their own internal divisions based for example on generation, on commitment or ability, on ideology, on social background or on geography.

Generational differences are most likely to manifest themselves in the form of pressures from younger elements against an 'old guard' leadership whom they see as lacking in vigour or imagination. One long-established Conservative leadership, for example, was seen by a younger critic as 'lacking the bottle' for necessary radical policies: for its own part the leadership saw such criticisms as a 'nettle' which had to be grasped.

To some extent, generational differences may partly relfect different degrees of experience. However, in some cases groups may also be divided, regardless of age groupings, over such characteristics as experience, commitment and ability. A sizeable 'tail' of inexperienced and unenthusiastic councillors, elected perhaps against expectation due to an unforeseen surge at the polls, or councillors whose prime claim to selection as candidates was their availability rather than their ability, can create a difficult situation for group leaders and for the more committed and able members of the group. In the authorities we visited, such problems were more frequently found in Conservative groups with a number of chief officers commenting on the 'dead wood' and the 'lobby fodder' which they reckoned to identify. If anything, Labour sometimes had the reverse problem, namely backbench councillors who were not necessarily experienced but who were extremely enthusiastic, arriving on the Council with great expectations and determined to be anyting *but* lobby fodder.

Ideological divisions within groups have always existed to some degree but the ideological polarization of the past decade or so has made them both sharper and more visible. Both officers and councillors were able, in the course of our interviews, to identify quite clear factions or tendencies within party groups particularly in the more politicized authorities. On the Conservative side a division between 'wets' and 'drys' was most commonly recognized, though degrees of dryness varied from those preoccupied with 'running a tight ship' to those keen to experiment with contracting out to the private sector. Labour's divisions tended to be seen in terms such as right and left, or moderate, soft left and hard left. To some degree these are relative terms and do not mean the same thing in all circumstances. Some hard left factions, for example, might differ in respect of the priorities they accorded to equal opportunities issues as distinct from so-called 'workerist' or trade-union issues. Right-wingers might be old-style Labour moderates or displaced soft leftists outflanked by more radical comrades. During the first half of the 1980s there seemed to be a widespread leftward trend occurring within Labour groups and this impression was confirmed in our interviews. It was perhaps most marked in London, though not confined to that city; it was least evident in some of the smaller and medium-sized industrial towns in the North of England. However the aftermath of the failed anti-ratecapping campaign, the exhaustion of the possibilities of creative accountancy and the failure to elect a Labour government in 1987 now seem to have curtailed that trend. Labour councils dominated by the left began to find themselves with little room for manoeuvre and forced to contemplate severe spending cuts. In the wake of this, influence and power seemed to be swinging away from the hard left and back towards the soft left and the right.

If there was a discernible trend within Conservative groups it was perhaps to be found in the gradual decline of paternalistic, quasi-feudal Toryism in the rural areas and its replacement by a Conservatism more concerned with management efficiency and, if necessary, privatization. To some extent, this reflects social changes within local Conservative groups. Chief officers in two such authorities spoke of a decline in the 'squirearchy' and in 'the old squirearchical government' as professional and executive newcomers gradually displaced the old Conservative gentry. Labour too has seen social changes have their impact on council groups, perhaps most notably in those areas where industrial decline and service-sector growth have changed the balance between blue-collar and white-collar workers within the party. Some at least of the right-wing versus left-wing conflicts within local Labour parties and groups can be traced back in part to just such shifts in the social base of the party (Goss, 1986).

Geographically rather than socially based divisions can also be encountered within groups, though atavistic loyalties to the pre-reorganization local authorities have by now largely vanished. Clashes between the different priorities of urban and rural members can be a particular problem for some Conservative groups, whilst in some of the larger shire counties factors of distance can prevent group members from opposite ends of the county from fully appreciating one another's problems.

Notwithstanding possible sources of internal division, virtually all majority groups are able to resolve their differences and vote as one at most council and committee meetings. The Widdicombe questionnaire survey revealed that 92 per cent of Conservative majority groups and 99 per cent of Labour majority groups 'usually' or 'always' voted as a cohesive group at full council meetings: at committee meetings the respective figures were 79 per cent and 85 per cent (Research Vol. I, 1986, pp. 28–30). These figures suggest a greater degree of discipline and cohesion within Labour groups than Conservative groups which in itself may be seen as a product of the former's greater stress on notions of solidarity and strength in unity.

For the most part the imposition of group discipline is aimed at issues which are seen as 'party political', which is normally interpreted as covering matters of major policy together with questions of council procedure or organization which might affect the interests of groups. Individual ward issues are not in most cases seen as suitable objects of group discipline unless they happen perhaps to exemplify some major issue of party policy: the Liberal model standing orders however do positively encourage Liberal councillors to support one another on non-political ward issues, a tactic not made explicit by the Conservative or Labour parties. In cases where councillors feel unable to abide by a group decision for reasons of conscience they may be permitted, in all parties, to abstain from voting but are expected not to speak or vote against the group at council meetings. The question of what constitutes a matter of conscience is left open by the Conservatives and Liberals but in the case of the Labour party the model standing orders refer to 'religion, temperance, etc.' and Labour councillors are urged to raise their conscientious doubts with the group before deciding to abstain.

Despite differing degrees of emphasis on the proper extent of group discipline its necessity is widely recognized. To Labour groups it is perhaps a natural component of the politics of solidarity and to that extent is seen as part and parcel of normal politics. For Conservatives the necessity for discipline is often seen as a necessary reaction to the Labour style, for 'if Conservatives are not equally well organised they will be defeated on major political issues' (Conservative Party, 1979, p. 1). Liberals have traditionally preferred to see 'Liberals voting together because they are convinced of the arguments', rather than because of a group whip, but it is now also recognized that 'Liberals are not just a bunch of Independents', and that 'the cause of Liberalism will be advanced better through the efforts of a united Group' (Association of Liberal Councillors, n.d., p. 4).

Political leadership

A review of political leadership in local authorities conducted in the 1970s came to the conclusion that:

A progression can be discerned through time to the more consensual and less heroic and self-centred type of leadership. Members have recently become less willing to contract out their power to the strong leader.   (Norton, 1978, pp. 220–1)

This perception is very much confirmed by our own findings. Although it is still possible to encounter a range of leadership

styles from the genuinely democratic to the robustly authoritarian the balance seems to be moving clearly away from the
latter and towards forms of leadership wherein group
consultation and discussion are integral parts of the decision-
making process and in which ultimately leaders may feel
obliged to bow to the wishes of the group rather than the
other way round. This trend is most clearly to be seen in the
Labour and Liberal parties. In the latter case in particular
great emphasis is laid on consultation and participation as a
fundamental political good which should extend into the
practice of leadership. Thus one Liberal group leader
virtually disclaimed the status of leader, describing himself
thus: 'I'm not the leader, I'm Peter!' The Conservative party,
in contrast, remains the chief stronghold of what remains of
'leadership from the front' as some of its exponents describe
it.

The selection of a group leader is a matter for the group
itself and is almost invariably conducted by a vote amongst
those councillors who make up the group. The only significant exception to this practice is to be found in some Labour
groups. Our Widdicombe questionnaire survey showed that
10 per cent of Labour majority groups extend the voting for
group leader beyond the ranks of councillors to include local
party delegates (Research Vol, I, 1986, p. 85). One method of
doing this is of course the electoral college referred to
previously, whereby a joint meeting of the group and the
local party choose a leader whose election is later ratified by
the group alone. Such a system ultimately depends on the
willingness of the group members to abide by the decision of
the joint meeting or electoral college: this cannot always be
guaranteed however. After the London borough elections of
1986, for example, just such a joint meeting nominated a
hard left councillor, Kate Allen, for group leader in Camden:
but at the subsequent meeting of the group itself, the post
was awarded to a 'softer' left councillor Tony Dykes, whose
supporters rejected what one of them described as 'an ill-
thought-out and ill-arranged attempt to put a caucus line
through, overshadowed by the cloud of sectarian policies'.

Once elected, leaders may expect to retain their position
for a number of years, although nominally they are subject to

re-election at annual intervals. Unless there is serious dissatisfaction with a leader on grounds of competence, or style or policy he or she is likely to be returned to office unopposed. In a few authorities, however, there may be a practice of allowing leaders only a finite term of office in order to avoid the concentration of power in one place for too long a period. Limiting the term of office may however strengthen the leader's position. Thus in one safely Conservative authority the operation of a three-year term for the leader, and indeed for the deputy leader and committee chairman was accompanied by the belief that incumbents should be allowed a fair degree of latitude once installed in office.

Although there is indeed a broad trend in the direction of more democratic and consultative styles of leadership than in the past, there nevertheless exists within that trend a wide range of styles and forms. These reflect the interplay of such factors as personality, internal group politics, local traditions, past experience, and the pressure of external events. The decline of the autocratic single leader has seen the rise not only of more consensually-oriented leaders but also in some cases of an inner circle of senior councillors – other group officers or a group executive or committee chairmen – whose dual allegiance to the group which elected them and the leader who leads them can make them key figures in relations between the leader and the group. Some idea of the range of approaches to leadership can be obtained from the following nine examples encountered in the interview survey.

In authority A, a traditionally Independent council, there has been resistance to the idea of power resting with any organized political grouping. There is little or nothing in the way of clear political leadership, with no majority group and with council chairmanship being seen as a mainly ceremonial role. There is no Policy Committee: the idea 'was thrown out in a pretty big way' when the chief executive suggested that it might be advantageous. This is partly because the members are firmly against any concentration of power in the hands of a few but also because of their reluctance to think in terms of policy for the council as a whole. Indeed, it is as much as officers can do to get the various committees to set down their own individual policy priorities: the tendency is for committee meetings to be discursive, not to say downright gossipy. In so far as there is any central co-ordinating role it falls partly on the finance committee, with its budget-setting role, and more generally on the chief executive, who for example, deals with councillors' preferences for committee places and makes his own recommendations to the council meeting.

In authority B a former long-standing Conservative majority has been replaced by a hung council in which the Alliance took chairmanships with the support of the Labour group. The former Conservative leader remains at the head of the group, a very srong individual, trusted and given considerable leeway by the group, and expressing a preference for 'crisp' decision-making. This is in contrast to the Alliance (Liberal) leader who sees himself as a chairman rather than a leader and lays great stress on the intrinsic virtues of proceeding by consultation. The Labour leader is a strong and respected individual who has to handle considerable pressure from the left-wing of the group. There is no general view within the authority as to where effective leadership now lies. In each committee the tripartite meetings of spokesmen try to iron out problems and make recommendations to their groups but these are not always accepted by the groups. The Policy Committee which had a major role in the previous administation, is now less sure of its role. The general impression is of parties proceeding with caution, uncertain how far they can trust one another and engaging in a war of manoeuvre whilst the officers try to gauge where the power lies: 'We are', said one officer, 'playing Blind Man's Buff!'

In authority C politics is fairly low key and the notion of clear political leadership not wholly accepted. The Conservative majority group was used to unquestioned dominance until a recent challenge from the Liberals and had not needed to exert itself to have its own way: indeed defence of local interests by some councillors occasionally prevented any agreement on a clear Conservative line. The emergence of the Liberals forced the Conservatives to organize themselves rather more effectively but it is clear that they have yet to endorse the idea wholeheartedly. The leadership of the

Conservative group has changed hands frequently since nobody seems very keen on occupying the post. The current leader sees himself more as a chairman than a leader; the group is run on a very loose rein, tightening up only when key decisions over chairmanships have to be made at the council's annual general meeting. In the leader's words, 'we haven't got an advanced leader concept here at all'.

In authority D the retirement of a long-standing and autocratic Labour leader provided the occasion for a radical change in leadership style to one more in tune with the changing character of the group. The outgoing leader had been, in his way, a charismatic figure who attracted considerable deference. He had, however, lost touch with the local party to some degree and was seen in some quarters as too reliant on the council's officers for ideas. He was succeeded by one of those councillors who had chafed against his authoritarian style and was determined to 'open up' decision-making. Labour group meetings are now long, open and participative, with the leader resisting any temptation to 'sew things up' beforehand, despite the emergence within the group of six or seven left-wingers whom he sees as a 'group within the group'. The latter element have persuaded the leadership to take a more interventionist attitude towards departmental management than perhaps might otherwise have been the case. On the other hand they have received retribution from the group – for example a loss of a vice-chairmanship and a withdrawal of the whip – when they have been seen to be stepping too far out of the agreed line. Meanwhile the leader curbs a certain impatience with this internal opposition, which is probably of more significance to him than is the official Conservative opposition, and allows everything to be argued through in the group before decisions are taken.

In authority E the left-wing Labour group is very clearly the focus of power. The leader receives a degree of loyalty from his members and can be particularly influential on issues of finance and overall strategy but he has neither the inclination, nor perhaps the personality, to command any automatic obediance. For the council's chief executive the absence of any single authoritative leadership makes it difficult at times to develop a clear line on corporate issues: instead he awaits the outcome of the three-weekly Labour group meetings, following which the group secretary meets with senior officers to outline the decisions taken. Decisions on committee places and chairmanships are the clear prerogative of the group rather than the leader. The leader himself is not a full-time politician although a handful of his colleagues are: because of a very large number of committees, sub-committees and working parties there are very few Labour councillors without some position in the hierarchy of chairmanship, vice-chairmanships and group offices. The overall impression is thus one of collective rather than individual leadership, of decisions debated rather than decreed. This clearly suits the mood of the party but as noted above it is not altogether welcomed by the officers of the council.

Authority F is safely Conservative, but with a somewhat fragmented Conservative group divided between 'wets' and 'drys', yet with the latter not proving a very coherent force. Although the group meets regularly, twice in each council cycle, it is not very firmly whipped and its decisions are not always clear. The latter is sometimes deliberate in order to mask internal disagreements but it makes it hard for officers who are seeking political guidance. The leader is eager to consult his group yet because of their indecisiveness sometimes feels he ought to give a lead. In their turn, and perhaps again because of their own dilemmas, the group members are willing to trust him and to accept that on occasion it will be his actions rather than formal group decisions which define Conservative policy. Yet although very able, the leader can also be somewhat indecisive and thus not provide great clarity. In the words of a chief officer 'policy lies in the leader's breast': the problem is to uncover it.

In authority G the pattern of leadership in the ruling Conservative group saw considerable changes over a ten-year period. Initially, the group was led by an extremely aggressive, partisan councillor, with a very clear, right-wing stance, who was very tough not only with the opposition but also with his own side. He was perhaps too tough in the latter respect since he was replaced by a less partisan, but also less decisive individual. When the latter lost his seat on the council the group turned to a leader who was neither dictatorial nor indecisive, who would lead but would not rise roughshod over his colleagues. This third leader is not an aggressive figure but he reconizes the need for leadership. He also recognizes that the composition of his group has been changing over time, with younger, less deferential membes coming on at successive elections. He thus tries not to presume too much on group loyalties and the group in turn allow him room for manoeuvre. He does not see his role as one of managing the authority; that is the officers' job. He is there to listen, to talk to people, to give political advice, to 'nurse' his group in the right direction and to give a lead when he feels it necessary.

In authority H a middle-of-the-road Labour majority group still inclines to strong leadership of a sort that is becoming increasingly rare. The group elects no inner executive and is happy to 'leave it to the leader to sort out' when any problems arise. It is left to him, for example, to advise the group on committee places and chairmanships. There is a general attitude of deference to the leader and this is underpinned by a very strongly disciplined group. The leader regards his position as council leader as a demanding one and does not hold any committee chairmanships himself, being content to let his deputy chair the Policy Committee. He is in the council offices at some point every day and involves himself in a great many issues, not only of policy but also of what might elsewhere be regarded as matters of detail and administration.

In authority I the Conservative leader had succcessfully navigated the change from being a well-established majority leader to that of leader of a minority administration. He operate as a strong leader, outwardly autocratic, but also supported and deferred to by his colleagues because of his experience, intellect and ability. He is allowed to select not only his own committee chairmen and vice-chairmen but also to allocate Conservative committee places himself. Over the years he has developed a very close relationship with the chief executive whom he tends to see every day. There is also a powerful management board of officers working within what the chief executive describes as a 'very centralized officer structure'. This pattern may have been a suitable match for a strong majority leader who could be relied on to 'deliver' his group. It is not clear how well it suits a minority administration in a hung council.

Clearly the instances cited above do not encompass all the possible approaches to leadership in local authorities. They do however cover a range of leadership styles from the non-existent or very low-key (A. B. C) through the group-based (D, E, F) to the more assertive or even authoritarian (G, H, I). The circumstances which have produced these styles clearly vary from those relating to the overall political situation (for example non-partisan politics in A) to changes within a group (for example in D) to factors of personality (for example in I). They also confirm the observations made by Madgwick (1978) in his attempt to identify the factors which produce different styles of local political leadership. He cited such features as personal qualities; group loyalty and cohesiveness; relations with council officers; and attitudes towards policies, for example differing emphases on continuity and stability, on reacting positively to problems as they emerge and on consciously determined radical innovation. The presence and interplay of such factors can be seen in varying patterns in the nine councils described above as also can the impact of past experience on the one hand and of social and political changes on the other.

Inter-party relations

Political parties, in local government as elsewhere, seek to implement policies deriving from their particular values and ideologies. In order to do so they seek to use these positions and procedures open to them to best advantage. Since these are the two prime preoccupations of parties it is not surprising that they colour the relations between them. Thus many aspects of inter-party relations within local authorities may be best understood by reference to the management of differences over values and ideologies and procedures.

Since the possession of a distinctive set of values and

ideologies is one of the basic features distinguishing political
parties from each other, it would not be surprising if this
proved a source of inter-party conflict; indeed, one might be
surprised if it were otherwise. In most authorities where
there is a party system there is indeed such a conflict: it tends,
however, to confine itself to the formal arenas of political
combat – the committee meetings, full council meetings, the
columns of the local press and the local elections. In these
arenas the traditional party lines are articulated and
defended, often with genuine passion and vigour. However,
this does not prevent the maintenance of civil relations
between individual councillors of different persuasions outside the council chamber or the comittee room in the neutral
territory of the members' lounge or the bar. Nor does it
unduly inhibit the operation of behind-the-scenes discussion
between group leaders and whips about expediting necessary
business with as little mutual inconvenience as possible. This
is especially true where one party seems destined to remain in
control for ever. Security of tenure gives a confidence which
allows not only a tolerant give-and-take by the majority
group, but also a degree of patronizing and condescension
which a minority group can exploit if it can overcome its
distaste. Thus in one metropolitan district where Labour has
always formed the majority party the Conservatives did feel
able to influence the Labour leadership through what they
called 'sensible' methods such as informal chats in the
members' room, talks in the corridor and post-committee
drinks. In those instances where difficulties do arise which
stem from conflicting values or ideologies it is nearly always
because polarization in one form or another has so widened
the political gap that mutual incomprehension is created,
resulting in and further compunded by genuine unease and
distrust on all sides. This is not a common phenomenon but it
can be found in a small number of the most highly politicized
authorities.

Clearly, an authority divided between hard left Labour
councillors and very dry Conservative councillors would
provide the classic illustration of this. Yet one of the starkest
examples we encountered concerned relations between a
Conservative group, long entrenched in power and with a

decade of broadly Thatcherite policies behind it, and an
insurgent Liberal group which had displaced Labour as the
major opposition and now saw itself in its leader's phrase as a
'majority in waiting'. The Conservatives were totally appalled
at the style of Liberal politics which confronted them and of
the approach to politics which they saw it as representing. To
them the Liberals were just 'not on the same wavelength',
they were 'juvenile; all sweatshirts and jeans', and could only
really be understood as 'left-wing socialists in disguise'. For
their part the Liberals were very iconoclastic, very publicity
conscious, very aggressive and supremely self-confident that
their hour was at hand. The Conservatives simply did not
feel they could trust the Liberals, even to the point of denying
them physical access to the town hall after working hours: the
Liberal response was that 'they are right not to trust us since
we are not a passive opposition'.

Such a degree of antagonism between groups is more
commonly encountered in the Conservative versus Labour
context, particularly where the majority group at least is
dominated by the Conservative right or the Labour left. In
these circumstances the particular ideological enthusiasm of
the majority group not only vexes the minority group; it also
tends to make the majority group view the minority group as
essentially an irrelevance, ideologically misguided and male-
volent in intent, and thus best ignored and excluded
wherever possible. The minority group in their turn respond
with equal vehemence to their treatment. Thus one Conservative leader complained bitterly that, 'the conspiratorial and
caucus politics of the Labour Party has now infected the
council' which had become 'like a one-party state concealing
all real decisions in smoke-filled rooms'. As that remark
implies, inter-party clashes over ideology may also manifest
themselves in disputes over the way council business is
organized. Disagreements on such issues are not, however,
confined to ideologically polarized authorities but can occur
in those with a more low-key politics.

One question basic to the operation of all local authorities
in Britain is that of the allocation of committee places both to
individuals and amongst party groups. The most common
presumptions are that any such allocation should pay regard

to the preferences of individuals and to the relative numerical strengths of the party groups. Translating the latter presumption into practice, however, can provide some fuel for inter-party disputes.

In authorities where there is a majority group in clear overall control, that group can, by its weight of numbers, determine the pattern of committee allocations. In doing so it may choose to depart from a strictly proportional numerical balance between the parties. It may, for example, give itself more than its fair share of seats on some major committee, perhaps taking less than its share on a minor committee. It may effectively inflate its majority on all committees by use of the *ex officio* device whereby one or more of the chairmen of the council, the vice-chairmen, the leader and the deputy leader, are automatically voting membes of all committees. It may also create a single (majority) party committee, notably in the form of a policy committee. Such practices are potential bones of contention and are usually particularly aggravating to the Alliance parties who tend to adhere to a strictly porportionalist line. In hung councils and in non-partisan councils the allocation procedure necessarily operates in a different fashion. In the former case, strict adherence to the principle of proportionality is likely to be in the interests of all concerned though its detailed application at the margin may still leave room for some disagreements. In the case of non-partisan councils committee allocations are by definition unlikely to be a focus of inter-party controversy: representation based on locality rather than party may be the chief principle here, particularly in the larger rural authorities.

Relations between parties are not solely determined by conflicts over ideology or over the organization of council business. Two other factors also merit recognition – the political climate and individual personality. The battles between central and local government since 1979 have clearly affected party relations at the local level but not in uniform ways. In some cases groups have felt able to share a common commitment to the defence of local government and to that extent may have been drawn closer together. That, however, is unlikely to be the case in the more polarized authorities where the issue of central-local relations becomes seen in purely partisan terms. In those circumstances, for example, a ruling Labour group can see its Conservative opponents as an outpost of the government: one Labour leader thus defended his withholding of information from the Conservatives on the grounds that 'it would be on the Minister's desk at the Department of the Environment the next morning'. The emergence of multi-party politics has also affected relations between groups. In some cases, with greater or lesser ease, new relationships have been devised and incorporated into the conventions or agreements between groups on hung councils in which entitlements and expectations are clearly defined. Elsewhere, however, where Alliance groups have, as it were, 'intruded' into but not displaced the two-party system, a common occurrence is one in which Conservative and Labour groups react with some bafflement. They understand each other and are accustomed to one another's ways but find it hard to come to terms with what seem to them the unpredictable attitudes and behaviour of Alliance councillors: relations may thus be easier between Labour and the Conservatives than between either of them and the Alliance. Carried to its logical conclusion such a situation could lead to a Conservative-Labour deal to exclude the Alliance from any power or infuence. In at least one authority this does indeed seem to have been the case: however, the possibility of such an arrangement was also facilitated by the very good personal relations between the Conservative and Labour leaders in that instance.

Such personal factors cannot be discounted as elements in inter-party relations. Leaders who dislike one another are not likely to facilitate good relations between their parties. Where particular interests require it they may on occasions be able to curb their own feelings but in terms of sustaining generally amicable relations an ability to get along well on a day-to-day basis is a great asset. For those commited to an intensely ideological politics, of course, such an ability might be seen not as an asset but as a weakness liable to sap the political will and to encourage accommodation and compromise.

6

Systems of political management

In Chapter 4 attention was drawn to the main areas of council activity in which increased member assertiveness has disturbed and challenged the traditional pattern of member-officer relations. In so doing, reference was made to certain aspects of the decision-making process, such as agenda-setting, pre-committee briefings and officer attendance at party group meetings. In this chapter attention is focused more directly upon the *decision-making machinery* of local councils, and the formal and informal procedures currently used to deal with council business. Three different forms of political control in local government are distinguished for this purpose: authorities in which the 'Independent' or *'low-partisan'* style of local government still prevails; politicized authorities in which one party has *majority control*; and *hung authorities*, or councils in which party politics is dominant, but where no one party has overall control. Majority control still predominates (in 1987 around two-thirds of all British local authorities were in this category) as examples of low-partisanship have continued to decline (to around one-eighth of all authorities in 1987). Hung authorities are currently experiencing a steady increase. (In 1987, just over one in five local councils were hung.) These three different types of political control involve different forms of political arithmetic and expectations, and present different pressures and choices for the development of political management systems.

In this chapter we look first at the changing role of council and committee meetings under these three different forms of political control, emphasizing the continuing dominance of the committee in local authority decision-making. The importance of the distinction between private arenas of debate (for policy formulation) and public arenas (for policy adoption) is then discussed with an analysis of the different types of setting which have been used for both purpose. Problems of facilitating the role of opposition parties in majority-controlled authorities are then highlighted. Finally, alternatives to the current system of political management in British local government are briefly discussed, and the changing role of the chief executive emphasized.

The changing roles of council and committee meetings

As outlined in Chapter 2, the formal settings of decision-making in local authorities have traditionally been the meetings of the council and the commitees (and sub-committees). Council meetings have taken on an increasingly ritualistic function in majority-controlled authorities in recent years, although they still have their value, particularly to opposition groups. In hung authorities (and some low-partisan authorities) council meetings have, however, taken on a new significance.

The committee system still dominates the formal machinery of local authorities, even though in majority-controlled authorities more and more of the effective decision-making now takes place outside committees, in party groups and elsewhere. However, 'the committee' still plays a dominant role in the average councillor's life. As Stewart has put it (1988, p. 6–7).

The main formal setting for the work of the councillor is the service committee, or a committee concerned with overall policy and resoures . . . councillors work with and through the instruments with which they are provided. The main instrument is the committee system. That system dominates the working of the authority, even where actual decisions are made outside it. It defines the role of the councillor. A councillor is known as the member of this committee and the chair of that committee. Committees and sub-committees and their work fill the councillor's diary.

Although as Stewart and other writers have pointed out, the dominance of the committee system is not congruent with all the major tasks of political management, there is little sign of a significant movement away from it, despite the existence in principle of alternative forms of machinery. The committee system has become one of the 'taken-for-granted' features of British local government.

Given the dominance of the committee system it is important to clarify the basis on which committee composition is decided, and the chairmen and vice-chairmen of committees selected. Material from the Widdicombe postal questionnaire and interview survey enables us to do so.

One major function of party groups relates to the allocation of councillors to membership of committees and the election of committee chairmen. In many cases there may be a formal procedure laid down in the council's standing orders specifying that committee places shall be allocated, for example, by a small selection committee made up of the chairman and vice-chairman and leader of the council, or on the recommendation of the chief executive, or the chairman of the council, and that committee chairmen shall be chosen by the respective committees. In non-party authorities such formal procedures may also represent reality, tempered perhaps by attempts to ensure that there is some territorial balance between different localities in the allocation of places. However, in party dominated authorities the formal systems of allocation and election of chairmen are essentially mechanisms for the ratification of what has previously been decided by the party groups.

The commonest practice is for each group to receive an allocation of places on each committee proportionate to its overall strength on the council and for the groups then to decide on how to distribute their own members amongst the committee places thus awarded to them: there is usually an attempt in doing so either to secure an equitable share of the workload amongst individual group members or to suit workload to personal circumstances. The mechanics of deciding, within groups, which councillors should sit on which committees may vary somewhat in detail but the broad outline is a fairly common one.

Councillors are asked to notify their group of their personal preferences for committee membership after each council election. These preferences are then considered, perhaps by the group leader alone, or by the leader and deputy leader or by a small number of senior councillors in the group with a view to making recommendations to the full group meeting. In making such recommendations, factors such as expressed preference, experience, ability, geographical representation and factional loyalty may all come into play. It will then be for the group meeting as a whole to approve the proposed allocations or perhaps to modify them by a certain amount of re-shuffling of names. Once the group have agreed their respective lists of committee members these can then be consolidated into final lists for each committee, to be duly ratified at the first meeting of the full council.

The choice of committee chairmen is again a matter which, in party dominated councils, is made through the group, more specifically of course, the majority group. The most common practice is for majority group members to vote on committee chairmanships and then to nominate and elect those thus chosen at the first meetings of the respective committees. In doing this, however, the group will not normally be taking part in a wholly open free-for-all. Group leaders are usually likely to have their own views as to desirable committee chairmen, to have discussed these with senior colleagues and to make their views known, perhaps during the process of nomination. In coming to a view leaders are likely to be influenced by such factors as experience, ability, the need for securing a balanced representation of different elements within the group, commitment to group politics and the existence or not of any conventions limiting tenure of chairmanships to a specific period of years. In most cases such leadership views will carry weight and the group will accept the suggestions put to it by the leadership. However, there is always room for the unforeseen to occur and in our interview survey we met with a small number of instances where the support of a leader had not been enough to secure the election of a favoured nominee, the post going instead to another contender.

Given that in most cases groups, in choosing committee chairmen, may be largely endorsing a leadership proposal it is hard to assess just where the balance is being struck between group democracy and leadership prerogative. The questionnaire survey suggests that 26 per cent of Conservative groups allow either their leader or an inner circle of senior members to choose the chairman rather than the groups as a whole: for Labour groups the figure is 9 per cent. However, our interviews suggested that these figures may be respectively under- and over-estimates, reflecting the difficulty inherent in determining whether the ratification of leadership nominations were a foregone conclusion or a matter for genuine debate.

Council and committee in low-partisan authorities

In authorities dominated by Independents, or in which low partisan approaches still predominate, meetings of the council and its committee are often the only arenas in which members and officers meet on a regular basis. In such authorities, these meetings have a significance which they invariably lack in majority-controlled authorities. There are no (or at most partial and sporadic) group meetings prior to council or committee although informal contacts, especially over the telephone, can be important. In principle, there is an open discussion over the agenda items, with officers speaking on the reports they have prepared, members asking questions and making contributions and deciding how they will vote on each issue (although in fact formal votes may be rare). In one or two such authorities visited it was claimed that over a significant range of decisions, members did actually make up their minds on the basis of the strength of the arguments put forward at the meeting itself (and in the light of their knowledge of the local circumstances and preferences in the ward/town they represent).

More typically in Independent-dominated authorities the voting patterns of members are more likely to be heavily

influenced by traditions of following the lead of certain key
influential councillors, and/or accepting the advice provided
by officers. In the former case, deference to experience,
ability or power of patronage may all be involved. In the
latter there often remains an awareness on the part of many
councillors of their own limitations of knowledge and
expertise *vis-à-vis* the officers. Either way, a greater predicta-
bility of decision-making than might otherwise be expected
would be the result.

In such authorities there may often be something of a
policy vacuum at member level. There will be a broad
consensus amongst members over perhaps three or four key
local objectives – for example, keeping the rates down,
conserving the local rural environment, promoting (or
avoiding) tourism in certain parts of the area, and so on.
Officers will be aware of these objectives as setting the
boundaries to what they can and can't do. Within these
boundaries much is left to them, and policy either operates
on a *de facto* basis, or through a process of officers
persuading members in committee (often relying heavily on
the chairman) that certain policies are a good thing, and
compatible with low rates/conservation, etc. Concern for the
local issue is very important in Independent authorities, and
the main 'political' division is often a *geographical* one,
between one town (or part) of the district and another.

In authorities like this the formal arenas more or less
suffice. They will be supplemented at most by chairmen's
briefing meetings, and a certain amount of contact between
chairmen and chief officers, and between the chief executive
and the council chairman or (more likely) the two or three
key influentials on the member side. In addition of course,
individual members would have a good deal of *ad hoc* contact
with individual officers over specific ward issues (for example
housing allocations). But with these limited expectations,
there is little perceived need for arenas where groups of
members can make contact with groups of officers outside
the formal arenas of council and committee.

Council and committee in majority-controlled authorities

In authorities dominated by party politics, and under

majority control, council and committee meetings play a quite different role. Council meetings provide opportunities for the opposition to criticize majority party proposals which they are well aware, however, will go through whatever the quality of the opposing argument used. In such circumstances, council meetings have a strong element of ritual about them. There is a good deal of 'playing to the gallery' from both majority and opposition parties, reflecting the fact that the local press are still likely to be present at council meetings (although increasingly no longer at all the committees). 'Notices of motion' are used, mainly but not wholly by opposition groups, to draw attention to the national or local issues from which political capital can be made. Flamboyant gestures such as the 'seizing of the mace' or the 'premeditated walk out' are becoming less uncommon as the temperature of inter-party political debate continues to rise. But it is rare, in the majority-control situation, for debate at council meetings to actually *change* a course of action which has already been decided upon by the majority group, who will have previously discussed the agenda in detail, and decided its voting strategy. In so far as much of the council business will be made up of recommendations from various committees, which the council is being asked to formally ratify, the voting implications for the majority party will normally be straightforward anyway. Many groups (particularly Labour) now decide beforehand who will speak, on what subject, and indeed what (in outline, at least) they will say. The proceedings only become significant in terms of decision outcomes if there are major divisions within the majority party and internal splits over particular issues are anticipated, or take place; or on the few occasions where a free vote is permitted.

Increasingly in such authorities committee meetings too are taking a similar ritualistic type of role, although the atmosphere of committees is usually more relaxed, and a more wide-ranging and genuine debate is more feasible. None the less, the function of the committee is, in majority-controlled authorities, similar to that of the council meeting: a formal mechanism for approving decisions which have already been agreed in more informal arenas, such as the chairman's briefing meeting, the inner circle or caucus, and the party group.

Decision-making systems in hung authorities

In hung authorities, the traditional arenas of council and committee have often become revitalized, and have developed a character very different from the staid formality of the Independent-dominated council meeting or the ritualistic points-scoring emphasis of the majority-controlled council. Discounting the few hung authorities where formal coalitions operate, decision-making in hung authorities is potentially always unpredictable. By definition, no one party can push through on its own any given policy or decision even in a minority administration situation, where one party holds all the chairmanships and vice-chairmanships. It is inevitably reliant on the co-operation of one of the other two parties. Sometimes this can be predicted, for example, in situations where a third party is working 'behind the scenes' with the party operating the minority administration (and in particular in the rare situations where there is an agreed 'programme of action'). However, more typically support cannot confidently be predicted, particularly in the not uncommon situation where a relatively small Alliance group holds the balance of power and is concerned to exploit it, by (*inter alia*) supporting policy proposals from either of the other parties 'on their merits'. In such situations, committee and council meetings take on a new significance. It may be the case, in any given committee, that a minority administration (and the officers concerned) genuinely do not know what decisions will be made during that committee. Indeed it may be that the Alliance group are 'open to persuasion', in which case the quality of the arguments made in the committee will actually make a difference! The same situation will often prevail at full council also. In most hung authorities there is a provision whereby any party group on a committee which is dissatisfied with a committee 'decision', over a matter formally delegated to it, can refer it to full council (i.e. 'take it out of delegation'). In other hung authorities, all committee decisions go to full council for ratification anyway. At the council meeting, the same uncertainty may prevail. The Alliance may, having reconsidered the matter, wish to change its stance. In a disorganized Alliance group, with a limited level of group discipline, it is by no means unknown for its members to vote on an individual basis, over certain issues at least. Whatever the details of intra-and inter-party politics, council (and committees) can become, in hung authorities, arenas in which decisions are actually taken, rather than ritual ratification procedures for decisions already arrived at. Many find this change refreshing and – in one sense – a symbol of enhanced democracy.

This is not to say that council (and to a lesser extent committee) meetings in hung authorities are not also prone to the ritualistic 'notices of motion' on national issues, the disruption of procedures, or a high level of inter-party invective. Some of the most conflictual hung authorities have provided some of the most extreme and newsworthy examples of such phenomena (including fisticuffs in the London Borough of Hillingdon). But the important point is that the element of unpredictability involved in the majority of hung authorities does lead to a different style and climate of operation in the formal decision-making arenas.

The distinction between public and private arenas

In relation to politicized local authorities, whether majority-controlled or hung, it is the private informal arenas of member and member-officer interaction which must be penetrated if decision-making processes are to be understood. Indeed, in the course of our Widdicombe research, a key distinction was frequently drawn by leading members of Conservative and Labour groups between *public* arenas where formal decision-making takes place and *private* arenas where policy was discussed and a common party line eventually agreed. Both arenas were considered essential: the former to retain the *legitimacy* of the local democratic system and to allow the opposition an adequate opportunity to play their distinctive role; the latter to enable party groups (or sub-groups) to weigh up the pros and cons of alternative courses of action *before* coming to a collective decision about them.

The Alliance are rather more ambivalent about this need for a distinction between public and private arenas. Certainly, they would acknowledge the primacy of the group meeting and the advantages of the confidential officer briefing. But they are invariably suspicious and critical of any piece of council machinery which is not open to opposition parties, the press and the public. Such criticism is most unqualified in authorities where the Alliance are a small minority. It becomes more muted where they actually hold or share power, and the benefits of the informal and private exploratory discussions with officers become apparent.

The key distinction between private and public arenas reflects, in majority-controlled authorities at least, the distinction between policy *formulation* and policy *adoption* (and *justification*). Policy is seen as appropriately adopted and justified (as indeed are detailed decisions of significance) in the formal public arenas of council and committee. Realistically, however, policy can only be formulated in private arenas.

Because many of the recent innovations in council machinery can only be understood in terms of the significance of this distinction, it is important to make clear why it is that the availability of suitable private arenas is considered so important, and why it is also seen as important that officers should be present at them. Although some party manifestos now have the appearance of a detailed programme of action, and indeed are sometimes treated as such (particularly by Labour groups who are strongly influenced by district parties) most manifestos are still more concerned to set out principles which will guide or shape policy rather than specify policies in detail. A process of refinement is therefore required whereby, once elected, the majority party group of councillors can 'work up' the manifesto into a set of policy initiatives which are legally sound, financially feasible and can be properly administered or implemented. It would be quite unrealistic to expect such a process to be carried out in the public arenas of council or committee. Consider, for example, a local Conservative manifesto commitment to a rationalization of schools provision at a time of 'falling rolls'. The party has been elected and wants to put this commitment into operation as a matter of urgency. It knows that the closure or amalgamation of schools is a highly contentious process, with strong local passions certain to be aroused. It knows also that the appearance of a school on a provisional list of possible reorganizations is likely to set in motion pressure-group action which may well turn out to be premature. It is likely to recognize before very long that there is no real alternative to some kind of majority-party only member-officer panel to discuss informally and in detail the pros and cons of different alternative schemes before coming to a conclusion about the best option to present to the education committee, and subsequently to the public for consultation.

Given the need for such arenas, the issue is raised of what the most commonly-used or appropriate types of private arena are for such policy formulation processes. In principle, at least six different private policy-formulation arenas – not necessarily mutually exclusive – can be identified. The *chairman's briefing system*, which can operate either at agenda-formulation or pre-committee stage; attendance by councillors at the meetings of the authority's *management team*; attendance by officers at *party group meetings*; informal meetings between (some combination of) chief officers and the *inner circle* of majority party councillors (including leader/ chief executive meetings); the operation of a system of *one-party working parties*, or panels, at which policies are worked up by majority party members and officers; and the meetings of *one-party committees* (or sub-committees) attended and serviced in the normal way by officers. All of these devices with the possible exception (since the 1985 Local Government (Access to Information) Act) of the last, are invariably exclusive of opposition, press and pubic. As appropriate vehicles for policy formulation, they have different strengths and weaknesses, which are discussed below.

The one-party committee or sub-committee

This device was a lot more prevalent at the time of our survey in 1985 than it is now. It has been overtaken by the provisions of the 1985 Local Government (Access to Information) Act which required the opening-up to the public of all council committees and sub-committees.

	All Cons. and Lab. majority administrations %	Conservative %	Labour %
Question: 'Are there any committees/sub-committees whose membership is drawn solely from the party or coalition of parties which form the 'administration'?'			
One-party committees			
2 or more	6	1	13
1	18	13	24
None	76	86	63
One-party sub-committees			
2 or more	21	14	29
1	17	15	18
None	63	70	53
Base	318	176	142

Source: Widdicombe Committee, Research Vol. 1, 1986, Tables 2.10 and 2.11, pp.35–6.

Table 23   *Prevalence of one-party committees and sub-committees (1985)*

But, in 1985, our survey showed that one or more 'one-party only' committees existed in just under a quarter of all majority-controlled authorities in Britain, and 'one-party only' sub-committees in just over a third. As there was a good deal of overlap apparent (i.e. authorities where one-party committees *and* sub-committees existed) our estimate is that in 1985, a total of perhaps two-fifths of all majority-controlled authorities employed this type of organizational device in some form or other.

What such committees (or sub-committees) typically provided was an arena for the majority party to discuss key items of business without the opposition, press or public being present. Both major parties made use of them, Labour somewhat more frequently than the Conservatives; and their perceived legitimacy was further illustrated by the fact that the predominant view of the opposition parties excluded from them (Alliance respondents generally excepted) was that they were an acceptable manifestation of 'the right of the majority party to govern'. Often the group currently in opposition had used – or even introduced – such a committee themselves, when they were in power.

It was very rare for such committees to have full powers of decision-making in their own right. Sometimes they had power to take emergency decisions: more often they were totally non-executive, in that all 'decisions' had to be channelled through a further all-party committee (or full council) before they could be acted upon. Only very rarely did one-party committees generate serious complaints from minority groups about effective exclusion from decision-making, although the Alliance always objected to them in principle, and no doubt still do.

Despite their relative popularity, it was our impression that one-party committees were not particularly effective in policy formulation terms. It was true that they provided an opportunity for private discussions between leading members and officers. However, their very status as committees often tended to act against the informality necessary for a genuine exchange of views. As with other (all-party) committees, discussion was typically reactive, in the sense that business was governed by an (often substantial) agenda, and the content of officer reports, not to mention the formalistic traditions and expectations of 'committee' behaviour. As a 'clearing house' prior to the proceedings of other committee, it had its uses. Indeed many examples of one-party committees (or sub-committees) were of the 'policy and resources' variety. As an effective confidential and exploratory discussion arena, they were less successful. Indeed several were not actually *intended* to be used in that way, as their openness to press and public (if not opposition) indicated.

Since 1985 there has been a reconsideration of the role of those one-party committees and sub-committees which were established as private arenas. In the light of the new legislation, they can no longer play that role, and alternatives have had to be sought.

Councillor attendance at management team

The extent of this practice was discussed in Chapter 3. All that needs to be said here is that nowhere did we find that the practice (on the rare occasions it was identified at all), represented a significant contribution to the kind of policy formulation process described earier. Where it did occur it was either a reflection of the mistrust which leading councillors felt about the management team, or it provided an opportunity for one-off discussions between the leader and the key officers about major or urgent issues.

Officer briefings of members

The regular briefing of committee chairmen before meetings is almost universal in British local authorities. Only five authorities (1 per cent) did not operate this kind of system. Patterns of briefing vary considerably. In many of the more policitized authorities there is an 'agenda callover' briefing, to discuss the contents of the agenda and of draft reports, before they go out to committee members, as well as the more traditional and widespread pre-committee briefings. In some authorities briefings are on a one-to-one basis (chief officer/ chairman). More typically both chairman and vice-chairman are involved. Indeed, there are signs within Labour groups of attempts to involve small groups of councillors in briefing meetings, a development not always to the liking of the chief officer. Sometimes a chairman and vice-chairman are faced with a whole phalanx of officers from the same department. Sometimes there are variations within an authority. Much depends on the preferences of the chairman (and/or chief officers).

The changing nature of the pre-committee briefing was discussed in Chapter 4. The point to emphasize here is that it is unlikely that this meeting can play an effective policy-formulation role. It is too tied to the items coming up at the next committee, about which reports will already have been written. Its restriction (in most cases) to the chairman and the vice-chairman means that 'elitist' processes by which an agreement over the policy decision of significance had been reached would make it unacceptable to all but the most autocratic of groups of majority party members on the committee. Such meetings have their functions: but they do not normally include policy formulation

Hung authorities often exhibit an interesting alternative to the pattern of pre-committee briefings. In most hung authorities an agreement has been reached between the three parties involved which gives each of the spokesmen the right to a confidential briefing on the agenda from the chief officer, before a committee meeting. In a few cases the briefing is a *communal* one (and hence of course non-confidential). More commonly the three party spokesmen see the chief officer separately. The briefings typically include the familiar attempts by the chief officer to persuade the councillor to support the cause of action which the chief officer favours; a good deal of detailed probing from the spokesmen on those agenda items regarded as controversial; together with some attempts (often unsuccessful) by the spokesmen to ascertain the stance of the two other parties on such issues.

There is no reason in principle why such facilities could not be extended to minority groups in majority-controlled authorities. Better-briefed opposition spokesmen would certainly lead to better-informed debates, more searching and relevant questions, and a greater public understanding of the issues and choices underlying any given policy decision. However, a device which allows an opposition to play its primary role more effectively is not necessarily going to be appreciated by most majority parties, and there is little sign of the practice of confidential agenda briefings for all parties that want them spreading to majority-controlled authorities. The best that an opposition spokesman can expect in such authorities is normally 'information' (usually verbal, sometimes only written) from a chief officer about a specified agenda item or items. In some authorities the quality of inter-party relations is such that the majority party would strive to minimize even this limited facility.

The 'agenda-callover' briefing does offer rather more scope for at least a broader discussion about policy issues, and we found some limited evidence of its use for this purpose in authorities in which the chairmen expected and were given a good deal of autonomy to make the running over policy formulation (within the constraints of the manifesto) in the particular area of activity covered by their committees. Such autonomy is granted more commonly to Conservative chairmen, although more traditional Labour councils also provide a few such examples. There is scope within this process, as we saw in Chapter 4, for major problems of agenda-manipulation and report-vetting by chairmen to arise.

Officers' attendance at party group meetings

Table 24 provides details of this phenomenon. It suggests that the significance of officer attendance at party groups has perhaps been over-estimated. In only four authorities (in the questionnaire survey) did the chief executive *always* attend party group meetings. In only 33 per cent of politicized authorities did he *ever* attend such meetings, and in the majority of these instances such attendance was only occasional. This pattern was confirmed by what we were told in the interview survey. The most common situation encountered was one in which the chief executive attended group meetings only in particular circumstances – usually in connection with the budget. Sometimes this was at the chief executive's own request: more typically at the request of the majority group leadership. In so doing, the chief executive would attend only for a part of the group meeting, during which he would present a verbal report, answer quotations and then leave before the group discussed the political implications of, and options in, the report. Often, there is an arrangement whereby other party groups in the authority are notified of majority group meetings which the chief executive (or any other chief officer) is to attend, and similar opportunities are always taken up.

Question: 'How often, if at all, do each of the individuals or groups listed below attend party group meetings?'

	All authorities %	Conservative %	Labour %	Minority and other forms of control %
Chief executive				
Sometimes*	6	3	14	1
Occasionally	27	15	41	29
Never	66	82	45	70
Chief finance officer				
Sometimes	3	1	4	4
Occasionally	27	12	48	25
Never	70	87	47	71
Other chief officers				
Sometimes	1	1	2	1
Occasionally	23	9	46	16
Never	76	91	52	83
Base	390	176	139	76

Source: Widdicombe Committee, Research Vol. I, 1986, Tables 5.4–5.6 (pp. 117–19).

Note: * includes four cases where the chief executive *always* attends party group meetings

Table 24   *Attendance of officers at party group meetings (1985)*

Attendance of chief executives at party groups is rarely a contentious issue. It is reserved for 'special occasions' – the budget, a school closures programme, a management restructuring – and takes place within known and agreed rules. As Table 24 shows, attendance at group meetings by the chief finance officer is less common than that of the chief executive, and by other chief officers less common still. In each case, it takes place on the same basis, and is viewed in the same way as attendance by the chief executive.

There are a number of reasons why officer attendance at group meetings is less prevalent than might be expected. By and large party group members do not welcome it; the group is seen as a specifically political arena which it is not appropriate for officers to attend, all other things being equal. Sometimes party leaders can see the value of bringing in an officer to explain the gravity of a situation, or put over an important technical argument, or to ensure that a party debate gets off on an informed and appropriate footing (for example, over a falling rolls/school closures issue). Sometimes chief executives feel the need to request the opportunity to attend – usually over similar sorts of issues. But it is almost always the exception rather than the rule.

Most chief executives and other chief officers prefer things that way. They are uneasy about the blurring of role which regular attendance at a specifically political gathering would imply. Some chief executives (although not all) do not like the idea (or experience) of talking to a group which contains non-councillor representatives, which would occur in almost all Labour and many Conservative groups. In the handful of cases where the non-councillors at the party group contain a member or members of the authority's own staff, then there is certainly a strong unease on the part of the chief executive about attending. Because, however, most chief executives not only rarely attend party group meetings, and party groups only rarely include an employer of that authority, there is no feeling that the problem is a significant, or indeed a growing one.

In hung authorities, it is normally ensured that if the attendance of an officer at a party group meeting is requested either by an officer or by the party group, then the same facility is explicitly offered to the other party groups also.

A few local authorities constitute party groups as formal sub-committees of the council, although this does not necessarily mean that officers always attend. The provisions of the Local Government (Access to Information) Act 1985 make it virtually certain that in these authorities group meetings will have to be reconstituted on another basis.

It will be apparent from the above analysis that officer

attendance at group meetings in its current form, clearly does *not* meet the need for an appropriate forum for informal officer-member deliberation over policy formulation.

Leadership group meetings

It is the 'leadership group' meetings, with officers present, which provides in the more politicized local authorities the most commonly-used mechanism for policy formulation (outside the district party/party group nexus, in the case of the Labour party). The first point to stress is the widespread acknowledged existence of such leadership groups. Of the authorities responding to a question which asked whether the party in power held meetings of an 'inner circle' composed of a small number of senior councillors, 64 per cent agreed that such meetings did take place. If the shire (including Welsh and Scottish) districts are excluded the proportion rises to 81 per cent. Such groups typically meet on an *informal* basis. In 1985 only 12 per cent of these groups were formally constituted as a committee or sub-committee of the council (typically as a 'policy advisory' sub-committee of the policy and resources committee). The remainder did not appear in the formal council structure, which was the most common basis of such criticism that was directed at them. The most common frequency of meetings of these inner circles is monthly, although about a tenth of them meet every week or fortnight.

It is when the pattern of attendance of officers at inner circle meetings is considered that their significance as a forum for officer-member policy discussions becomes apparent. Chief executives are much more likely to attend such meetings than they are to attend party group meetings. In authorities in which both inner circle and party groups exist, the chief executive *always* attends inner circle meetings in 27 per cent of the cases (cf. 1 per cent who always attend party group meetings). If the 'always' and 'sometimes', as opposed to 'occasionally' categories are combined, the proportions rise to 49 per cent and 10 per cent respectively. The relative likelihood of other chief officers attending inner circle meetings is also much higher than their tendency to attend party group meetings, being over 40 per cent (for the combined 'always' and 'sometimes' categories) for both chief finance officers and 'other chief officers'. In many politicized authorities, it is clear therefore that such officer attendance must overlap, and that groups of officers are present at inner circle meetings to discuss policy issues in an informal and private setting. Indeed in the interview survey, it becomes clear that the precise composition of the officers attending often depended on the context of the agenda.

Two examples of the kind of machinery involved may help clarify their function.

1   A Conservative controlled London borough, has a leader's co-ordinating committee, which consists of the nine chairmen. It is not an executive committee, and its agendas and minutes are restricted to its members. It used to function as an informal 'think tank' for chairmen, but was reconstituted as a committee to secure officer attendance. Its primary use is to think strategically rather than to take decisions, although the minority parties do not accept this as the reality. Opposition groups see it in fact as the key decision-making forum.

2   A minority-controlled Liberal administration in a shire district in the Midlands, have recently set up a 'leaders co-ordinating group' at which the leader and the committee chairmen meet regularly with the five management team members to review major issues of policy. These may be tabled either by officers or members. There is pressure from the group leadership to transform this piece of machinery into a 'management board' which would have greater executive powers, and would include one or two backbenchers. This change is being resisted by the chief executive as inappropriate in a minority-controlled authority.

The first example illustrates the unease which still exists in some authorities about the attendance of officers at informal groupings of members. Ironically it has been the subject of more criticism since it became a committee, than it was before.

The second example is of particular interest, because it is unusual in a hung authority for an inner circle to be permitted by the other parties to have this kind of privileged access to officers. It is much more common in hung authorities for there to be equivalent access for party spokesmen on all committees to the relevant chief officer, and equivalent access for leaders to chief executives. Indeed, the 'joint meeting' between all three party leaders and the chief executive (or between spokesman and service director) is a common feature of the informal machinery of many hung authorities, and provides a very useful means of progressing council business. What such meetings cannot provide are confidential member-officer policy explorations within one particular party. In hung authorities, where such facilities are felt to be required, they either take the form of a set of informal and confidential party specific working parties – typically to discuss and draw up budget proposals – *or* one-day or weekend seminars, usually held away from the town or county hall so that policy issues can be explored by members and officers in relaxed and convivial surroundings. Such facilities are invariably *offered* to all three party groups even if they do not all take advantage of the officer. Day or weekend seminars do of course provide similar potential advantages for ruling parties in majority-controlled authorities, and the members of such authorities making use of them, though currently small in number, is growing.

It would be wrong to suggest that there is not some resentment and suspicion of leadership groups, especially in majority-controlled authorities. Where the Alliance is a significant opposition force in an authority, it tends to object to any arrangements of this kind, although where it holds power it often sets up similar machinery. A Labour or Conservative opposition group is more likely to find either 'leadership groups', or 'strategic working parties' or indeed one-party policy committees acceptable, and would be likely to adopt similar arrangements when they achieved power. Most respondents – officers and members alike – found it hard to see, in the more policitized local authorities of the late 1980s, how they could operate satisfactorily without some arrangement of this kind. Indeed, officers, and particularly chief executives, were clear that it was, from their point of view, a necessity. They felt they needed an informal channel of policy advice to the key members.

Meetings between leaders and chief executives

One potential and exclusive variant of the inner circle/officer meeting is the meeting between chief executive and council leader(s). In the more politicized authorities this practice is, as might be expected, becoming commonplace. Of the authorities responding to a question about the frequency of informal discussions between chief executive and council leader(s), over 90 per cent reported that such discussions took place at least once a week. In 11 per cent of cases, meetings took place daily and in a further 43 per cent of cases, meetings took place 'several times a week'. The frequency of such meetings was considerably higher in counties, regions, London boroughs and metropolitan districts than in shire districts.

With one type of exception, it was our impression from the interview survey that such meetings were not generally used for the purposes of policy formulation, in the sense used in this chapter. They were much more likely to be used to discuss the 'urgent business' which is dropping in ever-increasing quantities into chief executives' (and leaders') in-trays, than to discuss detailed issues arising from the implementation of policies already agreed.

The one exception to this generalization can be found in those authorities where the 'strong leader' syndrome still prevails. It is still the case in many Conservative groups and indeed several Labour groups that the leader is expected to give a lead in policy, especially in relation to the new issues which emerge, and have to be responded to, during the lifetime of a local administration. In such circumstances, particularly if the strong leader co-exists with a 'strong' chief executive (as often seems to be the case), then the regular meetings between the two can in effect operate as a policy formulation arena. Accommodations reached here have of course to be sold to the group and management team. But if there is a predisposition amongst the majority group to accept guidance from the leader, then any difficulties which the chief executive might have can potentially be overcome, through political channels, even if the management team is not enamoured by what is proposed. Although the prevalence of the 'strong leader' does seem to be declining, in all types of party group, there are still some of them around.

The frequency with which chief executives meet with minority party leaders is predictably much less than meetings with majority party leaders. None the less, such meetings are more prevalent than might have been anticipated. In about 20 per cent of all politicized authorities, the chief executive sees the opposition leader weekly or fortnightly. This kind of frequency is most common in those authorities where something of the old bi-partisan tradition still survives, and inter-party relations are relatively cordial. Indeed, it is not unknown for moderate and experienced Labour leadrs, faced with a growing left-wing minority within their own party group, to feel they have more in common with similarity moderate and experienced Conservative leaders, whom they know well personally, than with the more radical members of their own party. In such circumstances, not only are chief executive/opposition leader meetings not discouraged by the majority party leader, but the latter may be happy (and wecome) to attend them himself!

Member-officer policy groups

Leadership groups and leader/chief executive meetings both provide, in certain circumstances, appropriate arenas for policy formulation. But because of the nature of their composition and the scope of their brief, they do not always provide adequate opportunity to work at *specific* policy issues in detail, particularly for party groups with a strong commitment to strategic thinking and policy development. For such groups a set of mechanisms *additional* to the leadership group may be required. Although 'strategy' and 'policy' groups involving both members and officers are to be found in only a few authorities, where they are found they are typically viewed positively by both sets of participants. A number of examples will help convey something of the flavour of such arrangements.

1   In one English county council there is a strategic policy working group system, which was introduced by a Conservative administration in 1977, and extended when Labour came to power in 1981. It comprises a wide range of subject-specific working party sub-groups, and an umbrella 'strategic working party' which concentrates on budgetary issues and major policy items. The strategic working party and its sub-groups are one-party only. Relevant officers attend and are encouraged to express their views on the policy options being discussed openly and honestly. The quality of debate in these arenas is highly rated by officers and members alike. The system 'does not exist' as far as the official council structure is concerned. It is *par excellence* an informal system for deliberation about and formulation of majority party policy. All 'recommendations' stemming from the system are taken through the formal council decision machinery.

2   In an English metropolitan district, a new piece of central machinery for the formulation of policy has been introduced recently to replace the previous haphazard pattern of contact between chief executive and the majority party leadership. Key issues are thrashed out informally in this arena between leading politicians (the majority party group executive plus one or two backbenchers) and leading officers. The precise composition of the officers attending varies with the agenda. The strategic working party does not make decisions, but can make recommendations. If these require urgent decisions, they can be formally ratified by the strategic policy sub-committee (which is also one-party).

3   In a large Scottish region considerable use of joint officer-member groups is made. In these groups, both senior and backbench members participate on an informal basis to develop new policies and review existing practices. One participant felt observers would be unable to tell officers from members at such meetings. Representatives of both Labour and Conservative parties participate, although the SNP were excluded 'because they had a commitment to have the region dismantled and weren't interested in making the region work'. One service director was somewhat worried by this development, as he felt it reduced his ability to give professional advice, over the selection of topics for working

groups, or on the recommendations for changes. Members were generally enthusiastic as it allowed them to get into the depth of issues in a way conventional committees do not. The main criticisms made of such 'strategy groups' are in relation to their very informality. Some opposition groups, particularly the Alliance but also Labour or Conservative groups long accustomed to opposition, tend to be critical of any set of arrangements in which members and officers discuss policy issues but which are *not* explicitly part of the organizational chart or formal decision-making machinery. Opposition groups which have had more recent experience of power tend to be more accepting of such arrangements, knowing that they would wish to make use of them in future (or indeed had done so in the recent past). If the need for informal policy discussions between groups and officers in private arenas is accepted, then policy/strategy working groups appear a particularly effective means of meeting this need, so long as their existence does not pre-empt the opposition groups from playing their 'critical scrutiny' role effectively.

Single party member-officer policy groups, meeting in private, can be viewed as one variant of a more widespread phenomenon to be found in local government the 'working party' or 'panel' which is comprised of members of all political parties represented on the council. The advantage of such working parties is that they provide a forum in which policies or specific problems can be thought through in a less politically-polarized setting, with the benefit of officer advice which is often provided on a less formalized basis than in committee. Whilst the most politically-divisive issues (for example, the implementation of the sale of council houses) would normally be avoided, such groups would be felt to be appropriate in principle for a wide range of other tasks and problems. They have a particular role in relation to ongoing projects which require political input or supervision at a greater frequency than the committee cycle, such as a town centre development scheme. In some cases they may be given suitably circumscribed emergency decision powers. In hung authorities they provide a forum to which problems which cannot easily be resolved in committee can be referred, and from which they can be referred back to the committee when a majority agreement has been forged.

Such groups are most effective in authorities where something of the old bi-partisan tradition has survived. In authorities where political divisions are deeper, there will normally be less scope for working parties with an all-party composition. For example, in relation to working parties connected with the 'new' functions of, for example, race relations, equal oportunities and police monitoring, although . minority parties are almost always allocated seats (together with a number of co-opted members), opposition members often choose not to attend, because of a lack of sympathy either with the objectives of such working parties, or with the tone of discussion or atmosphere at the meeting.

In many authorities, particularly where traditional concepts of member/officer roles prevail, working groups are few and far between. They are in general less common in Conservative-controlled authorities, where much of the potential business would be regarded as the responsibility of officers, than in Labour-controlled authorities where they provide one manifestation of the tendency to embrace a wide range of policy issues and an increasing concern with the detailed impact of policy and delivery of services.

Some members and officers find such working parties frustrating: 'talking shops' is an epithet commonly used. Sometimes officers (and members) find it hard to adjust to a non-committee format, and committee conventions and assumptions continue to prevail. The working group seems to work best where there is genuine political commitment to it: where the task is a relatively specific one; where there is a time limit to the group's activities, and where officers have the capacity, if they are involved, to talk freely. In these circumstances they are seen as a valuable adjunct to the formal channels of decision-making.

The role of the opposition

In the Widdicombe interview research, the case for private policy discussion and formulation arenas was widely recognized and accepted. Problems occur however if the deliberations which take place in such arenas, and the provisional policy decisions reached within them, are not then open to critical scrutiny by opposition parties before a formal decision is reached. If adequate time is not available to opposition groups to work up critical responses to majority party policy proposals, and then to question the majority party in detail and in public upon them, then the legitimacy of the arenas within which such proposals were generated becomes more questionable. It is rare, in local government as in central government, for opposition arguments to deflect the party in power from its chosen course. But it is important that their attempts to do so are publicly debated and on public record.

It has been argued that although some opposition groups are intrinsically suspicious of supposedly non-executive arenas such as leadership groups and strategy working parties, the majority regard them with a wry acceptance, as a necessary 'fact of political life'! Where this is the case, the key issue is seen as one of *access to information*. Complaints were made in situations where either no agendas or mintues of such meetings were ever published, or, if they were published, this happened too late for them to be of any use in preparing arguments for public debate in committee or council. It was apparent that in some authorities – particularly those where the opposition was either regarded with contempt, or viewed with unease as a real potential challenge for power – adequate time for the opposition to prepare its counter-arguments was often *not* made available (in such authorities opposition access to officers for confidential briefing was often also heavily constrained).

Thus the minimum requirements of opposition groups are typically as follows: first, adequate representation in arenas where decisions are formally reached; second, adequate information (for example agenda papers and reports) on which to develop an informed and (potentially) critical response to the proposals of the majority group; third, adequate lead-time to prepare such responses; fourth, the opportunity to supplement the written information made available with confidential briefings on specific items from relevant officers; and finally, an adequate opportunity at the formal meetings involved (for example council, committee, sub-committee) to put over their arguments and question the majority party's spokesmen in detail about their proposals.

How common is it for these 'minimum requirements' to be accepted by a majority party? Not surprisingly the answer is that it varies. Much depends on the recent political history of the authority and the quality of inter-party relationships involved. Certainly, in the interview research examples were discovered of failure (deliberate or otherwise) to meet each of these minimum requirements (although not normally all five together). Key aspects of those requirements are discussed below.

Representation

The extent and nature of one-party committees have already been discussed. Athough their capacity to act as private deliberative sessions has now been removed, in that such meetings have now to be held in public (which means that there is nothing to stop members of the opposition from *attending* such meetings), they can still effectively exclude opposition members from the decision-making process, if they are empowered to take decisions. The right of attendance as an observer is not, of course, equivalent to the power to participate. Also the flexibility over the definition of business from which the press and public can reasonably be *excluded*, means that part of the agenda of such one-party commitees can still take place in private.

Although as we have seen the majority of one-party committees and sub-committees are not empowered to take formal decisions, but can simply 'recommend' courses of action to other multi-party arenas, there were a small number of instances discovered in the 1985 survey of one-party committees or sub-committees which were empowered to take decisions under delegated powers. Where this practice occurred, unless such decisions were perceived to be of a genuinely 'emergency' nature, it was roundly (and on most plausible criteria of democratic accountability, rightly) condemned. The recommendations of the Widdicombe

Committee in this area would prelude such practices (see Chapter 8). More common were complaints of *inadequate representation* of opposition groups on decision-making committees, and inadequate time availability at meetings where opposition groups *were* represented, for there to be a full debate about the recommendations of a one-party committee.

Although proportional representation, in terms of overall party strength on the council, is the norm in both majority-controlled and 'hung' local authorities the practice is not universal. Several instances were discovered of an opposition group being allowed a token number of places on an important committee (for example Policy and Resources) which did *not* reflect their numerical strength on the council. This was of particular significance if the number of seats which an opposition group was permitted to hold was one, rather than two or more. If only one seat is held, and its incumbent wishes to propose a motion critical of the policies of the ruling group, then he or she is unlikely to elicit the support of a seconder. If on the other hand there are two members of an opposition group represented, then it becomes almost certain that any critical motion will be seconded and hence discussed and voted upon. Thus the limitation of opposition representation to one has important implications for procedure, and public debate. Examples were also discovered, however, of majority groups which were prepared to give opposition groups a *higher* than proportional number of seats to enable opposition motions to be seconded and debated.

Time availability

The issue of the availability of adequate time for the opposition to probe the majority party's case and present alternative arguments is of particular significance in relation to council meetigs. Council meetings, although often ritualistic in nature, do provide important opportunities for opposition groups to operate in this kind of way. Indeed they are widely seen as being 'opposition-oriented' occasions. But what if the duration of such occasions is inadequate (or deemed to be inadequate) for this role to be effectively performed?

There are two potential problems here. First, despite the generally accepted 'opposition' emphasis in the council meetings, such meetings have their uses for the majority party also, particularly in relation to press coverage (for backbenchers, over specific issues, as well as the leadership). Particularly if relations between the parties are conflictual, time allocations between majority party and opposition contributions may not always be seen by the opposition as fair, especialy in the light of the fact that the mayor, or chairman of the council is highly likely to be a majority party member. In such circumstances the role of the chair is a demanding and thankless one. He or she is unlikely to be able to satisfy both (or all three) party groups in the way in which time is allocated.

The second problem stems from the amount of business to be discussed. For the many local councils which use their council meetings as a mechanism for formally ratifying the (provisional) decisions of the full range of council commit-tees, the potential scope for debate – particularly when other types of item such as 'notices of motion' are taken into account – is enormous. What happens if a council meeting has gone on for four or five hours and a significant number of items (for example sets of commitee minutes) remain to be discussed? The same issue is often also pertinent to commit-tee meetings.

There are three possibilities: long council meetings, con-tinuing until all business has been fully discussed (to the satisfaction of opposition parties); adjourned council meet-ings which are reconvened within the next day or so; and guillotined council meetings. The first two options are common in hung authorities, where it will not normally be acceptable to a majority of the councillors concerned for committee minutes to be ratified without a proper debate. The first option is unpopular in many of the counties, where the long travelling distances involved may create real problems for councillors, if meetings progress beyond, say, 10 p.m. The third option – guillotining – occurs only in majority-controlled (or Independent-dominated) councils. What it involves is the assumed passing of any committee business (i.e minutes) *not* reached by a particular point in time. Sometimes this provision is uncontentious. In a few politically-conflictual councils however, it has been a subject of major disagreement and indeed violent action including 'mace-grabbing' and other forms of demonstration by opposition members. Sometimes such actions are intended as political theatre; on other occasions however, they represent deeply-felt grievances about the lack of opportunity to discuss important issues in public.

There is also the issue of whether there is adequate time for opposition groups to prepare their arguments. All members of the council, or relevant committee, receive copies of the agenda at the same time. Key members of the majority party in a majority-controlled council will already be familiar with the content of the agenda from earlier informal discussions with officers and pre-agenda meetings (or until recently in many authorities previous discussions in one-party committee). In a few authorities visited, opposition members felt that adequate time was not available to prepare counter-arguments. This feeling of discrimination was highlighted in authorities where opposition members also felt that they were denied other important aids in playing their oppositional role effectively: for example access to the agenda and adequate briefing/information facilities.

Access to agendas and information

Of these two issues, access to the agenda was the less important. In most authorities, officers are still the final arbiters regarding what does or does not go on to the agenda. 'Reasonable' requests from opposition members for items to be included on an agenda will typically be accepted, so long as they are received in adequate time for a report to be prepared, and the requisite amount of officer time is deemed to be available. Problems are more likely to arise in authorities where inter-party relationships are poor, and in which chairmen have a more pro-active role in agenda-setting. But even if opposition groups are not allowed access to agendas, there are usually other methods by which they can raise those issues which they wish to raise, for example by raising verbally under 'any other business' an issue at a committee meeting, and requesting a report for the meeting in the next cycle, or – as a last resort – through the right to submit notices of motion at full council meetings.

The issue of briefing is potentially more problematical. In the vast majority of majority-controlled councils, it is not normal for opposition spokesmen to receive an agenda briefing prior to a committee meeting; nor, typically, would they expect one. In these majority-controlled authorities where inter-party relationships are relatively consensual there may be no objection to a chief officer discussing with an opposition spokesman a specific agenda item. That is normally as far as it will go, and, even in this case, the officer has to be careful not to provide the opposition spokesman involved with ammunition to embarrass the party in power (or at least ammunition which can be traced back to the officer). Chief officer/chairman relationships are important to both participants and are rarely lightly disrupted.

More typically, there is an arrangement whereby opposition members can request information, in writing, from chief officers, which may be in relation to specific current agenda items or may not. The problem (for many opposition members) is that typically the reply provided by the chief officer is copied to the committee chairman. This practice, of course, allows the latter to anticipate occasional questions or new lines of argument from the opposition, and to make sure he or she is well-armed in advance agains them. It is a practice also carried out in relation to backbenchers from the chairman's own party, in which case it provides a parallel early-warning system.

The automatic copying to the chairman of information provided was a source of great annoyance to many opposition representatives of all parties. In a few authorities which adopted this practice, it was possible to request that the information required be provided on a confidential basis. In the majority, however, this 'exception' clause was not available. The main substance of opposition complaints lay in the very effect of the copied information in alerting and forewarning, and the potential loss of 'political capital' involved.

In hung authorities, as we have seen, confidential briefings are normal although not universal. There seems no reason in principle (apart from increasing the public discomfort of the majority party!) why this practice should not be adopted in all types of authority. It was noteworthy how often, in authorities in which opposition groups felt themselves otherwise to be well-treated, the non-confidentiality of information provision was the one exception which was singled out.

The issues set out above illustrate the potential range of procedural issues through which a majority can, if it so wishes, discriminate against minority parties. The list could be easily added to. The Widdicombe research revealed isolated instances of named opposition councillors being excluded from specified committees (although typically opposition parties are allowed to decide for themselves who sits on which committee); small 'third parties' being excluded totally from all or most committees; chief officers being actively discouraged from speaking to opposition members; the misuse of urgent business procedures to avoid before-the-event opposition comment; and the chairing of committee (or council) meetings in such a way as to limit opposition contributions, either generally, or from specific individuals.

It should be stressed, however, that these practices, and indeed those discussed in more detail earlier, are very much the exception rather than the rule. There is very little evidence of widespread or systematic discrimination against minority parties even in highly politicized authorities. In a few (although probably increasing number of) London boroughs, fewer metropolitan or shire districts, and a mere handful of shire counties was there to be found serious and sustained opposition argument that their ability to play an effective oppositional role was being materially constrained. None the less, it can be argued that a limited number of adjustments – for example, in relation to confidential briefings, access to agendas, time applicability in debates and representation on formal committees – would further strengthen the legitimacy of the system.

Alternatives to the existing political management system

The procedural innovations so far discussed in this chapter all represent changes which are possible within the present legal framework of local government. There are others which are also worthy of mention: the *management board* consisting of leading members and officers in Alliance-controlled Hereford; the devolution of power to *area committees*, responsible for the full range of services in their area, which is currently being instituted in the London Borough of Tower Hamlets; the formal division between committees responsible for *policy* and committees responsible for *executive action and performance review* (London Borough of Bexley); and the small *executive committee* concerned with a specific project, which is given fully delegated authority, and which can achieve a speed of decision-making beyond the powers of the traditional committee (Portsmouth has a three-person executive committee with the responsibility for the establishment of a ferry terminal). John Stewart (1988) illustrates the extent to which the limitations of traditional committee-bound decision procedure can be escaped from if the will to do so exists, and the scope of alternative arrangements which are possible within existing legal constraints.

There also exists, however, a series of alternative systems of political management, which would require *legislative change*. In particular, in many other countries there is a much clearer separation between the *representative* role of the local council (with responsibility for policy-making and resource allocation) and the *executive* role, through which policy is administered and implemented. The latter can take several different forms: the Oberburgermeister in Southern Germany; the strong (elected) mayor in America; the county (or city) manager as in Ireland; and the small Executive Board (Sweden). Thus the executive can be a single person (elected or appointed) or a small group of politicians either directly elected, or elected from within the larger representative council. In British local government there exists one current attempt to separate powers in this way. The relationship between Passenger Transport Authorities and Passenger Transport Executives is legally much more closely prescribed than the relationship between the typical local authority committee and department. In addition, in Police Authorities, although the Police Force is formally resopnsible to a committee of a local authority the Chief Constable is, in fact, permitted in law a much greater degree of operational autonomy than a Director of Social Services, for example, has.

In the course of our research, we found little evidence of lukewarm support, let alone enthusiasm, for any of the array of 'separate executive' alternatives set out above. Nor was the British central government system of cabinet governments and departmentally-based ministries favoured either. A few chief executives, in authorities where political power was centralized, and five or six leading councillors in effect already cited as a cabinet, were in favour of the idea of formalizing such a system into a 'cabinet' or 'separate executive' of one kind or another. Interestingly, the political leaders in their authorities rarely shared this view. Current conceptions of the role of party leader, particularly in the Labour party, militate against formal cabinets, etc. The overwhelming body of opinion amongst chief executives and (particularly) councillors was for a retention of the current arrangements: executive authority to remain with the council (and to continue to operate in practice through the committee system); the council to continue to be formally responsible for all decisions, unless delegated to officers; and the rights of access and representation of opposition groups to remain broadly as they are at present.

Neither does the separation of powers embodied in the PTA/PTE relationship have any support from councillors, although the Audit Commission and a small number of chief officers who feel themselves to be politically beleaguered support this idea. As we saw in Chapter 2, the main complaint of councillors in this connection is that the compensation system which currently operates severely constrains the capacity of (leading) councillors to carry out their political management role effectively in the current highly politicized conditions of central-local relationships (and of inter-party relations at the local level). There is nothing, it is argued, that a more sensitive system of councillor remuneration and 'time-off from work' provisions could not, in principle, overcome. Thus the *mis-match* between the reality of political change, and the set of structures, processes and procedures which currently operate in British local government (identified by the Widdicombe Committee amongst others) is seen as capable of redress by means of incremental changes to the existing local government system, with major changes of a constitutional nature deemed as unnecessary, not only by the vast majority of respondents to our survey, but by the Widdicombe Committee itself (1986, pp. 71–6). Other influential writers (Stewart, 1988, pp. 11–14) would question the appropriateness of this type of response.

Conclusions

Whatever changes are deemed to be appropriate, the sense of formidable stress on the current political management systems of local government is widely felt. Nowehere is it more keenly felt that amongst chief executives who as we saw in Chapter 3 play, in most authorities, the key role of mediation between members and officers. The extent to which pressures have increased from this source upon chief executives in the 1980s is considerable, particularly in London, the major metropolitan conurbations, and in hung authorities, wherever they are to be found.

In the two decades prior to 1974, the role of the chief executives (or town clerks as they were the known) was secure. Their credibility as the source of legal advice in the authority was unchallenged; their rulings on procedural issues and the interpretation of standing orders were rarely questioned. Even-handedness, in terms of serving with equal commitment whatever political party happened to be in power was relatively unproblematical, given the limited range of policy differences between these two major parties, and the generally good relationships which prevailed (with only a few exceptions) between them. 'Political management', particularly when the annual budgetary growth increment was an unquestioned fact of life, was not necessarily a major priority for town or county clerks.

In the past few years, however, the demands placed on the political management role of the chief executive have intensified, and his or her position in the highly-politicized authorities now often seems far from secure. There are potential problems of identification with a particular political administration, particularly if its policy priorities have required the chief executive to operate in a public, pro-active and entrepreneurial style. There are political problems of deciding what kind of role to play in the first few weeks of a newly-hung authority. There is the growing problem of trying to find legally-varied ways of doing what a radical administration of the left or of the right wants to do, whilst retaining the support of that administration on the occasions when the required legal provisions genuinely cannot be found. It is hardly surprising, therefore, that the extent to which chief executives have left or retired early from posts in which they would in less frenetic circumstances have almost certainly continued much longer, has clearly increased recently. The problematic relations of the leaders of Lambeth and Westminster with their respective chief executives have been much publicized. Similar problems have been experienced in Ealing, Wirral and Liverpool (where the chief executive threatened resignation over the lack of preparedness of the Labour administration to seek a redetermination of the 1988–9 rate support grant), whilst less publicized rumblings of mutual discontent have been apparent on a much wider basis.

It is this increased role-strain which has led several commentators to argue that the *structural* role of the chief executive within British local government merits a major reassessment. There are three separate types of solution which have been put forward. The first is that proposed by the Widdicombe Committee itself – to strengthen the position of the chief executive by providing him or her with a range of new statutory duties and safeguards. This option (discussed in more detail in Chapter 8) has already been rejected by the chief executives' own professional organization SOLACE. The second is to replace the present 'politically-neutral' method of appointment of a chief executive, by the use of more explicitly political criteria, in which case the position would become akin to the American elected mayor or politically-committed city manager. In either case the appointment would have to be fixed-term (with the term corresponding to the period in office of the party which appointed them). In neither case is there any significant level of support currently from either local politicians or (with one or two exceptions) chief executives. The third option implies a separation of powers within the role of the chief executive itself. This idea was forcibly argued recently by Rodney Brooke (Leach, 1986, p. 68):

What Widdicombe does is to move the *arbitration* role very much up front as almost a major priority of chief executives. I do ask myself whether in some councils the various roles (professional manager; policy adviser; arbiter) can be combined or whether or not there are alternatives. You could for example *separate out* the town clerk's job from that of the chief executive . . . and have the town clerk with the right of adjudication upon the procedures of the authority, with the chief executive being responsible to the majority party.

A redefinition along these lines would certainly remove some of the role conflict currently being experienced by chief executives, and also some of the sheer work pressure involved.

The present climate of uncertainty in central–local relations should, however, make us wary of any attempt to be too specific about appropriate political management structures. The impacts on local authority political management systems of the 'opting-out' provisions in housing and education, as well as the requirement to put out to tender an ever increasing range of council services, have not yet become clear. Until they do, or until the next set of major centrally influenced changes emerges, pragmatism and 'seat-of-the-pants' management are likely to remain the only feasible responses.

7
The involvement of the public

Public attitudes to local government

1   Local councils exercise control in one degree or another over the houses people live in, the streets and roads along which they pass, the food and drink they consume, the factories in which they work, the schools in which their children are educated, and the cemeteries in which they are buried. There are ... tens of thousands of Councillors and tens of thousands of officials. Yet the vast majority of the ratepayers have very little knowledge of how Local Government is worked, even in their own districts ...

Most ratepayers are unable to mention the names of more than two or three members of their Local Council. Quite a number are unable to mention any .... Under these circumstances it can hardly be wondered at that the percentage of electors exercising the franchise at local elections is small ...

2   Local democracy is a farce .. only about 25 per cent of people ever vote in a local election, and those who *do* simply regard it as a popularity poll for the real political leaders in Westminster. Who do local councillors represent? Nobody knows who their councillor is ... Do you know who your councillor is?

These twin portraits of ratepayer ignorance and electoral apathy seem almost interchangeable. As it happens, though, they derive from two sources, separated by a period of nearly forty years, who could hardly be more different. The first is Eugene Hasluck (1948, pp. 37–40), the 1940s historian to whom we referred in Chapter 2. He was not a great deal more impressed by what he calls 'the mental calibre of the electorate' (p. 41) than he was by that of the councillors seeking to represent them.

The second quotation, on the other hand, is completely contemporary – from the country's most popular Prime Minister at the time of writing: The Rt Hon. James Hacker, MP, of BBC's *Yes, Prime Minister*. Local government is one of the topics on which Hacker and Sir Humphrey Appleby tend instinctively to see eye-to-eye, and Hacker's dismissive views date back at least to his days as Minister for Administrative Affairs. On this particular occasion, though, they were addressed to his Private Secretary, Bernard Wooley, who, it might be added, proved quite incapable of naming his local councillor.

The first quote, then, is dated; the second possibly exaggerated for dramatic effect. Both, however, have at least a ring of authenticity to them, and it is the purpose of the opening section of this chapter to present a statistical investigation of that authenticity. We do so with particular reference to the survey of public attitudes to local government carried out on behalf of the Widdicombe Committee by NOP Market Research Ltd, the findings from which are reported by Ken Young and William Miller in Research Volume III of the Committee's Report.

The NOP study was the largest govenment-sponsored national survey of attitudes to local government for twenty years – since the rather differently focused Government Social Survey conducted for the Maud Committee in 1965 (Maud Committee, Vol. 3, 1967). Interviews were carried out in November–December 1985 at the houses of 1144 electors, on the basis of a stratified random sample in 112 parliamentary constituencies throughout Great Britain. The questions covered five broad themes:

1   public awareness and knowledge of local government;
2   the extent to which people are satisfied with the standard of their local services;
3   their experience of complaining about local decisions;
4   their views on the relationship between local authorities and the national government;
5   their opinions in respect of local elections and the operation of the local democratic system.

We shall endeavour to address each of these themes at least summarily in the remainder of this section.

Public awareness of local government

The NOP survey asked respondents a series of sixteen factual questions about their knowledge of local government, of their own local authorities, of their councillors, and of the political complexion of the party (if any) in control of their local and county or regional councils. Ken Young's review of the responses to these questions was fairly upbeat in tone:

Overall, the level of knowledge displayed by our respondents in what was a fairly exacting series of questions appears to be quite high . . . It is apparent that for the most part the scope of local government provision is fairly well understood . . our own findings point towards a reasonably well-informed electorate. (Widdicombe Committee, Research Vol. III, 1986, pp. 28, 31)

So have Hasluck and Hacker got it all wrong? Do the NOP statistics refute their unsubstantiated aspersions? Well, partly perhaps, but by no means entirely. As so often, one's conclusion depends on one's definition and interpretation of, in this case, phrases like 'quite high', 'fairly well understood' and 'reasonably well-informed'. You pays your money and you takes your choice, as the saying goes. The basic evidence is set out in Table 25.

Both Hasluck and Hacker, it will be recalled, draw attention to the inability of most people to name their own local councillors; in fact, depending on one's point of view, 'as few as' or 'as many as' 30 per cent of the NOP respondents were able to do so. There were some major variations: regionally, from 42 per cent in Scotland down to a mere 15 per cent in London, and in age-groupings from 39 per cent among those over 55 down to 20 per cent among the under-35s. Interestingly, and most unusually with knowledge-based questions, social groups DE were slightly *more* likely to be able to name a local councillor (33 per cent) than were AB and C1 respondents (30 per cent), and the non-employed were much more likely (35 per cent) than the employed (25 per cent).

		% of respondents able to name correctly			
		All respondents %	London %	Metrop. England %	Rest of England and Wales %	Scotland %

		All respondents %	London %	Metrop. England %	Rest of England and Wales %	Scotland %
1	Name of county/ regional council	52	38	45	57	52
2	Name of city/district/ borough council	70	81	65	73	52
3	Name of (any of) the councillors(s) for your ward on. . . local council)	30	15	22	33	42
4	Party of your local councillor(s)	54	50	62	51	62
5	Party in control of. . . (local council)	61	68	80	53	62
6	Party in control of. . . (county/ regional) council	56	77	72	45	62

*Type of authority –
county/regional
council (CC), local
council (LC), or
'some other body'
(OB) – responsible for:*

7	Schools (CC/LC)	67
8	Council housing (LC)	73
9	Hospitals (OB)	33
10	Street cleaning (LC)	80
11	Electricity supply (OB)	63
12	Home helps for the elderly (CC/LC)	45
13	Rubbish collection (LC)	79
14	Unemployment benefit (OB)	60
15	Dealing with planning applications (LC)	69
16	The fire service (CC)	57

	% of respondents able to name correctly				
	All respondents %	*London* %	*Metrop. England* %	*Rest of England and Wales* %	*Scotland* %
'Well informed' (13–16 correct answers)	18				
'Quite well informed' (10–12 correct)	34				
'Not very well informed' (6–9 correct)	36				
'Uninformed' (0–5 correct)	12				

Source: Widdicombe Committee, Research Vol. III, 1986, Tables 2.1, 2.6, 2.7, 2.8 and 2.10 (pp. 25–34).

Table 25 *General knowledge of local government (1985)*

Although the question was not included in the NOP survey, all these councillor-identification figures are significantly below the MP-identification figures of around 50 per cent that have been found in other studies (for example Crewe, 1985, p. 59; Heald and Wybrow, 1986, p. 78). The same is true of party recognition. Between a half and two-thirds of the NOP sample were able to identify the party of their local councillor(s) (where they had one) and/or the party in control of their local councils – which compares with the three-quarters who can name their MP's party (Heald and Wybrow, 1986, p. 78).

Finally, among this initial group of factual questions, only just over a half of all NOP respondents were able to name correctly their county or regional authority, and only just over two-thirds their 'local' council. Reversing the councillor-identification figures, Londoners were the most familiar with the names of their borough councils (81 per cent), while Scots were the least familiar (52 per cent).

The remaining questions included in the aggregate 'knowledge of local government' measure required respondents to allocate a set of ten services between the two levels of local government and 'some other body, such as the central government and nationalised industries'. This, it should be noted, it a relatively undemanding form of service-allocation question. It is less testing, for instance, than one of the forms used in the Maud Committee Survey, in which people were asked spontaneously to name 'some of the things that their local/county council provides in this area'. Placed in this situation, over a quarter (26 per cent) of the Maud respondents had been unable to think of any service provided by their local borough or district council, and very nearly half (49 per cent) of those living in areas served by county councils could not mention any service provided by their county authority (Maud Committee, Vol, 3, 1967, p. 7).

Not surprisingly, the more closed form of the NOP question produced a more positive set of results. Most of the seven local government services on the list were correctly located by between two-thirds and three-quarters of respondents, the principal exception being home helps for the elderly, which in both Scotland and non-metropolitan England and Wales tended to be linked to the district councils rather than the appropriate upper-tier authorities. The three non-local government services on the list, however, were also located with local authorities by many repsondents, most spectactularly hospitals, which 59 per cent imagined were (still) run by local government.

On the basis of their 'correct' answers to this set of sixteen questions, respondents were then coded into one of four categories, from 'well-informed' to 'uninformed', as in the final section of Table 25. This categorization is inevitably somewhat arbitrary: different breakpoints between categories would obviously yield different proportions of, say, 'well-informed' or 'uninformed'. Nor did cross-tabulation with personal, social and regional variables produce any great surprises. The highest proportions of the well-informed were found among social classes AB (29 per cent), the 55 to 64 age-group (27 per cent), men (26 per cent), and Londoners (23 per cent), with the lowest proportions among social classes

DE (11 per cent), the under-35s (10 per cent), women (12 per cent) and, perhaps most unexpectedly, the Scots (8 per cent).

Ken Young, in evaluating these NOP findings, ventured to suggest that, when they are compared with the figures from the Maud Committee's Government Social Survey:

There are . . . some indications that the level of confusion as to the operation of the local government system is in some important respects lower today.   (Widdicombe Committee, Research Vol. III, 1986, p. 31)

It is, admittedly, a tentative conclusion and, as Young points out, direct comparison of the Maud and Widdicombe figures is impossible, not least because of the differently structured questions used in the two surveys. Nevertheless, with a small amount or re-analysis, some comparisons are possible, particularly of the service-location data. Table 26 relates the Maud findings to those of the NOP/Widdicombe survey in Table 25 (asterisked): the figures offer little support to Young's thesis.

Having been asked if they could spontaneously name some local government services, the Maud respondents were then presented with a list of nine services and asked to locate them with either their borough or district council or their county council. For those people living in county boroughs – unitary authorities responsible for the management of all local government services – this constituted a relatively undemanding task. Among respondents in the two-tier county authorities, on the other hand, there were definite signs of both uncertainty and confusion, which manifested themselves not least in a tendency to think that 'local' councils were responsible for county authority services. This, of course, was what many in the NOP survey had apparently done with home helps for the elderly; and was similar too to the patterns of response found in a recent MORI/INLOGOV survey of residents in the six former metropolitan county council areas (Game, 1987d, especially pp. 15–17). The confusion would seem to stem, therefore, from the very existence of a two-tier or non-unitary system of local government. That system, virtually nationwide until the abolition of the GLC and the metropolitan county councils, is still more widespread than it was in 1965 – which may help to account for the fact that *none* of the five directly comparable services in Tables 25 and 26 was 'correctly' located by as high a proportion of all respondents in 1985 as it had been in 1965.

Question: 'I'd like you to tell me which authority is responsible for providing each service – the borough/district council or the county council'

	County borough residents			County residents		
Service	Borough/ district %	County council %	Other/ don't know %	Borough/ district %	County council %	Other/ don't know %
Street lighting (B/DC)	85	7	8	<u>77</u>	9	14[a]
*Street cleaning (B/DC)	89	7	4	<u>91</u>	4	5[b]
*Refuse collection (B/DC)	94	4	2	<u>92</u>	5	3
*Housing (B/DC)	86	8	6	<u>75</u>	11	14[c]
Public libraries (both)	81	8	11	<u>45</u>	<u>40</u>	15[d]
*Schools (CB/CC)	76	12	12	21	<u>66</u>	13
*Fire brigade (CB/CC)	73	13	14	30	<u>51</u>	19
Old people's homes (CB/CC)	75	9	16	41	<u>27</u>	32
Welfare clinics (CB/CC)	77	10	13	37	<u>40</u>	23
Base		629			1,555	

Source: Maud Committee on the Management of Local Government, *Vol. 3: The Local Government Elector* (by Mary Horton), 1967, Tables 6–15, pp. 10–14.

Notes: * = services also included in the NOP/Widdicombe Committee survey

<u>77</u> = correct answer

[a] excludes the 436 county residents in rural districts, where street lighting was sometimes the responsibility of the parish council and sometimes non-existent.

[b] excludes the 436 respondents in rural districts, where street cleaning was often the responsibility of the county authority.

[c] excludes the 131 respondents in London metropolitan boroughs, where housing was also the responsibility of the London County Council.

[d] libraries were run by both local and county authorities in county areas.

Table 26   *Allocation of local government services to types of local authority (1965)*

This comparision, it must be stressed, is far too partial and speculative to support any firm conclusion. But it does at least cast some doubt on the idea that people today are significantly more aware of and factually knowledgeable about the workings of local government than they were either twenty years ago, or even forty years ago at the time Hasluck was writing. They may be slightly better able to put a name to their local councilllors than Jim Hacker would give them credit for, and certainly, as we describe later on in this chapter, some councils are nowadays making strenuous efforts to improve their public communications and information provision. The signs are, though, that at least a sizeable minority of the public has so far remained relatively resistant to such blandishments.

Satisfaction with local councils

It would be quite wrong, however, to equate any lack of factual knowledge with either dissatisfaction or unconcern. Being uncertain as to whether a particular service is run from the county hall or district council offices – often located in the same town – is by no means the same as being dissatisfied with the quality or standard of that service. Indeed, it could be argued that the opposite is more plausible: active dissatisfaction would necessitate finding out precisely who was responsible.

The NOP/Widdicombe survey added to the now substantial body of evidence suggesting that the general level of public satisfaction with local government and with local authority services is in fact relatively high. As can be seen in Table 27, more than 70 per cent of all respondents were satisfied with the performance of both levels of local government, with slightly more reservation being expressed about the district and borough councils (Research Vol. III, p. 39). Even the lowest levels of satisfaction recorded were still comparatively high: among those in social class E (63 per cent), the 55 to 64-age group (63 per cent), council tenants (63 per cent), metropolitan residents (62 per cent), and, interestingly, *non*-ratepayers (59 per cent). Contrary to what is sometimes supposed, payment of rates does not itself appear to bring about a sense of dissatisfaction with the rating authority.

One of the most intriguing findings thrown up by Young's analysis of the NOP data was the very weak relationship beetween respondents' partisan sympathies and the political control of the local council. Conservative supporters did prove rather more positive about their local council in those areas where it was controlled by their own party, but Labour supporters were actually slightly *less* satisfied with Labour authorities than with those under other, or no, control. It would seem from this finding that the increased party politicization of local government in recent years has impinged considerably more upon the politicians involved than upon the local electorate. For the latter, partisan sympathies are frequently not the principal criteria by which they judge the performance of their local councils, which perhaps makes it less suprising that, as we shall see, they are not always the criteria which determine their voting behaviour either.

The NOP survey did not attempt to devise any parallel question asking people about their satisfaction with the performance of *central* government. Indeed, it might be urged that no precisely parallel question is devisable. All the same, frequent attempts have been made in recent years, for obvious political reasons, to compare the electorate's perception of both central and local government, and the results are undeniably illuminating. Table 28 is drawn from a national survey of voters in England and Wales carried out by MORI for the Audit Commission in May 1986. The phrasing of the relevant questions is slightly different from that employed by NOP – and possibly slightly leading – which may account for the rather lower proportion of respondents describing themselves as satisfied with their local council. That lower proportion, however, is twice that of the dissatisfied respondents, and also a great deal higher than those saying they were satisfied with the national Government. As would be expected, there are considerable variations in some of these figures: dissatisfaction with the local council being greater, for example, among the residents of metrpolitan areas (32 per cent), of Wales (30 per cent), and most especially those

Question: 'On the whole, do you think that . . . (county/local) council runs things very well, fairly well, or not at all well?'

	County regional council runs things:		Local council runs things:		
	'Very' or 'fairly' well %	*'Not at all' well* %	*'Very' or 'fairly' well* %	*'Not at all' well* %	*Base*
All respondents	72	16	71	21	1,144
By locational characteristics					
Region:					
London	70	18	64	25	123
Metropolitan England	62	24	60	27	235
Rest of England and Wales	76	13	77	17	677
Scotland	68	20	68	22	108
Housing tenure:					
Owner occupier	74	15	75	20	815
Council tenant	63	20	61	26	234
Ratepaying:					
Pays rates in full	73	16	73	19	812
Rates partly rebated	76	16	68	25	118
Does not pay rates	59	19	60	27	122
By partisan sympathy (majority party supporters only)					
Conserv. supporter in Conserv. locality	–	–	72	14	143
Conserv. supporter in non-Cons. locality	–	–	63	20	217
Labour supporter in Labour locality	–	–	65	16	195
Labour supporter in non-Lab. locality	–	–	70	20	198
Politically sympathetic to local council	–	–	68	15	338
Politically unsympathetic to local council	–	–	66	21	415

Source: Widdicombe Committee, Research Vol. III, 1986, Ch. 3, pp. 40–3.

Table 27 *General satisfaction with local councils (1985)*

of Inner London (41 per cent), while dissatisfaction with the government was particularly high among the under-35s, the unemployed (62 per cent), and council tenants (61 per cent). In the case of *every* single cross-tabulation, though, satisfaction with the local council is higher, or dissatisfaction lower, than it is with the government. The same is true of every published study in which this pair of questions has been included: irrespective of the political complexion of the survey area, the political control of the local authority, or the popularity of the government at the time, the comparison consistently comes out to the advantage of local government.

Satisfaction with local services

Satisfaction with the majority of individual local government services tends also to be relatively high, as was found by both the NOP/Widdicombe and the MORI/Audit Commission surveys. The latter study, being both more recent and covering a more extensive range of local service, is the one summarized in Table 29.

Overall, of all the seventeen services asked about, an average of 54 per cent of this national sample said they were satisfied – which, as it happens, is almost precisely the same as the 53 per cent who said they were satisfied with the local councils in Table 28. But in all such studies individual ratings vary enormously from one service to another. Road maintenance in particular, as highway engineers will need no reminding, wins few plaudits from the public; but, together with street cleaning, this was the only service which did not enjoy greater public satisfaction than dissatisfaction. Of the remainder, five services were regarded as satisfactory by more than three-quartes of respondents – refuse collection, the fire service, street lighting, libraries and the police – and a further two by more than three in five – parks, playgrounds and open spaces, and swimming pools/sports facilities. Both of these services, on the other hand, also received comparatively high dissatisfaction ratings, along with care of the elderly, council housing and secondary schools.

Few of the services on this list, however, are actually used 'regularly' by even half the general population. So while the

Question: 'Overall, how satisfied or dissatisfied are you with the way your local district or borough council/the government is running this area/the country?'

	Local council %	The government %	Relative satisfaction with local council %
Very/fairly satisfied	53	32	+21
Very/fairly dissatisfied	26	52	+26
Neither/don't know	21	16	
Net satisfaction	+27	−20	+47

Base = 1,659

Source: MORI, *Attitudes to Local Authorities and their Services:* Research study conducted for the Adult Commission, May 1986, pp.1–4.

Table 28 *Satisfaction with local council vs. the government (1986)*

extent of public satisfaction may be an interesting statistic, the more significant one, and the one of greater concern to the providers of the service, may well be *user* satisfaction. It is notable, therefore, that in just about every case in this MORI survey, satisfaction with a given service proved to be considerably *higher* among users of that service than among the public as a whole. For example, while 78 per cent of all respondents say they are satisfied with libraries, the figures rises to 92 per cent among regular library users. Similarly, council housing is considered satisfactory by barely one-third of the sample as a whole, but by more than three in five (61 per cent) of regular users – presumably tenants (figures which, incidentally, match very closely those in the NOP/Widdicombe survey, Research Vol. III, p. 45). But at the same time, regular users are at least as ready as other respondents to express *dis*satisfaction with a service – and rather more so in the case of education and housing.

The final columns of figures in Table 29 focus attention on one of the key local government debates in recent years: the preparedness of people to pay higher rates in order to

Questions:
1. How satisfied or dissatisfied are you with . . . in this area?'
2. 'Which, if any, of these services do you or members of your family use or
3. (i) 'In which of these service areas, if any, do you think more money should
4. (ii) 'In which of these service areas, if any, do you think costs can be reduced

Service	Public satisfaction all respondents	
	Satisfied %	Dissatisfied %
Fire service	82	1
Libraries	78	5
Police service	77	12
Refuse collection	85	13
Museums	41	11
Street lighting	80	14
Swimming pools, sports facilities	61	22
Primary schools	43	12
Child care facilities	31	13
Further education	48	14
Care of the elderly	45	23
Parks, playgrounds and open spaces	63	24
Care of the handicapped	37	16
Council housing	34	20
Secondary schools	34	19
Footpath and street cleaning	44	50
Road maintenance	29	63
None of these	–	–
Don't know	–	–
Base	*1,659*	

Source: MORI, *Attitudes to Local Authorities and their Services:* Research study conducted for the Audit Commission, May 1986, pp.9–22. 1986.

Note: None of the pairings of figures add up to 100 per cent, because of the exclusion of 'Don't know' responses.

Table 29   *Satisfaction with individual council services (1986)*

benefit from on a regular basis?'
be spent, assuming the money comes from local ratepayers?'
without reducing the quality of the service?'

User satisfaction Regular users only			*Higher/lower spending* all respondents	
(% of all respondents) %	*Satisfied* %	*Dissatisfied* %	*More money spent* %	*Costs reduced* %
(81)	94	2	9	1
(44)	92	4	5	3
(9)	91	7	15	4
(81)	86	11	6	4
(7)	84	10	5	5
(59)	83	11	8	3
(31)	78	19	13	3
(20)	76	20	24	2
(7)	75	17	17	1
(11)	71	21	15	3
(8)	71	23	34	2
(36)	69	25	14	3
(5)	68	28	29	1
(17)	61	32	15	5
(15)	60	31	24	3
(55)	43	51	17	3
(48)	29	66	30	4
	–	–	9	52
	–	–	9	21
Regular users only			1,659	

maintain or improve the standard of local services. Respondents in this MORI/Audit Commission survey were asked in which areas they felt costs could be reduced without reducing the quality of the service, and also where they felt more ratepayers' money might be spent. An overall majority of the sample (52 per cent) thought that there were *no* areas in which costs could be reduced without the quality of the service being affected, compared to only 9 per cent who felt that no money should be spent on any service. As many as one in three (34 per cent) said that more money should be spent on care of the elderly, and more than one in four said the same for road maintenance (30 per cent), care of the handicapped (29 per cent), and both secondary and primary school (27 per cent and 24 per cent) respectively. Moreover, as the authors of the MORI report emphasize, there was 'almost no difference between the answers of respondents who are ratepayers and those whose rates are paid by the state' (p. 21).

This preference for rate increases over service reductions is one that has been gaining steadily in strength throughout the 1980s, as can be seen from the Gallup Poll summary in Table 30. By April 1985, when the Conservative government in fact held a small lead over Labour in voting intentions for the coming county council elections, very nearly half of all respondents wanted more spent on local services, even at the acknowledged cost of rate rises (*Daily Telegraph*, 2 May 1985). It would seem, as we noted at the start of this section, that some people at least may be rather more appreciative and supportive of local government and its services than they are factually informed about them.

Satisfaction with councillors and officers

Support for local services, particularly those bringing some kind of personal or family benefit, is easily understandable; support for the councillors and officerrs who provide those services, and to whom one complains when something goes wrong, is quite another matter. In this section, therefore, we look at the reactions people have to their contacts with these local government personnel.

Question: 'People have different views about whether it is more important to reduce rates or keep up local government spending. How about you? Which of these statements comes closest to your own view?'

	April 1980 %	Feb. 1982 %	April 1985 %
'Rates being cut, even if it means some reduction in local services such as schools, housing and welfare services'	26	22	14
'Things should be left as they are'	29	32	30
'Local services such as schools, housing and welfare services should be extended, even if it means some increases in rates'	36	38	49
Don't know	10	8	7
Balance in favour of rate increases to extend local services	+10	+16	+35

Source: Gallup/*Daily Telegraph*, 2 May 1985; Game, 1987a.

Table 30 *Rates vs. services (1980–5)*

The NOP/Widdicombe survey asked their respondents whether they had ever contacted or complained to either a councillor or their council office 'by phone, visit or letter'. As can be seen in Table 31, roughly a half reported to have been in touch with their council offices, while one-fifth had contacted their councillor. This latter figure is consistent with that found in other studies, and is perceptibly higher than that usually recorded for contact with MPs (for example Crewe, 1985, pp. 54–64; Moss, 1980), reflecting councillors' generally easier accessibility, living as they invariably do either in or close to their wards. The regional variations in the patterns of contact are striking, with particularly low levels of contact with officials in Scotland and with councillors in London. Council tenants are considerably more likely than any other social group to have communicated with their councillor, but, rather surprisingly, slightly *less* likely than

Questions:
1. 'Have you ever complained to or contacted one of your councillors/a council department on . . . (local council) by visit, phone or letter?'
2. 'How satisfied or dissatisfied were you with the way your councillor/the council dealt with the matter?'

	Contact with councillor %	Contact with council offices %	Base
1 All respondents	20	49	1,144
By region:			
London	14	49	123
Metropolitan England	20	52	235
Rest of England and Wales	22	50	677
Scotland	21	32	108
By housing tenure:			
Owner occupier	18	50	815
Council tenant	32	47	234

2 Respondents who had contacted or complained

Satisfaction with the way the councillor or council officers dealt with the matter:

'Very' or 'fairly' satisfied	61	54	
'Fairly' or 'very' dissatisfied	33	39	

Source: Widdicombe Committee, Research Vol. III, 1986, Calculations based on figures in Tables 2.12 and 3.9 (pp. 36–48).

Table 31   *Contact with councillors and council offices (1985)*

owner occupiers to report any contact with their council offices.

The lower section of Table 31 summarizes respondents' reactions to their contacts with councillors and officials. In both cases, the majority declared themselves generally satisfied, with councillors receiving the slightly higher satisfaction rating. It is likely that the relatively small difference is accounted for mainly by the differing reasons that prompted the contact in the first place – council officers being faced with a higher proportion of apparently insoluble problems or unresolvable complaints. It is also true, though, that there are better and worse ways even of saying 'No', and it can be instructive to look in a little more detail at the ways in which people describe having been treated by officials. This was something that was beyond the scope of the NOP/ Widdicombe questionnaire, but that has been investigated in a number of the surveys undertaken by MORI. One such national survey was conducted by the Association of Metropolitcan Authorities (AMA) in August 1985, and those respondents who reported ever having contacted a council official were presented with the sets of paired questions outlined in Table 32.

Question: 'When you *last* contacted a council official, did you find them . . .?'

	%
Helpful	69
or Unhelpful	27
Friendly	80
or Unfriendly	10
Efficient	57
or Inefficient	31
Interested in your problem	62
or Uninterested in your problem	30
Quick to respond	50
or Slow to respond	44
Easy to get hold of the right person	64
or Difficult to get hold of the right person	31

Base = all who have ever contacted a council official = 645

Source: MORI, *Attitudes Towards Local Government:* Research Study conducted for the Association of Metropolitan Authorities, Oct. 1985.

Table 32 *Treatment by council officials (1985)*

As was found in the NOP survey, a majority of those who have contacted a council official about a problem or a matter to do with the council came away with a fairly positive impression. Officers are considered to be friendly and generally helpful and interested in the problems or issues brought before them. On the other hand, nearly one-third of those who had tried to contact a council official had experienced difficulty in getting hold of the right person, and then, having done so, had found that person to be inefficient and/or uninterested in their problem. Finally, and rather in conformity with popular myth, as many as 44 per cent felt that council officials were slow to repsond. As we shall see later on in this chapter, it is findings like these – as well as the service-satisfaction figures of the type described earlier – that have helped inform the development of the concept of a 'public service orientation'.

We shall see also, however, that there has been an element of defensiveness behind local authorities' search for higher quality service delivery and improved client relations. Local government has felt itself under attack from central government: financially constrained, and with its activities subject to increasing central scrutiny and control. As central-local government relations have become visibly more stressed, it is worthwhile examining where the instincts and sentiments of the electorate lie.

The NOP/Widdicombe survey included several questions on this general theme, of which the two summarized in Tables 33 and 34 are representative examples. Confirming the findings of other studies that have asked similar questions, Table 33 shows that while the largest group of respondents are satisfied with the status quo, there is more than twice the support for a reduction in central control than there is for an increase. Not surprisingly, these views correlate strongly with respondents' party political sympathies, but there are significantly more Conservative sympathizers in favour of less central control than there are Labour supporters in favour of more. There is a loose relationship between respondents' knowledge of local government – as reported earlier in this chapter – and their attitudes to central control, with the more knowledgeable

Question: 'Do you think local councils ought to be controlled by central government more, less, or about the same as now?'

	More central control %	About the same %	Less central control %	Base
All respondents	14	46	33	1,144
By party identification:				
Conservative	23	59	15	359
Labour	9	38	47	390
Alliance	14	48	34	196
By 'knowledge of local government':				
'Well informed'	12	42	45	209
'Quite well informed'	14	45	36	387
'Not very well informed'	16	50	28	407
'Uninformed'	12	45	21	141

Source: Widdicombe Committee, Research Vol. III, 1986, Ch.5, pp.76–80.

Table 33 *Preferred degree of central control over local councils (1985)*

generally favouring less control.

Table 34 focuses on a slightly different aspect of the central-local relationship: the range of powers and duties thought appropriate to local government. Respondents were asked, for a range of services – some traditional mandatory duties (roads, parks and housing) and some permissive powers in more innovatory areas (playgroups, grants to voluntary organizations, and job creation) – whether councils should be required to do them, allowed to do them, or not allowed to do them. Interestingly, the great majority of the NOP sample thought that *all* these services were the legitimate subject of local government activity, while a clear majority in the case of job creation and a near majority in the case of playgroups felt that these services too should be not merely permissible, but mandatory. In its own way, this response would seem to be as strong an endorsement of the institution of local government as the more direct expressions

Question: 'People have different views on what councils should or should not do. For each of these, can you say if local councils should be required to do them, or should be able to do them if they wish, or should not be allowed to do them?'

Service	Have to do %	Be allowed to do %	Not be allowed to do %
Maintain road surfaces	77	16	6
Provide playgroups for young children	48	43	6
Give grants to voluntary organizations	17	58	17
Provide council housing	81	15	2
Provide parks and open spaces	77	19	2
Spend money to create jobs in the area	59	29	8

Base = 1,144

Source: Widdicombe Committee, Research Vol. III, 1986, p.60.

Table 34   *The powers and duties of local councils (1985)*

of support and satisfaction noted earlier. There is more than an echo here of the view of an active and wide-ranging local government taken by the Bains Committee in the early 1970s:

Local government is not, in our view, limited to the narrow provision of a series of services to the local community . . . . It has within its purview the overall economic, cultural and physical well-being of that community . . .   (Bains Committee Report, 1972, p. 6)

Local voting behaviour

A sceptic, of course, might easily mock such a suggestion: if people really are supportive of local government and want its role enhanced, why do so few of them seem to show it in their local voting behaviour? It is an observation that, while it certainly cannot be refuted, needs at least to be set in context.

First, there is the issue of local election turnout – the percentage of the registered electorate casting a valid vote. As Michael Goldsmith and Ken Newton show in their review for the Widdicombe Committee of *Local Government Abroad*:

local election turnout in Great Britain is almost at the bottom of the international league table. Setting aside those nations in which voting is technically or actually compulsory (Italy and parts of Australia), turnout ranges, for the most part, between 60% and 80%. In Sweden it approaches 90%, in Denmark it is over 70% . . . A comparative study of twelve western nations shows a turnout of roughly 70% in city elections. (Widdicombe Committee, Research Vol. IV, 1986, p. 146)

By way of contrast, as can be seen in Table 35, local turnouts in Britain during the 1980s have averaged consistently around 40 per cent – with little variation between metropolitan and shire county areas. It is obviously well below the international average. Yet, as William Miller point out in his overview of the literature for the Widdicombe Committee:

. . . other comparisons are possible. Turnout in British local government elections is not a great deal less than at American Presidential elections and somewhat more than the turnout for off-year Congressional elections in America, or European Parliament elections in the U.K. . . . Moreover, while turnout in American national elections is much lower now than in the last century, turnout in British local government elections has never been high. Complaints about apathy towards local government elections were frequent in the 1920s, 1930s and 1940s . . . (Widdicombe Committee, Research Vol. III, 1986, pp. 113–4)

It was these years, of course, that Hasluck was describing – and Jim Hacker apparently imagining – in our opening quotations. They were years in which, moreover, as we saw in Chapter 2, as many as half of all candidates would be returned unopposed – without anyone voting for them. By these standards – and taking account too of the fact that

turnouts in British parliamentary elections also come almost
equally low in any international league table – local democracy today is not perhaps in quite such a moribund state as
is sometimes suggested.

		%
1982	Metropolitan districts	37.6
1982	Scottish regions and islands	42.9
1983	Metropolitan districts	41.2
1984	Metropolitan districts	38.6
1985	English counties	41.4
1985	Welsh counties	47.0
1986	Metropolitan districts	39.3
1987	Metropolitan districts	44.0

Source: Rallings and Thrasher, 1987, p.i, Karran
and Bochel, 1986.

Table 35   *Turnouts at metropolitan district
and county council elections (1982–7, contested
seats only)*

The second issue that we need to address is the idea that
local elections constitute little more than a 'sort of annual
general election' (Newton, 1976, p. 16), or, as Prime Minister
Hacker less modestly put it: 'a popularity poll for the real
political leaders in Westminster'. Hacker's view has been lent
added weight by the fact that this is apparently precisely how
the local elections of both 1983 and 1987 *were* treated by our
non-fictional Prime Minister in her search for a propitious
general election date. All the same, it is a generalization that
needs some qualification. That qualification can take essentially two forms: an examination of how people actually *do*
vote, and how they *say* they vote. Fortunately, both types of
information are now available to us in a way that they were
not, for instance, at the time Newton was writing in the early
1970s.

By far the best chance to compare actual voting patterns in local and national elections came in May 1979, as the result of Prime Minister Callaghan's largely enforced decision to call a general election on the same day as the English and Welsh district council elections. It was a decision that may not have been welcomed by the political parties, who found themselves at short notice having to run two campaigns simultaneously, but it offered a unique opportunity to students of local politics. If local elections really were, to quote Newton again, 'determined overwhelmingly by national political considerations' (p. 16), then on this occasion there should have been two sets of near-identical results. Discrepancies would have arisen only where local parties failed to contest individual wards in constituencies fought at the national level.

The figures show, in fact, that the local and national results were far from identical. In a striking number of constituencies, particularly in the more rural parts of the country, there were unmistakable signs of what Americans would call 'split-ticket voting' – voters splitting their votes between candidates from different parties in the two elections, and even between local candidates on the same party ticket. Thus, Robert Waller, summarizing the two sets of results from some 100 constituencies, found that 'it was not unusual for a candidate to poll over twice the vote of a ward running mate' (Waller, 1980, p. 445).

More generally, there was the widespread tendency for Liberal candidates to do better in the local elections than at the general election. In Liverpool, for example, where the Liberals had formed the largest group on the city council for much of the 1970s, they won nearly 28 per cent of the local vote, yet barely 14 per cent of the parliamentary vote (Cox and Laver, 1979, p. 386). In other places too, where a full local and general election comparison was possible, the Liberal share of the local vote was several percentage points higher, mostly at the expense of the Conservatives. Given the closely corresponding turnout figures in the two elections, the only way in which such results could have been produced is by considerable numbers of voters 'splitting their tickets' and supporting the Liberals locally and Conservatives or Labour nationally (Cox and Laver, 1979; Game, 1981).

These electors, in other words, brought different considerations to bear on the two types of electoral decision they were being asked to make. In voting for their council candidates, they were obviously taking some account of the respective parties' local records, their stands on major local issues, and the personality and performance of their local councillors. In their general election vote, by contrast, they were presumably giving more weight to the national parties, their leaders and manifestos, and to the record or promise of the parliamentary candidates. In many cases these differing considerations must nevertheless have resulted in local and parliamentary votes for the same party. But in many thousands of cases they demonstrably *did not*, and votes were cast for different parties in the two elections.

Common sense suggests that if local considerations can prove a decisive local electoral influence in the circumstances of 1979 – at the culmination of a general election campaign, with two ballot papers to be marked at the same time in the same polling booth – they must surely be at least as influential at other local elections. However, it requires the literal coincidence of local and parliamentary polling dates to furnish what Cox and Laver describe as this 'unequivocal evidence' of the impact of local factors (p. 338). In the absence of such coincidence, we have to rely on how people report their behaviour or intentions in differing electoral situations.

There has been plenty of relevent opinion poll evidence gathered in recent years, of which only a small selection can be presented here. First, we have in Table 36 the responses given to pairs of voting intention questions that have been put to samples of voters during recent local election capaigns. The figures show only the *net* differences in voting intention in the two types of elections, rather than the complex pattern of inter-party variations which go to produce those net differences. But the findings of these and several other similar polls over the past five years (see Game, 1987b) are remarkably consistent. They all report proportions of voters saying that they would vote differently in local and general elections; and, furthermore, that the net effect of this

behaviour is a local advantage of several percentage points
to Labour.

'Which party are you most inclined to support?'	Conserv. %	Labour %	Alliance %	
1984				Lab. lead over Cons.
'in next Thursday's local elections'	35	46	18	+11%
'if there was a General Election tomorrow'	39	42	18	+ 3%
Local electoral advantage to Labour				+ 8%
Base = 434				
1987				Cons. lead over Lab.
'in next Thursday's local elections'	36	35	27	+ 1%
'if there was a General Election tomorrow'	40	32	27	+ 8%
Local electoral advantage to Labour				+ 7%
Base = 951				

Source: MORI/*Sunday Times*, 29 April 1984; NOP/*Independent*, 7 May 1987.

Notes:
a All questions were asked *only* of respondents living in areas where local elections were due to be held.
b The figures exclude those who said they would not vote, don't know, or refused to say.

Table 36 *Local and general election voting intentions (1984 and 1987)*

'If you are voting in a *general election,* do you vote more for an individual candidate or more for the party he or she is from?'

'If you are voting in a *local election,* do you vote more for an individual candidate or more for the party he or she is from?'

'If you are voting in a *local council election,* are you influenced more by local issues or more by national issues?'

Base = 1,144

*Respondents by coincidence of their
local/national voting preferences:*

Respondents whose local preferences are *in accord* with their general election preference

Respondents whose local preferences are *not in accord* with their general election preference

Respondents whose local preferences are *in accord* with their Con/Lab/Alliance national party identification

Respondents whose local preferences are *in direct contradiction* to the Con/Lab/Alliance national party identification

Respondents whose local preferences are for an *'other' party/ candidate,* but who have a Con/Lab/Alliance national party identification

Respondents who *do not have* a Con/Lab/Alliance national party identification

Source: Widdicombe Committee, Research Vol. III, 1986, pp. 163–5.

Table 37   *Basis of local and general election| voting choice (1985)*

Table 37   *Basis of local and general election voting choice (1985)*

	Candidate %		Party %	
	11		79	
	32		52	

	National issues %		Local issues %	Both equally %
	22		54	13

All respondents with a local election voting preference %	% claiming local voting on basis of candidate %	% claiming local voting on basis of local issues %
83	77	69
17	23	31
79	71	64
7 ⎫ 5 ⎬ 22 10 ⎭	9 ⎫ 9 ⎬ 28 10 ⎭	9 ⎫ 13 ⎬ 36 14 ⎭

Other recent and confirmatory evidence of the influence of local factors on local election choices comes from the analysis of the NOP/Widdicombe survey data by William Miller. The top half of Table 37 summarizes the responses to two types of questions in voting choice. As in previous surveys, the Widdicombe sample of voters reported being much more influenced in local elections by the identity of the candidates and also by local, rather than national, issues. But 'being influenced' is, of course, very different from actually changing one's vote. Many, indeed most, of these locally-influenced voters will, quite understandably and consistently, come to the conclusion that the party they identify with and/ or vote for nationally also has the better candidate and the more appealing local policies. Many, however, do not, as can be seen in the lower half of Table 37, which looks at the reported voted inclinations of all those in the NOP sample who expressed a local voting preference for any political party or party grouping.

The figures show that for 17 per cent of these respondents their local voting preference was different from their current general election voting preference, while in over one-fifth of cases it was different from their national party identification. In some instances their local preference directly contradicted their party identification, with one major party (Conservative, Labour or Alliance) being favoured nationally and a different one locally. Fifteen per cent of this group, however, either had no national party preference at all, or supported 'other' local candidates – for example, Independents. Not unexpectedly, all these latter figures proved to be higher for those respondents who had previously claimed to vote locally on the basis of local issues or for the candidate.

William Miller's analysis of these NOP data, barely touched upon here, is sophisticated and subtle. It permits a balanced and informed evaluation of local electoral behaviour. It quantifies the extent to which 'national choice factors of one kind or another dominate local election choice', but it emphasizes also that 'there is some slippage between national and local choice' (Research Vol. III, 1986, p. 167). If 'over four-fifths of local voters vote exactly in accord with their national party identification or current national preference for the Conservatives, Labour or the Alliance' (p. 169), it obviously follows that nearly one-fifth *do not*. For this one-fifth and for the many more whose votes are also influenced by local issues, policies and candidates, local elections are clearly about a great deal more than Jim Hacker's Westminster popularity poll.

A variety of publics

In the previous section of this chapter we were concerned almost exclusively with the attitudes and behaviour of the public at large. The statistics presented were drawn from national surveys of adult respondents, and we therefore talked mostly in terms of 'voters', 'the electorate', or 'the general public'. By itself, however, information at this level of generality is of limited value to the individual local authority. For the public with which an authority has to deal has not one, but several manifestations. There *is* a local 'public at large', but there are also its component individuals and groups, each of whom may stand in rather differing relationships to the council. This reality was highlighted for example in the case brought by the London Borough of Bromley against the GLC over the latter's 'Fares Fair' policy. Giving judgement on the case in 1983 Lord Diplock referred to the need for weighing 'one against the other . . . all those categories of persons to whom a [council's] collective duty is owed'. In this particular instance Lord Diplock identified three relevant 'categories of persons', namely the residents of Greater London in general, those who paid rates within Greater London, and the potential passengers on London Transport services subsidized by the GLC. Those categories he observed 'overlap but do not coincide'. Leaving aside for the moment Lord Diplock's analysis of what duty the GLC owed to each category it will be convenient to pursue his three-way division of the public. Modifying his terminology slightly we may refer to the general public, the ratepayers and the users of services. Relations between local authorities and each of these three manifestations of the public vary considerably and in each case have become subject to change and experiment in recent years.

The general public

Traditionally the main means of communication between a council and the general public, outside of the electoral process, has been the local press through its reporting of council business and, sometimes, through exchanges of comment and argument in its correspondence columns. However local press coverage of council affairs has often attracted criticism for its lack of depth or insight, its concentration on personalities or trivia, its failure to develop any investigative journalism and its tendency towards a bland and harmonious view of life in the community. Such criticisms are perhaps less fairly made of some of the provincial daily newspapers, able for example to employ a specialist town hall reporter, and would rarely apply to most of the, sometimes short-lived, radical 'alternative' local press which has existed for the past two decades. For many of the local weeklies however it would be hard plausibly to disclaim the 'silent watchdog' epithet which they attracted in the mid-1970s (Murphy, 1976).

Since that period there is little evidence that much has changed in that respect. Greater potential access to background information under the Local Government (Access to Information) Act 1985 has provided an opportunity which may not be fully realized. The possible reasons for this are suggested by Franklin (1986) – the growth of the commercial weekly free press and the concentration of ownership of the local paid-for press into a small number of groups. The effect of these developments has been to place financial interests above journalistic interests in the struggle for advertising, circulation and revenue. This reduces the incentive to improve standards of reporting; perhaps more significantly it also tempts the local press to rely on the cheap and easy practice of reprinting free copy from local authority public relations officers.

The expansion of public relations activity in local government has been a major feature of the last decade. This may be attributed partly to the desire of newly-created authorities to define their public image after re-organization and partly to the wish to defend the cause of local authorities in an increasingly troublesome political climate. The increasing emphasis placed on such activities is symbolized by the creation in the mid-1980s of the Local Government Public Relations Awards sponsored by the *Local Government Chronicle* and organized by the Institute of Public Relations, which now possesses its own specialist Local Government Group. The character of local authority public relations work can be gauged from the categories of the awards – leaflets, booklets, posters, press advertisements and newspapers. The political impact of such work will clearly depend in part on the status which public relations staff have within their local authority. The Institute of Public Relations (1986) thus urges that they should enjoy 'direct access to and the support of the leader of the council, committee chairmen, the chief executive and all Chief Officers' if their efforts are to be successful.

Evidence of the impact enjoyed by some local authority public relations work became apparent during the political debates about rate-capping and the abolition of the GLC and the metropolitan counties in the period between 1983 and 1986. It may be a matter for debate how far the authorities concerned increased their levels of public support in this period; and it may be significant that perhaps the most successful campaign, in terms of moulding opinion, namely that of the GLC, owed much to the work of hired, rather than in-house, experts. None the less such endeavours clearly had an impact on the government of the day which in 1985 asked the Widdicombe Committee to make an early report on 'overt political campaigning at public expense'.

The committee in due course accepted the argument 'that public funds should not be capable of use for party political gain' but in framing subsequent legislation in the form of the Local Government Act 1986 the government seemed keen to draw the reins even tighter, limiting councils' publicity powers to the provision of information on local government functions and services as against 'matters relating to local government' or 'local government matters affecting the area' as in the Local Government Act 1972.

Allowing for the constraints of prevailing legislation at any given time, communications between the council and the public need not be wholly a one-way affiar. Clearly the public may feel that it has something to say to the council at certain times. To cater for this possibility a number of experiments have been launched aimed at giving the public certain rights of presenting petitions and/or deputations and of asking questions at council and/or committee meetings. A survey carried out by the Community Rights Project discovered fifty-nine councils which accommodated petitions or deputations and sixteen which had introduced some form of Public Question Time at meetings of the council or its committees. The survey also disclosed seven authorities which were experimenting with various forms of regular public meeting for discussion with, and questioning of, councillors (Taylor, 1986).

Ratepayers

It has been said that the form of local government bequeathed to us by the Municipal Corporations Act 1835 was 'more suitable for a local authority seen as the trustee of the rate fund than for one whose primary duty is the development of major social services' (Keith-Lucas and Richards, 1978, p. 18). This situation arose from the fact that historically the law had not distinguished municipal corporations from any other form of corporation: the corporate property and corporate income existed for the benefit of the members of the corporation. Such a view of the nature of a municipal corporation was carried over into the relationship between the corporation as a rate-levying body and those who paid the rates. This now expressed itself in the notion of the corporation holding the rate income in trust for the ratepayers: as such the corporation was held to have a specific fiduciary duty to its ratepayers on whose behalf it administered the rate fund. What this might, and indeed does, mean in practice is clearly seen if we return to Lord Diplock's judgement in the case of the GLC's 'Fares Fair' policy. Having weighed 'one against the other' the claims of the three 'categories of persons' to whom the GLC owed a collective duty he came down on the side of the ratepayers. The GLC's policy, he concluded, involved 'a thriftless use of money obtained by the GLC from the ratepayers . . . . It was thus a breach of the fiduciary duty owed by the GLC to the ratepayers.'

In the case of the GLC the domestic ratepayers comprised some 40 per cent of the resident population; to their rates could be added the non-domestic or commercial ratepayers who subscribed some 62 per cent of the total rate income. The ratepayers were thus by no means synonymous with residents or voters. Indeed it was not until 1945 that the local election franchise was extended from domestic ratepayers and their spouses to all adults; non-resident ratepayers however still retained the right to vote in elections until 1969.

There has thus been a continuing history of council-ratepayer relations which differ in important respects from council relations with the general public or with the users of its services. Most important of all perhaps has been the specific fiduciary duty owed by the council to the ratepayers, the duty to avoid a 'thriftless use' of their money. The concept has been denounced as 'anachronistic and unworkable' and it has been suggested that a possible alternative interpretation of the relevant sections of the Municipal Corporations Act 1835 would have established that the corporation 'existed to promote the interests of its inhabitants rather than that of its ratepayers' (Elliott, 1983, p. 43; Loughlin, 1986, p. 197). None the less the prevailing legal interpretation has been one which has placed the ratepayer in a legally privileged position in relation to the other 'categories of persons' to whom councils may owe their duty.

However, being in such a position does not necessarily solve all the problems to which ratepayers may regard themselves as being subject. In particular they have expressed resentment at what has been described as 'representation without taxation'. Thus the chairman of the National Union of Ratepayers has complained that only 15 per cent of local government electors pay domestic rates in full, the other 85 per cent either receiving rate rebates or not being rateable occupiers (Hayton, 1985): non-domestic ratepayers, for example industrial firms, do not of course form part of the electorate.

The issue of accountability to the ratepayers became politically significant in 1974 when a combination of inflation, changes in grant distribution and the impact of reorganization in England and Wales produced abnormally high rate increases, which in turn provoked a so-called 'rates revolt' by protesting ratepayers. The reaction of the then Labour government was to increase domestic rate relief, to raise the amount of central government grant and to appoint the Layfield Committee to inquire into the whole field of local government finance. Of more long-term significance however was the reaction of the Conservative opposition, whose Environment spokesman, Margaret Thatcher, set up a working group which went on to recommend the abolition of the rating system. Increasingly the Conservatives came to see themselves as committed to the active rather than the rhetorical defence of the ratepayer interest. The defence of the ratepayer interest, combined with a general strategy of reducing public spending, led the government into a series of measures including changes to the rate-support grant system and the introduction of machinery for limiting, or capping, the level of the rate, both for individual councils and potentially for all local authorities. Other measures geared more specifically to the defence of ratepayer interests were the requirement for councils to consult non-domestic rate-payers before determining the level of the rate, introduced in the Rates Act 1984, and the setting up of the Audit Commission in the Local Government Finance Act 1982.

Statutory consultation with non-domestic ratepayers began in 1985, though some authorities had been engaging in various informal discussions with commercial interests in earlier years. The initial experience of the statutory procedure suggested that there was a fair amount of learning to be done on both sides before any positive benefits could be achieved. The commercial ratepayers were often represented by local chambers of commerce or trade, or by local branches of the CBI or the National Federation of Small Businesses and the Self-Employed. A National Chamber of Trade survey of the first year's consultations found that nearly 80 per cent of local members had regarded it as a worthwhile exercise but that there were problems over the availability and intelligibility of the council's documentation, over the short time-scale of the procedure and over the council's appreciation of the submissions from the business community (Tennant, 1985). Our own interview survey suggested that local authorities were, if anything, rather less sanguine about the virtues of the consultations. They felt that they and the commercial rate-payers were often operating on the basis of very different premises – the need for services versus the need to restrain the rates – and that the increasing complexity of local government finance created formidable gaps in understanding between the expert consulter and the lay consultee. Comments such as 'no real dialogue', 'a farce', 'a terrific waste of time' and 'they didn't understand local government finance', outweighed any more positive evaluations from the local authority side. However, as one chief officer observed, the commercial ratepayers were 'at the bottom of the learning curve' so that matters might improve with time.

Among the issues identified by the National Chamber of Trade in its review of consultation procedures was the need to address problems of cost-efficiency in council spending. By the terms of the Local Government Finance Act 1982 this issue had already been placed within the ambit of the Audit Commission. The work of the Commission, through its studies of local authority practice and the work of the auditors it appoints to examine individual council accounts, is in each case intended to secure 'economy, efficiency and effectiveness' in the use of resources and the provision of services. Commending the Commission to the House of Commons during the Second Reading of the Bill in January 1982 the then Minister for Local Government and Environmental Services, Tom King, argued that 'the importance that the Audit Commission will attach to greater value for money is probably the most important single ingredient in the Bill'. In the same debate, Michael Heseltine, as Secretary of State, linked the issue of value for money to the interests of the ratepayer arguing that 'in the final analysis it is a local authority's responsibility to give its ratepayers value for money'. In that respect therefore the Commission would be on the side of the ratepayer; it may thus be appropriate that the first chairman of the Commission commended its work in its third annual report (1985–6) as a matter of 'interest and concern' not to the general public or to the voters or to service users but to 'all ratepayers'.

The users of services

A major problem with strategies designed to secure value for money or to improve economy, efficiency and effectiveness is that they do not rest upon any universal agreement as to the meaning of those terms or on how they may be best interpreted in a public, rather than private, sector context. In particular the distinction between cost-cutting and cost-effectiveness may not always have been clear (Kline and Mallaber, 1986). This confusion for example led the National Consumer Council (1986, p. i) to fear that '"Value for Money" had become a euphemism for providing services at the lowest possible cost, with scant regard for what services actually achieve' and that 'service effectiveness was being neglected in favour of economy and efficiency' (Potter, 1986).

A similar concern for service effectiveness has also been expressed by the Local Government Training Board, notably in work carried out on its behalf by John Stewart and Michael Clarke (1987). One outcome of the shared concern of the Local Government Training Board and National Consumer Council for effective service delivery was the joint preparation of a guide on *Getting Closer to the Public* (1987) which outlined some of the practical implications for local authorities of Stewart and Clarke's concept of a 'public service orientation'. The basic propositions behind this concept are that councils exist to provide a service to the public; that they will be judged by the quality of that service; that service has value only to those for whom it is provided; that the latter demand high-quality service; and that high-quality service demands closeness to the customer.

To some extent the search for higher-quality service delivery might be seen as something of a defensive measure. As it is pointed out in *Getting Closer to the Public* local government has been undergoing close public scrutiny, with declining resources and problems of morale. One way for such a beleaguered institution to rebuild its confidence and its public image is to attempt to improve the quality of its service delivery. This however represents the occasion, rather than the justification, for such an attempt. The justification lies in the recognition that the 'essential rationale of public service . . . lies in service for the public' (Stewart and Clarke, 1987, p. 161).

The implications of such an approach are encapsulated in one of the guiding principles of Sheffield City Council's policy statement *Improving Service Delivery*, published in 1986, namely that 'the user should be at the centre of our thinking in planning, managing and providing services'. What this might mean in practice can be seen from a checklist of possible council actions in *Closer to the Public*, including regular surveys to establish customer attitudes to services received; market research on customer reaction to proposed changes in services; reviewing premises and reception areas for ease of access; ensuring that senior management visit customers and that chief officers spend some time on reception duties; inviting suggestions for service improve-ment; and ensuring that council committees regularly review service quality in the light of experience. One small example of the sort of initiative which might thus be undertaken is the practice of Braintree District Council of inviting every tenant to return a form giving their view on the adequacy or otherwise of any repairs done to their house. More ambitious has been the work of Newcastle-upon-Tyne's Performance Review and Efficiency Sub-committee in undertaking a substantial consumer survey in the West City Ward exploring patterns of service use, levels of satisfaction, perceptions of service quality and opinions on service developments.

The notion of putting service quality at the top of the agenda may prove politically difficult for some authorities. Conservative authorities committed to cutting back costs might for example cavil at re-designing reception areas or commissioning user surveys: the notion that 'if it costs anything, we're not going to do it', as one Conservative leader put it to us, could clearly constrain any new moves of that sort. On the Labour side the desire to defend trade union interests might be a similar problem: not all Labour council-lors would readily accept the warning of Margaret Hodge, leader of Islington, that quality of services 'must take precedence over trade union interests, or even jobs'(*Local Government Chronicle*, 3 July 1987).

Apart from the possibility of political foot-dragging in some quarters the thrust of public service orientation has also been queried from a rather differerent perspective. Although its proponents see it as being more than just consumerism, with a due regard for the user's role as citizen, it has been criticized on the grounds that it 'permits people to have a say in *defining* their needs but stops short of their involvement in *meeting* them' 'and that it sees users as customers rather than partners (Smith and Chanan, 1986, p. 2, emphasis in original). The emphasis of a public service orientation is on 'service *for* not **to** the public' (Stewart and Clarke, 1987, p. 167); the critics are concerned about providing services *with* the public. Indeed they might argue that to see local government primarily in terms of the services it provides is to risk overlooking its role in 'creating a free society through citizen participation' and its 'corresponding duty to foster citizenship' (Rhodes, 1987, pp. 71–2).

Involving the people

The passive reader of the local press, the cost-conscious ratepayer and the quality-conscious service user do not exhaust the possible manifestations of a local authority's public. As our preceding remarks indicate there is also the notion of that public as a body of concerned and, at least potentially, active citizens.

If we had been writing twenty years ago we would almost certainly at this point have felt obliged to introduce the notion of 'public participation'. However the experience of two decades of experiment in this field has resulted, not in a total abandonment of the general concept but in its absorption and refining into a series of specific procedures and practices relating to particular services and/or localities. In the words of one review of the experience of the late 1960s and the 1970s:

The high tide of enthusiasm for public participation is now in ebb: but attitudes have not settled into their previous pattern. People are less willing than they were to accept authoritarian styles of leadership. Action groups and public protest have become a regular feature of policy development. The receding tide leaves pools of interest where new initiatives are taken . . . (Boaden *et al.*, 1982, preface)

This measured, and, some might think, slightly pessimistic judgement surely contains two basic truths, one explicit, the other implicit. The explicit truth concerns the change in attitudes amongst the public, with a decline in deference towards authority and a greater assertiveness of individual and group claims or rights. The implicit truth is that two decades of experiment with public participation have produced no sure and certain rule to success, though some blind alleys may have been identified: instead a variety of initiatives of greater or lesser promise have been embarked upon.

One specific set of responses to a greater public assertiveness has been to extend and built upon the pre-existing practices of co-option of and consultation with representatives of particular interests in the local community. The co-option of non-councillors onto council committees has for long been a statutory requirement in the cases of education committees and police committees (other than in Scotland). Co-optees onto education committees normally represent church, professional and other educational interests; those on police committees represent the magistracy; in both cases co-optees are guaranteed full voting rights by law. Councils cannot co-opt anyone onto the council itself, nor onto its finance committee; nor may any one committee contain co-opted members in excess of one-third of the committee's membership, though sub-committees are exempt from this restriction. Within these limits the actual arrangements for co-option can and do vary but our questionnaire survey reveals certain clear patterns. In terms of types of committee (other than education and police), social services and leisure and recreation are those most likely to have co-opted members, this being the case for 48 per cent and 25 per cent of those committees respectively. As for types of authority, committees with co-opted members are most common in metropolitan authorities outside London, all of whom had at least one such committee, and least common in Scottish and shire districts where 72 per cent had no such committees; one other noticeable phenomenon was the presence of co-optees on nearly half the London Borough housing committees, a proportion not matched anywhere else. In political terms Labour-controlled authorities tend to be more ready to practice co-option than do Conservative or Independent councils. Over and above co-option to main committees there also exists a greater level of co-option to sub-committees, advisory committees and working groups; here again it is the Scottish and shire districts which show least enthusiasm for the practice.

The sources of co-optees naturally vary considerably, given the variety of committees and authorities that may be involved. Social services committees tend to draw heavily on representatives from voluntary organizations, notably those involved with different client groups; similary housing committee co-optees are most likely to be drawn from tenants organizations, whilst those on leisure and recreation commit-tees often come from local sporting and cultural organiza-tions. Where local authorities have set up race relations and women's committees these bodies and their sub-committees, etc., normally tend to draw heavily on co-optees from the various ethnic and women's organizations in the locality.

A number of possible problems are presented by the practice of co-option. One concerns the granting of voting rights to co-optees. This is most common in the case of leisure and recreation committees and given the generally low political temperature of such bodies it is rarely seen as a problem there. However in the case of education and police committees, where co-optees' voting rights are automatic, and in social services and housing committees where much may be at stake politically, fears are sometimes expressed that voting co-optees may be a device used to create or inflate a particular party majority. This can sometimes happen, as it did on the Warwickshire Police Committee in 1985 where the magistrates combined with the Conservatives to overturn what could otherwise have been a Labour-Alliance majority and thereby elected a Conservative chairman. There is however little evidence of the conscious selection of co-optees by a majority or near-majority party with the specific intent of 'improving' the political arithmetic. If it occurs at all, and imputing such motives is inevitably a somewhat speculative exercise, it seems confined to one or two education committees where a wafer-thin majority on the council might otherwise have been endangered on an education committee with unsympathetic co-optees.

The desire to defend a majority arising from an election raises a second problem sometimes associated with co-option, namely that it in some way dilutes the democratic principle if people are in a position to vote on public issues by virtue of appointment rather than of election. There is a strongly held view amongst councillors of all parties that any deviation from the principle of answerability through the electoral process risks blurring the lines of accountability and responsibility to the public. There may in any event be some problem in determining the exact nature of the accountability of co-opted members. Are they to regard themselves as accountable to the general public, as councillors may do, or to the specific interest or organization which they represent? They may also find themselves facing the difficult problem of being expected to act in two conflicting roles – representing their interest group to the council and the council to the interest group. In some cases the definition of interest group or of the true nature of the interest may not always be uncontested and questions may arise as to a co-optee's legitimate right to claim to represent a particular interest. Thus in relation to one or two race relations committees there have been controversies over how and by whom ethnic minority co-optees ought to be chosen, whether by public meetings of individuals or of black organizations, or by direct nomination from black organizations, or by an open-nominations system or by council selection from black organization nominees (Prashar and Nicholas, 1986).

Despite the possible difficulties which it presents however co-option does have its supporters. Indeed, without such support it is clearly unlikely that the practice could continue outside the cases required by statute. Not un-naturally it finds support from those sections of the community who see it as a useful means of influencing events through the

activities of their co-opted representatives: but it also receives
some backing from those within local government. Although
most councillors are sceptical or even hostile to the principle
there are a minority who will defend it on the grounds that it
provides an avenue of representation open to those groups
whose voices may be submerged or overlooked in the
electoral process, for example the elderly or the disabled or
ethnic minority groups who are not incorporated into the
world of conventional politics. Council chief officers tend to
be rather less hostile to co-option than do councillors: they
often claim for example to appreciate the inside knowledge
and expertise which co-optees can bring into committee
work. They may also derive some benefit from having their
clientele represented in person at committee meetings when
hard decisions have to be taken about resource allocation.

Co-option with voting powers on major committees clearly
allows interests within the community a measure of access
into the decision-making process. However, much co-option
involves co-optees sitting in advisory sub-committees or
working groups with no powers of decision or resource
allocation. This is particularly true of those authorities which
are favourably inclined to co-option on a large scale: they
tend to generate a considerable network of such non-
executive bodies with co-opted members. In the absence of
any decision-making powers such bodies are only able to
express views or to make recommendations to the appropriate major committees: they are thus essentially exercises in
consultation and as such they may be only one form among
many.

Consultative practices by local authorities vary widely in
part at least as a consequence of statutory requirements and
political inclination. Thus parish councils in England and
community councils in Wales have a statutory right to be
consulted about planning applications whereas community
councils in Scotland do not. Planning issues thus come to
form a major element of district-parish relations in England
for example, though the problems of accommodating parish
views within the provisions of the districts' lawful planning
powers sometimes means that consultations may generate
rather than dissipate conflict.

In political terms, Independent councils and councillors are particularly likely to be enthusiastic about consulting with parish and community councils whom they see as genuine voices of local opinion as distinct from interest groups whose more narrow concerns they rather distrust. The Liberals tend to see procedures of consultation, whether with parishes or interest groups, as inherently virtuous and thus to encourage them as a matter of principle. On occasions they seem more preoccupied with how decisions are arrived at than with the actual content of the decisions: consequently it is the consultative process rather than the executive product which concerns them. Conservative councils tend to stress the desirability of consulting with local ratepayers and commercial organizations, a practice which of course has now become a statutory obligations as far as commercial ratepayers are concerned: they are likely to be suspicious of any dealings with organizations which they identify as leftist, such as women's groups or campaigning bodies such as Shelter. Labour councils are likely to stress the need to consult with trades unions, tenants' associations, client groups and ethnic minorities: indeed some such councils have gone beyond the requirements to consult non-domestic ratepayers by incorporating various community and client groups into the procedure. Labour does not however have a wholly uncritical fondness for such groups, being particularly wary of those it regards as dominated by sectarian leftists or white racists or as trojan horses for middle-class interests.

Such patterns of discrimination between acceptable or unacceptable consultees are not new. Twenty years ago Conservative councillors in Kensington and Chelsea could clearly distinguish in their own minds between 'helpful' and 'unhelpful' groups, the former being those who either did not 'make claims on the council' or did not conflict with 'the councillor's own views as to the proper scope of council activity' (Dearlove, 1973, p. 168). What may be new are the more overtly political stances of some interest groups and of the parties' reactions to them, and also the more vigorous level of claim and counter-claim in an era when as one council leader put it 'we have pressure groups coming out of our ears'.

One of the more notable features of local political life over the past twenty years has been this emergence of a much more clamorous and determined body of interest groups seeking to bring pressure to bear on local authorities and demanding the right to consultation if not full participation in the council's decision-making procedures. The party politics which grew to dominate local government in the post-war decades has now become compounded and complicated by what can be called a sectional politics based on the interests of particular groups identified by their locality, by their social characteristics such as race, culture or gender, by their relationship to particular council services, or by their promotion of single-issue causes (Gyford, 1986).

Council responses to this sectional politics have taken varied forms of which co-option is only one. The need to respond to the claims of specific localities with an authority's boundaries, for example, has led to a series of experiments since the 1960s, with area or neighbourhood-based structures of which the most recent are the decentralization schemes of some forty or more mainly Labour and Liberal councils. In some cases these concentrate on improved service delivery at the local level, for example by decentralizing housing repair work; in others there are provision for area-based committees or forums within which local opinion can be expressed to the council; in a few cases there are provisions for such local bodies to have modest powers of executive decision over a small area-based budget. A major issue concerns the question of how far and how fast such experiments should move from a preoccupation with better service delivery to an emphasis on a greater democratization of the services themselves (Hoggett and Hambleton, 1987).

Whatever their ambitions in the latter direction decentralization schemes do pose certain problems to local authorities accustomed to more traditional ways of working. They may raise fears amongst the officers of disturbance of career patterns, changed working conditions, closer public scrutiny and challenges to the normal hierarchy of professional departments. Councillors may wonder about how to relate their own political responsibility and accountability to new neightbourhood institutions claiming to represent local opinion: political parties may sense a challenge to their power from local organizations. It is perhaps not surprising that devolving service delivery has seemed easier than devolving effective power (Gyford, 1986).

Responding to the politics of race, culture and gender has sometimes taken the form of setting up special council committees to address the issues raised and co-opting individuals from particular sections of the community onto such committees. The provision of translation facilities, of creches and of transport has also been undertaken in order to encourage participation in whatever consultative machinery has been set up. In the case of groups based on receipt of council services, here again co-option has been one device used to accommodate sectional pressures. More innovative however have been schemes for user participation in the running of leisure facilities and community centres. Tenant involvement in housing management has been another area of experiment, with some fifty or more tenant management co-operatives, dealing with maintenance, repairs and allocations, having been established in cities including Birmingham, London and most notably Glasgow (Stoker, 1987).

Responding to pressure from groups campaigning for particular causes may often be the most problematic element of sectional politics. Such groups may not be interested in any procedures of consultation or participation on an on-going basis. What they want is likely to be a change in council policy rather than procedure and they may prefer to campaign vigorously on, for example, environmental issues from outside the council rather than risk being absorbed into the council's own workings. Moreover, they may be ill-disposed to the idea of compromise or meeting the council half-way and their views may be countered by groups campaigning equally vigorously for an opposing point of view.

Involving people in the workings of local authorities and their services implies that one of the routes to a fuller citizenship lies within local government and the public sector. The practicalities of, for example, co-option or decentralization, may be problematic but the principle behind them is clear if implicit. This approach is sometimes quite explicit, as it is in the aspirations of the Liberals' community politics and

Labour's local socialism both of which seek, albeit in differing ways, to explore the potential of a decentralized and democratized local government as a vehicle for raising levels of political consciousness and activity.

There is however a different view, namely that the best way to secure the involvement of the people in services is to take those services out of local government altogether. This is the view of the present Conservative government and it can be seen expressed in two main forms. First, there is the move to transfer an increasing amount of council provisions into the private sector where market relations are dominant. This is canvassed not only on the grounds that greater value for money will thereby be obtained but also on the basis that widening the scope of the market-place enhances the role of the market as a mechanism of accountability to the public. Second, there are the proposals to dismantle the established structures of local authority education and housing. It is argued that these will create opportunities for greater teacher and parent involvement in the running of schools which 'opt out' of council control and also allow for greater tenant choice of landlord and for the creation of tenant co-operatives in housing.

Such initiatives in the direction of maximizing popular involvement outside rather than inside the local public sector do of course reflect the New Right tendency to see involvement in politics as inferior to involvement in the market-place both as a means of accountability and as a maximizer of welfare (cf. Butler, 1985). They may thus be seen as attempts to encourage what Brittan (1975) described as 'participation without politics'. The challenges that they pose to local government are therefore of a different order from those presented by demands for a consumer-conscious public service orientation or for the decentralization and democratization of services.

8
Political change since Widdicombe

By far the most important source of the material discussed in the preceding chapters of this book has been the research programme commissioned by the Widdicombe Committee, the results of which were published in Research Volumes I–IV. In particular, our own work on the political organization of local authorities (Research Volume I) and the SCPR survey of councillors (Research Volume II) has been drawn upon extensively. This emphasis is an appropriate one for, as Rodney Brooke, Chief Executive of the City of Westminster, noted:

Whatever may be thought of the Widdicombe Report, its five volumes represent the most extensive and authoritative examination of the internal workings of local government for two decades.
(Brooke, 1986, p. 40)

Up to this point in the book, however, the reader will have learnt rather more about the content of the four research volumes than about either the content or the context of the Report itself. A few of the Committee's individual recommendations have been touched upon in passing; but we have said little about why the Committee was set up in the first place, what it concluded, what was thought of those conclusions, and what has happened since. The main aim of this penultimate chapter, therefore, is to redress that balance: to examine some of the principal political changes and developments that helped give rise to the Committee and that have taken place in the period since it reported.

Origins of the Widdicombe Committee

It is rarely easy to know precisely where to begin any examination of political change, to identify the best point at which to break in to the process of change. But in this instance it is possible to pinpoint one particularly significant and appropriate week: the one commencing Monday 8 October 1984. It was the week of the 101st Annual Conservative Party Conference, held that year at Brighton; the conference that was to culminate so dramatically with the IRA bombing of the Prime Minister's hotel. As is invariably the case, the priorities and concerns uppermost in the minds of the party activists attending the conference were strikingly reflected in the motions that had been previously submitted by the local constituencies and other party organizations. There were 875 in all, classified in the conference agenda under thirty-one different subject headings. The most popular subject by a very long way, as can be seen in Table 38, was local government, attracting more than one in every seven motions submitted.

Subject	No. of motions
Local government	126
Employment and industrial relations	72
Public relations and party organization	72
Law and order	63
Education	60
Food, farming and fishing	51
Economy and taxation	42
Electoral law	30

Total = 875

Table 38 *Most popular subjects of motions submitted to 101st Conservative Party Conference, October 1984*

Subject	No. of motions
Rate reform	55
Abolition of the GLC and MCCs	24
Support for abolition	13
Regret of lack of more effective government publicity campaign	5
At least qualified criticism of abolition	6
'Abuses of local democracy':	19
Councils' funding of publicity campaigns	6
Councils' funding of voluntary organizations	1
Councils' funding of 'other political purposes'	10
Other 'abuses of local democracy'	2
Rate-capping and Rate Support Grant system:	14
Support for rate-capping	5
At least qualified criticism of rate-capping	3
Criticism of operation of grant/penalty system	6
Other local government finance reform	4
Privatization	2
Miscellaneous	8
Total	126

Table 39 *Specific subjects of local government motions, Conservative Party Conference, October 1984*

The detailed concerns of those local government motions, as summarized in Table 39, are equally revealing. Rate reform alone was the subject of nearly as many motions as that perennial Conservative Conference favourite, law and order. Most of these motions were prefaced by clauses regretting or even deploring 'the Government's continuing failure to honour the Conservative party's repeated commitment to reform local government taxation' (Eastleigh). Some spelt out what they felt should be the objectives of such a reform: 'a system of local taxation which bears more fairly on a wider spread of the population' (Rushcliffe); 'a more equitable means of levying local government taxes, so that the amount paid by each household bears closer relationship

to the income of that household' (Nuneaton). This latter
motion might be seen as at least implicitly advocating a local
income tax (LIT), as did the motion from Stirling quite
explicitly, calling for the replacement of domestic rates by
'local income tax as a fairer means of raising local revenue
according to the ability of people to pay, and as a means of
improving the financial accountability of local authorities to
a wider number of their electorate'. By way of balance, there
was also one specific call for a poll tax (Ashford), and it
received a favourable mention also from Nigel Cutts,
proposer of the Rushcliffe motion actually selected for the
Conference debate. Interestingly, though, Cutts' conception
was apparently of a tax that would merely reduce the burden
of rates, rather than completely replace them: his case
resting on the argument that 'most people would be able to
pay £30 a year poll tax without difficulty' (*Local Government
Chronicle*, 12 October 1984), or roughly one-sixth of the
government's estimated average payment, had its community
charge been in place in 1987–8.

Rate reform of some description, however, was an almost
universally supported cause. Rate-capping, on the other
hand, which had just entered the statute book in the form of
the Rates Act 1984, was viewed rather more coolly, as were
some of the government's ongoing attempts to control local
spending by means of targets and grant penalties. There
were expressions of 'concern as to the application of rate-
capping where it penalizes authorities that have previously
been prudent' (Sevenoaks); of opinion 'that the present
formula for determination of rate support grant has inade-
quacies which penalize some authorities who are operating efficiently at service levels within the Government
guidelines' (Ruislip-Northwood); and of warning of the
'severe effects [that] the cutting of the RSG may have on the
next county council elections' (W. Herts.).

The second great topic of concern at that 1984 Conference
though, was not rate-capping but rather the government's
abolition of the GLC and the six metropolitan county
councils, as outlined in its White Paper of the previous year,
Streamlining the Cities. The majority of the motions on this
topic were supportive of the government's policy, 'in accord-

ance with its commitment in the 1983 Conservative Manifesto' (Liverpool, Broadgreen). But there were also some expressions of reservation and criticism, deploring 'the Government's decision to scrap the elections for those councils, scheduled for May 1985' (Crawley), or emphasizing 'the need for a London-wide body, directly elected, to provide an effective voice and direction for the specific and defined tasks that must be done for London as a whole' (Chipping Barnet). There was also a clutch of motions addressed specifically at the anti-abolition publicity campaign being conducted most prominently by the GLC – with apparently rather too much effect for some party supporters, and rather too little counter-publicity from the government itself. References were thus made to the 'adverse impact of the "Save the GLC" campaign on the European Election results in London' (City of London & Westminster South), and the government was asked 'to be mindful of its failure to inform and convince the electorate of the advantages of abolition, and to take immediate steps to counter the propaganda campaign launched by the Leader of the GLC' (Walthamstow).

Though not selected for debate, this motion interestingly articulates an apparent double-standard that was explored in some of the Widdicombe Committee's early deliberations. X's 'provision of information to the electorate' is Y's 'propaganda on the rates'. Alternatively, while it was legitimate and laudable for the government to publicize the merits of abolition, it was illegitimate for local councils to publicize the value of their threatened services. But double-standard or not, political propaganda was the subject of other motions too, addressed at alleged 'abuses' of local democracy: 'using ratepayers' money to attack Government policy and support left-wing causes', for the funding of 'political campaigns and extremist groups', and 'overt political and dubious social activities'.

These, then, were the key party concerns which confronted the government ministers responsible for replying to the two scheduled conference debates on local government: the recently appointed Kenneth Baker, who had replaced Lord Bellwin as Local Government Minister, and the Secretary of State for the Environment, Patrick Jenkin. The ministers were prompted early on in that Conference week too by the timely publication of a booklet provocatively entitled *The New Corruption* by the Centre for Policy Studies, the think-tank organization set up in 1974 by Sir Keith Joseph. The booklet was actually compiled by Dr Charles Goodson-Wickes, a Conservative party research worker. He concluded, after a study of twenty-four exclusively Labour-controlled, and predominantly London, councils, that there were some

disturbing trends which have emerged recently in Local Government, which have serious implications for democracy in Britain. Indeed, the combination of these trends may be so sinister as to warrant the description 'The New Corruption'.   (Goodson-Wickes, 1984, p.5)

'Corruption' is not an allegation to be levelled lightly, particularly in the world of local government. It is important, therefore, to understand the nature of the 'disturbing trends' Goodson-Wickes had in mind. He was not, it should be emphasized, using the term in its conventional sense, as a synonym for bribery: the offering of gifts or financial inducements to influence the actions of politicians or officials (Doig, 1984, p.25). Rather, his concern was with what he described as the erosion of 'certain conventions' in five main spheres of local government:

1   *Manipulation of Standing Orders* by a majority group, to deprive opposition members of their rights;
2   *Politicization of officers* – the appointment of officers who are politically sympathetic to the majority group;
3   *Cross-employment* – local government officials in one authority serving as councillors in a neighbouring one, with a resulting conflict of interest (also known as 'twin-tracking' – see Chapter 2);
4   *Relationships with Trade Unions* – exemplified by some councils' financial support of industrial disputes, and the deliberate favouring and protection of their Direct Labour Organizations (DLOs) when faced with competitive tendering for council contracts;
5   *Political propaganda* – the use of public money to fund campaigns attacking the central government's policies and to reward or secure party political support.

The examples cited by Goodson-Wickes to illustrate his

case were inevitably one-sided – drawn as they were from Labour authorities only – and frequently, on the face of it, unexceptionable. In the present context, however, it is his recommendations which are of the greater significance. He recommended in particular

that a Public Inquiry be set up by the Secretary of State to assess the basis, extent and consequences of the growth of Local Government's activities, inasmuch as these activities may encroach upon and frustrate Central Government's policies; and to examine the role of the Audit Commission and District Auditors in improving accountability to the general public. (Goodson-Wickes, 1984, p.26)

Within days of those words being published, the Secretary of State, Patrick Jenkin, endeavoured to placate some of his party conference critics by announcing to them that he would in fact be setting up not just one local government inquiry, but two. The first inquiry would take the form of a ministerial review, carried out by Kenneth Baker and a junior Environment Minister, William Waldegrave, of the whole system of council financing. It was this review which was to result in January 1986 in the government's Green Paper, *Alternatives to Domestic Rates*, with its proposals for a community charge or poll tax.

The second inquiry, however, would take very much the form called for by Goodson-Wickes: a public inquiry into the perceived 'abuses' of local democracy being perpetrated by certain left-wing authorities. The Minister's vehemence of phrase and his listed concerns echoed closely those of *The New Corruption*:

There is a cancer in some local councils which runs much deeper than extravagant spending. In some cities local democracy itself is under attack . . . The conventional checks and balances are scorned. Councils squander millions on virulent political campaigns. Officers are selected for their political views; the rights of minorities are suppressed; standing orders are manipulated to stifle debate; the conflicts of interest which can arise when an officer of one authority becomes an elected member of another are left undeclared. (*The Guardian*, 11 October 1984)

This public inquiry, understandably enough, took rather

longer to set in motion than the ministerial review of local finance. It was not, therefore, until the spring of 1985 that its terms of reference were laid down and its membership finally confirmed – by which time it had become not one inquiry, but two linked ones. The vehicle of investigation was to be a departmental committee, chaired by David Widdicombe, QC, with the following terms of reference:

To inquire into practices and procedures governing the conduct of local authority business in Great Britain, with particular reference to:
   (a)   The rights and responsibilities of elected members;
   (b)   The respective roles of elected members and officers;
   (c)   the need to clarify the limits and conditons governing discretionary spending by local authorities;
and to make any necessary recommendations for strengthening the democratic process.

Having announced these terms of reference to the House of Commons on 6 February 1985, the Secretary of State went on to say that:

In view of the growing public concern about the use made by some local authorities of their discretionary powers to engage in overt political campaigning at public expense, I am asking the Committee to submit an early Interim Report on this question. As far as the report as a whole is concerned, I am asking the Committee to aim to report within a year.   (Widdicombe Committee Report, 1986, p.18)

What was seemingly visualized, then, was a wide-ranging investigation of the party politicization of local government, to be preceded by a short specific examination of the topic of local authority spending and advertising out of public funds: two inquiries with possibly two somewhat differing sets of purposes.

   Given the phrasing of the Secretary of State's announcement in the Commons, it is difficult to conclude that the principal purpose of the interim inquiry was anything other than what Loughlin has referred to as 'a device of camouflage. The Government knows what it wants to do and sets up a Committee to secure approbation for its policy' (Loughlin, 1987, p. 65). In this instance it would seem that the government had already decided that 'overt political cam-paigning at public expense' *was* taking place, that it *was* a cause of 'growing public concern' and that it should be stopped. If confirmation of this view were needed, it was to be provided, as we shall see, by the government's swift legislative response to the Committee's Interim Report.

The government's aims in setting up the main inquiry, on the other hand, were not quite so palpable. Camouflage may again have played its part, but accompanied perhaps by a recognition of the usefulness of the Committee as information-gatherer and pacifier. In Loughlin's words again:

. . . the Committee may have been established simply to inform. . . . In the context of local government, where practices vary, a committee of inquiry might be the best mechanism for acquiring the necessary information . . . We must not ignore the possible role of the Committee as pacifier . . . as a sop to the right-wing of the Conservative Party, in order to disguise a partial failure of nerve by the Government in its attempt radically to restructure local government. (Loughlin, 1987, pp. 65–6)

In view of the relatively short time-span allotted to the inquiry, the Committee was almost inevitably small, its five members comprising a mixture of what might be termed 'experts' and 'representatives'. David Widdicombe himself was a specialist in planning and local government law, who in 1973–4 had served on the Redcliffe-Maud Committee on Local Government Rules of Conduct. Sir Lawrence Boyle was currently a partner in a firm of financial and management consultants, but a former City Chamberlain of Glasgow and then Chief Executive of Strathclyde Regional Council until he retired in 1980. Peter Newsam was Chairman of the Commission for Racial Equality, having previously spent twenty years at ILEA and elsewhere in local authority educational administration. George Russell, managing direc-tor of British Alcan Aluminium and a past member of Washington Development Corporation and of the Northern Industrial Development Board, could be seen as a represen-tative of business and corporate interests, and Diana Eccles, Vice-Chairman of the National Council for Voluntary

Organisations (NCVO), as representing the voluntary sector. There was not – as there had been, for instance, on the Layfield Committee on Local Government Finance – any academic representation; nor, much more significantly, any serving, or even former, elected councillors.

In summary, therefore, it can be seen why the launching of the Widdicombe Inquiry was described by one informed observer as being 'inauspicious':

> There could be no finer illustration of central hostility to local government than the atmosphere surrounding the appointment of the Widdicombe Committee. It . . . was announced at the Conservative Party conference and was widely seen as an attack on the political activities of Labour controlled councils. The committee could have been forgiven if it had failed to recover from such an inauspicious start.   (Rhodes, 1987, p.199)

In Rhodes' judgement, however, the Committee did recover – partly through its decision to commission and make use of an extensive programme of independent research, and partly through its refusal to deliver up to ministers the kinds of censorious denunciations of local government practice for which they were apparently looking.

The Interim Widdicombe Report

The Widdicombe Committee's Interim Report on *Local Authority Publicity* was submitted, as requested by the Secretary of State, by the end of July 1985. It was a request acceded to, as the Report makes clear, with some reluctance:

> Many of those who have given evidence have considered it unfortunate that we should have been asked to prepare an Interim Report on local authority publicity ahead of the rest of our remit. We have some sympathy with this view . . . . any consideration of 'political campaigning' by local authorities needs to be considered alongside wider evidence of the politicization of local government. . . . publicity needs to be set in the wider context of the present role of local government. (Widdicombe Committee, Interim Report, 1985, p.2)

In the limited time available to it, the Committee was not able to commission any formal research into local authority information and publicity. The Report was based, therefore, on a combination of written and oral evidence, and on the more detailed information provided on request by a sample of thirty two local authorities. Nor did the Committee members find it possible to present the Secretary of State with a unanimous set of conclusions. They were agreed upon five general principles, but not upon the course of action (or inaction) to which those principles pointed.

The principles themselves are, however, worth examining, not least because they represented the first public indication that the Committee's view of the role of local government and its place in the country's political system was by no means a narrow one:

1 *Local government is more than the sum of the particular services provided.* It is *not*, in other words, 'simply there to deliver and administer the statutory services' (p.5);

2 *Local government should act within the law.* Local authorities may properly lobby for changes in the law, but in their day-to-day conduct of affairs they must act within the law as it stands;

3 *The relationship between central and local government should be an open one*, and changes affecting local government should be the subject of consultation;

4 *Local government has a duty to inform the public* within its area as to the exercise of its functions and on local government matters generally. Specifically, 'local authorities should be able to use their powers, with incidental persuasive effect, in support of or opposition to legislative changes' (p.8);

5 *Local government publicity should not be used to promote the interests of a political party.*

These principles were expanded upon in the main body of the sixteen-page Report, which contained numerous positive affirmations about the legitimacy of local authorities expressing views on matters of political controversy (pp. 36–7); about the positive value of publicity in, for instance, increasing public awareness of local services and contributing towards greater openness in local government (pp. 45–6); and about the desirability of at least approximate equity between central government's already wider legal powers to inform and advertise and those of local government (p. 45). At the same time, at least a majority of the members of the Committee felt that there were some particular points of potential concern – about the impact, scale, tone and presentation of 'a small proportion' of local authority publicity material – that needed to be addressed. Accordingly, they proposed a set of recommendations, designed 'to establish a proper and workable framework in which local authorities can issue publicity . . . and continue to play a full part in debate on matters affecting them . . . without any question of the mis-use of public funds' (p. 61). The most important of these recommendations was that there should be an express statutory prohibition on publicity of a party political nature – i.e. publicity which promotes the interests of a particular politician or political party. The general scope of local government publicity powers should otherwise remain unchanged – enabling an authority to continue to provide *'information on matters relating to local government'* (emphasis in original) – but these powers should in future be contained in a single section of the relevant legislation, with local authorities required to keep a separate account of their advertising and information expenditure.

Two of the five Committee members, however, felt unable to give their unqualified assent to this Interim Report. Peter Newsam appended a Note of Reservation, regretting the prominence given at points in the Report to what he felt were damaging proposals for 'controlling' local authority publicity. Sir Lawrence Boyle went further still, arguing in a Memorandum of Dissent against any change in local authorities' powers until after there had been 'a complete re-appraisal of the role, purpose and nature of local government' (p. 83) – any 'problem' of advertising being, in his view, merely a symptom of these wider and more fundamental questions.

It was the Committee's majority verdict, though, that the Environment Secretary, Patrick Jenkin, seized upon, welcoming specifically the call for the statutory prohibition of party political advertising. By the start of the new parliamentary session in November 1985, Jenkin had been displaced as Secretary of State by Kenneth Baker. But, as if to give credence to Loughlin's 'camouflage' thesis, the very first legislation to be published in that session – despite having been unaccountably omitted from the Queen's Speech – was a Local Government Bill containing, along with other provisions, the government's version of a political publicity ban.

This government version went substantially beyond, and in some instances directly contradicted, the Widdicombe Committee's proposals. Whereas, for example, Widdicombe's concern had been with the *con*tent of any publicity, the Bill was aimed at its *in*tent, or even its possible intent. Thus the publicity prohibition would apply to any

material which, in whole or in part, appears to be designed to affect, or can reasonably be regarded as likely to affect, public support for (a) a political party, or (b) a body, cause or campaign identified with or likely to be regarded as identified with a political party, (Clause 2)

The scope of councils' publicity too was to be significantly restricted – to material relating only to their functions or to the services of other local authorities in their area (Clause 3). Authorities were thus to be prevented from publishing information 'as to local government matters affecting the area' and on 'matters relating to local government', which the Widdicombe members had seen as entirely reasonable and legitimate publicity concerns. As was pointed out, the combination of these provisions would have been to outlaw not only anti-abolition and anti-rate-capping campaigns, but also presumably publicity encouraging council house sales, or opposing comprehensive education, and conceivably the campaigns run by certain councils to attract jobs or industrial development, to increase the take-up of welfare benfits, or to publicize the availability of cervical smear tests.

A further contentious provision of the Bill was that giving the Secretary of State power to issue codes of recommended practice as regards the content, style, distribution and cost of local authority publicity (Clause 4). These were matters which the Widdicombe Report (p. 66) had felt strongly could best be dealt with 'by self-regulation within local government, or through the agency of the local authority associations'. The content of the Outline Code of Practice produced by the Department of the Environment (DOE), on the other hand, was all-embracing, applying not only to advertising, but also to unpaid publicity. Committee reports, council minutes, press releases, recruitment advertising, consultation documents and media interviews would all become subject to the proposed ministerial codes and controls.

Widespread though the criticism was of some of these proposals, the Local Government Bill emerged from its Commons Standing Committee virtually unamended. As was to happen with some regularity during the 1983–7 Parliament, it was left to the House of Lords to come to the at least temporary rescue of local government. To the patent annoyance of government ministers, Lords amendments were carried with all-party support deleting the subjective test of the 'likely effect' of publicity (Clause 2), and requiring any ministerial codes of practice to be approved by both Houses of Parliament, and to be merely advisory, not statutory and binding. Anxious to get its Bill, even in this somewhat emasculated form, given Royal Assent, the government did not seek to overturn these amendments to what then became the Local Government Act 1986.

The reprieve, however, was to be shortlived. The Local Government Act 1988 contained clauses seeking to introduce again a mandatory code of practice on local authority publicity, and to define what constitutes legal publicity even more restrictively than in the 1986 Act. In the light of this legislation, therefore, councils would be prevented from commenting on any matter which 'promotes or opposes a point of view on a question of political controversy which is identifiable as the view of one political party and not of another' – which would cover, presumably, most of the government's legislative programme.

The Final Widdicombe Report

If the government's response to the Widdicombe Committee's Interim Report was one of almost unseemly haste, precisely the reverse was to be true of its reaction to the Final Report. Submitted to ministers in early May 1986, there was no official government response to the Report until over two years later. Meanwhile Environment Secretary Nicholas Ridley, was 'carefully scrutinising and analysing Widdicombe and the responses to it – which is why it is all taking rather a long time' (*Local Government Chronicle*, 13 November 1987). Others, as we shall see, were more precipitate in their judgements.

Unlike the Interim Report, the Committee's Final Report was unanimous. It made extensive reference throughout to the findings of the various research studies it had commissioned, and it produced no less than eighty-eight separate recommendations. Those recommendations are conveniently summarized at the end of the Report itself (pp. 235–48). They have also been collated, together with a summary of some of the official responses, by one of the present authors (Game, 1987e, pp. 3–28). The most that can be attempted here is to convey something of the flavour of the Report's key themes and its major proposals.

The principal themes are spelt out in Chapters 3 and 4 of the Report. Chapter 3 discusses three of the interlocking attributes and values of local government: *pluralism*, or the dispersal of power, 'providing political checks and balances, and a restraint on arbitrary government and absolutism' (p. 48); *participation*, both in the expression of community views and in the actual delivery of services (p. 49); and *responsiveness*, or effectiveness in meeting the needs of the local community (p. 50). If local government is to be able to demonstrate that it is a more effective system for the provision of services than is local administration, the Report argues, these three attributes need both to be fostered and kept in balance. That, indeed, could be seen as the overall objective that the Committee set itself: 'to help to maximize the potential of local government to provide major services, and meet other local needs, within a local democratic framework' (p. 57).

Chapter 4 of the Report outlines the principles underpinning the Committee's recommendations for strengthening that democratic framwork. It is here that the Committee sets down those references noted in our opening chapter to the need to reflect and accommodate politics – 'the essential currency of representative democracy' (p. 60) – in the organizational arrangements for local government. The Report then identifies the main unifying themes of its recommendations, acknowledging especially the systemic strength which results from the diversity of local political systems, and also the need to narrow – through evolutionary development rather than institutional change – the increasing gap between the statutory local authority framework and political reality.

The actual recommendations of the Committee are summarized briefly below, under the headings of the five chapters in which they emerge:

The decision-taking process (Chapter 5)

This section of the Report opens with an endorsement of the existing corporate local authority system, in which officers serve the council as a whole, and decisions are taken openly by the whole council, without – as in central government – any separate source of executive authority. Committees and sub-committees with powers to take decisions for the council as a whole should reflect the overall composition of the council. Co-option to such committees should end, decisions being taken by elected councillors only. Non-councillor advisers from a variety of bodies can attend those committees, but they should not be able to vote, and their identity should be known publicly. Purely deliberative committees, on the other hand, should not be subject to such strict legal regulation: they could be one-party and could meet in private, with neither the public nor other councillors having the right to inspect documents or attend meetings.

Councillors and officers (Chapter 6)

This section, easily the longest in the Report, also accounts for half of its recommendations. It looks first at councillors and then at officers, particularly senior officers, with the aim of clarifying their respective roles. As we noted in our own chapter on councillors, the Committee was not keen to encourage the phenomenon of the full-time member, but it did propose a simpler and more generous system of remuneration. There should also be a statutory register kept of both the pecuniary and non-pecuniary interests of councillors, with councillors declaring a pecuniary interest at a meeting being required to withdraw from the room.

In one of its most publicized and controversial recommendations, the Committee proposed a complete ban on 'political activity' for all local authority employees on Principal Officer grade or above. Political activity in this instance is given an extremely broad definition, similar to that applying to senior civil servants subject to the Civil Service Code. It would include not simply standing for or holding public elected office, but also holding any party office, election canvassing, and 'speaking or writing in public in a personal capacity *in a way that might be regarded* as engaging in party political debate' (Recommendation 51(iii) – our emphasis). It is perhaps paradoxical that the subjective test, which was eschewed by the Committee in its Interim Report on council publicity, should be seen as an appropriate means of judging the behaviour of individual officers.

Another highly contentious set of recommendations related to the enhanced role proposed for the chief executive. In future, it was proposed, local authorities should be required by law to appoint a chief executive as head of their paid staff, with overall managerial responsibility for the discharge of functions by officers. This chief executive would have, in addition to the 'traditional' roles of adviser and professional manager – responsible, for example, for the discipline and dismissal of all staff and also for the appointment of staff below the rank of principal officer – the new role of 'arbiter'. All statutory functions relating to the proper conduct of council business would be vested in the chief executive, including the new arbitrating duties of deciding whether a councillor has a need to inspect a document or attend a meeting; deciding whether a matter is urgent, before a committee chairman can act on it; and, probably most controversially of all, deciding on the detailed application of the rules for party balance on committees – a matter hitherto gratefully left by most chief executives to elected members and their respective political parties.

Electoral arrangements and council size (Chapter 7)

The Committee's proposals under this section were directed towards the establishment of uniformity throughout Great Britain, based on single-member wards and all-out council elections every four years. In addition, the government should review council size, 'in the light of the current variations in the numbers of councillors per council and per head of population' (Recommendation 55).

Discretionary spending (Chapter 8)

The Committee's terms of reference had identified specifically 'the need to clarify the limits and conditions of discretionary spending by local authorities'. In particular, the Committee was invited to examine the use made of s137 of the Local Government Act 1972 (s83 of the Local Government (Scotland) Act 1983): the general discretionary power under which local authorities may incur, up to the product of a 2p rate, expenditure which is in their opinion in the interest of their area, or of some or all of its inhabitants. Unlike some of its predecessors – the Maud Committee, for example, and the Redcliffe–Maud and Wheatley Commissions– the Widdicombe Committee rejected the case for a general competence power for local authorities, unlimited by any financial ceiling. Rather, it was proposed that the financially limited general discretionary power should continue, but calculated in future on the basis of the population of an area, instead of its rate product. As an interim measure, London boroughs and metropolitan districts – now single-tier authorities, following the abolition of the GLC and the MCCs – should have their 2p rate product limits immediately doubled, to make up the lost s137 spending capacity in these metropolitan areas.

The Committee's research had revealed that by 1984–5 over two-thirds of all s137/83 expenditure was being directed towards measures designed to tackle unemployment, to assist industry, or otherwise promote the local economy (Research Vol. IV, p. 18). This contrasted with just 4.4 per cent being spent on the publicity and promotion with which the government was so concerned and which it had recently outlawed in the Local Government Act 1986. Responding to these figures, the Committee recommended that the government should review the proper economic development role of local authorities, 'with a view to identifying any areas in which additional local authority statutory powers should be introduced' (Recommendation 58).

Apart from publicity and campaigning, the type of local authority discretionary spending which tends to cause the greatest consternation is probably the funding assistance given to various voluntary groups and organizations. The Committee acknowledged that, to their critics, the objectives and activities of such groups could be regarded as 'sectional, divisive, socially unacceptable or even plain ridiculous' (p. 193). But it argued that, rather than attempting to proscribe support for such activities, which would be neither desirable nor practicable, it was more important that local authorities be made to account to the electorate for such support. Authorities should, therefore, be required to maintain and public annually a register of all grants to voluntary bodies, and indicate the purpose for which the grant was given.

Public challenge (Chapter 9)

This final substantive section of the Report was aimed at clarifying and strengthening the mechanisms through which members of the public can challenge possible breaches of the law, procedural abuse and maladministration on the part of local authorities. While acknowledging that the existing mechanisms for local authority challenge – the audit service, the ombudsmen and various courts and tribunals – are already more rigorous than those applying in certain other contexts, the Committee felt there were still weaknesses which could be remedied.

It was proposed, for example, that the Audit Commission in England and Wales and the courts in Scotland be given new statutory powers to seek an interim injunction restraining a council from incurring unlawful expenditure. Local ombudsmen should be able to consider complaints direct from the public, and to investigate individual cases on their own initiative. Individual citizens, for their part, should have the right of assistance through the ombudsmen to challenge in the courts decisions of their local authority.

Reactions to the Widdicombe Committee recommendations

It is a reflection of the modern-day transcience of cabinet ministers that, during its lifetime of little over a year, the Widdicombe Committee found itself responsible to three different Environment Secretaries. By the time the Final Report was published in June 1986, Patrick Jenkin's successor, Kenneth Baker, had himself been superseded by Nicholas Ridley. Launching the Report in the House of Commons, Ridley chose to describe it, somewhat enigmatically, as 'radical in content', without indicating either which particular elements he found 'radical' or, indeed, whether he felt they were radically good or radically bad.

Other instant commentators on the Report were rather less guarded, and there was certainly no shortage of criticism from the world of local government. Labour party and trade union reaction was especially hostile – most notably towards the restrictions on the political activities of senior officers, the proposed far-reaching powers given to chief executives, and the Committee's opposition to the principle of full-time salaried councillors.

Subsequent judgements, it is probably fair to say, have been rather more favourable. They have also been more wide-ranging, trying, as David Widdicombe himself exhorted in his Foreword to the Report, to assess the 'whole, balanced, closely inter-related package' of recommendations, instead of focusing on simply one or two of them in relative isolation. As already noted, we have sought elsewhere (Game, 1987e) to collate and summarize the responses of local authorities and other local government bodies to the Committee's individual recommendations. What follows is an attempt to synthesize the reactions of those same organizations to the Final Report as a whole. It is inevitably a subjective and selective exercise, but in so far as it is possible to identify any overall local government view of something as complex and detailed as the Widdicombe Report, this is probably what it would look like.

There was a widespread, if hardly surprising, welcome for what was felt to be a forthright endorsement of the value of local government, of its place in the political system, and of its present institutional and decision-taking structure. The Committee had clearly and positively recognized the inherently political nature of local government; it had acknowledged its readiness and ability to respond innovatively to new pressures and new demands; and it had confirmed, through its exhaustive research programme, that local government generally is held in high regard by the electorate.

At the same time, it was regretted that the Committee's terms of reference had been so narrow, and that any resulting changes would inevitably be made without adequate consideration having been given to factors such as structure, functions, finance and the electoral system. In particular, there was a consciousness that the Committee had been quite unable even to pass comment on any violations of local democracy that might have been perpetrated by central, as opposed to local, government.

As for the overall tone and direction of the recommendations, there was felt to be something of a divergence between the expressed aims of the Committee and some of its actual proposals. Thus, there were frequent references in the opening chapters of the Report to the need to strengthen local democracy, and to avoid prescriptions of national uniformity. Yet many of the recommendations seem designed to impose precisely such a uniformity, frequently by means of statutory rules and central controls. In the same way, having talked positively of the centrality of politics to representative democracy, the Report could be seen as weighted rather against councillors and towards officers, and particularly towards the chief executive. As Loughlin concludes:

The two themes which pervade the Widdicombe Report are the formalization of certain conventional practices and the reassertion of officer control. For Widdicombe these themes provide the key to solving problems which arise from the sharpening of political intensity in local government'. (Loughlin, 1987, p. 81)

If confirmation were needed of at least the broad validity of some of these latter points, it is perhaps provided in Table 40. The table provides a classification of all eighty-eight of the Widdicombe recommendations in terms of the type of action they primarily advocate. It will be seen that nearly 70 per cent of them do indeed impose some new statutory requirement on local authorities or call for an amendment to existing legislation. By comparison, only a small minority of the recommendations opt for non-statutory action – in the form of, for instance, voluntarily developed codes of conduct, or standards of practice monitored and policed by the local authority associations.

Type of Action	No. of Recommendations
New legislation/statutory instrument/ statutory requirement	38
Amendment to existing legislation	23
New conventions/code of conduct/ code of practice	4
Amendment to existing code of conduct/ conditions of service	6
Other form of non-statutory action	6
Government to undertake review	8
Affirmation of existing practice	3
Total number of recommendations	88

Table 40   *Classification of the types of action required to implement the Widdicombe Committee's recommendations*

There can be no doubt, therefore, that there is plenty of scope for the government to legislate on Widdicombe if it wishes to do so. But the major delay in the appearance of any official ministerial response to the Report suggested some hesitancy by the government. Its eventual response, in the 1988 White Paper *The Conduct of Local Authority Business*, did identify subjects for future legislation. These included restrictions on twin-tracking, the enforcement of fair party representation on committees, the limitation of co-option and the banning of council staff serving as political advisers. Introducing the White Paper however, the Local Government Minister, Michael Howard, warned that its proposals 'won't all be legislated for at once' (*Independent*, 22 July 1988), suggesting a rather piecemeal approach. It is an approach which obviously conflicts with the Committee's wish to see its Report treated as a whole package. But it might also be viewed as something of a backhanded compliment to the Committee: having been presented with a much more substantial, subtle, and comprehensively researched report than they were initially anticipating, government ministers may have been at a loss to know precisely how to respond.

The impact of abolition

There is, however, an alternative explanation of the government's slow response to the final Widdicombe Report. If, as we have suggested, it was the Interim Report on Publicity in which ministers were primarily interested – as 'camouflage' for their own already planned legislation – it may be that the functions of the main Inquiry were rather to pacify and distract (Loughlin, 1987, p. 83). At that Brighton Conference in October 1984 it had been Conservative party activists who had needed pacifying and distracting – in particular from the government's failure to have abolished domestic rates, and from the embarrassingly effective impact of the anti-abolition and anti-rate-capping campaigns being waged by the GLC and other affected councils.

By the time the Committee's Final Report was delivered, the political climate had changed dramatically. The government's Green Paper, *Alternatives to Domestic Rates*, had been published in January 1986, foreshadowing the replacement of domestic rates by the flat-rate community charge. Abolition was history, the seven metropolitan authorities having been wound up on 31 March 1986 and their functions dispersed across a range of joint boards, joint committees, metropolitan districts, residuary bodies and 'arm's length' companies. The councils may have won their publicity battle with the government, but they had lost the war.

The same was true of rate-capping, only more so. The early unity, in the summer and early autumn of 1984, of the sixteen rate-capped Labour authorities, campaigning collectively behind a policy of 'not setting a rate', had crumbled and finally collapsed in what David Blunkett describes as 'a disorderly retreat' (Blunkett and Jackson, 1987, p. 181) and Ken Livingstone, more brutally, as a 'fiasco' (Livingstone, 1987, Ch. 9). One by one all the defiant councils had fixed rates, although not soon enough in the case of the Lambeth and Liverpool members to prevent their being taken to court by their district auditors, surcharged and disqualified from public office. At the time of writing it is still possible that a similar fate may eventually face members from the London boroughs of Camden and Islington, both of whom deferred making a rate until roughly two months into the 1985–6 financial year.

The second year of rate-capping, 1986–7, involved almost twice as many authorities as in the previous year, since the nineteen new joint boards and the new directly elected ILEA were all subject to selective rate limitation under the abolition legislation. This time, though, there was no collective non-compliance, and several of the capped authorities applied to the Environment Secretary for, and were granted, redetermined spending levels. It was an early indication, more of which were to follow, of a growing pragmatism among Labour councils, and of a growing recognition that the local political landscape was being quite fundamentally transformed. In these changed circumstances, government ministers found themselves in much less need of a 'distraction' like Widdicombe than they had been two years earlier.

The origin of the abolition proposals and the convoluted

process of the legislation have been described in detail elsewhere (Flynn *et al.*, 1985; Forrester *et al.*, 1985; O'Leary, 1987). The new organizational arrangements in the former MCC areas have also been the subject of a study by an INLOGOV research team including two of the present authors (Leach *et al.*, 1987). What is relevant in the context of this book is an evaluation of the effect which the disapperance of the GLC and the MCCs has had upon the dynamics of local politics in the seven conurbations.

Three major effects can be identified: the relative depoliticization of a number of important service areas; an associated reassertion of officer influence; and the strengthening of inter-district political networks, sometimes in quite surprising ways which cut across party political divisions.

Depoliticization

Reference to depoliticization brings us back to our discussion in Chapter 1, in which we sought to emphasize the intrinsically political nature of Local government decision-making. The observations of Widdicombe Committee member, Sir Lawrence Boyle, to which we referred in that chapter, are equally relevant here:

. . . all governments, be they central or local, have a two-fold function to perform. They have the service function and they have the political function.

The service function consists of the provision of those goods and services which for one reason or another are supplied through the public sector. The political function, on the other hand, is the management and reduction of the conflict which arises out of the issues involved in the public provision of goods and services. It embraces such questions as the scope, the scale and the quality of the public services and the manner in which their costs should be met. And it should be noted that it is easier in fact to remove the service function from local government than it is to remove the political function. Because the service function, as we know, can always be privatized, but the political function cannot and should not be delegated. *If the political function is removed from local government, it ceases to be local government.* (Boyle, 1986, p. 33, our emphasis)

Depoliticization, then, can be viewed as the attempt to remove the political function from local government, and to make the service function predominant. The outcome, as Boyle notes, would be that 'the role of the politician is subsidiary to that of the administrator, and the position of the political process inferior to that of the administrative machine' (ibid.). Loughlin argues that precisely this objective – depoliticization – lies at the heart of the Thatcher government's whole local government strategy (Loughlin, 1987, p. 65), and certainly it would appear to be true of its approach to abolition.

Depoliticization has manifested itself in two principal ways: one imposed by central government, in the form of 'precept-capping'; the other a consequence of the fact that the members of the new joint boards and joint committees are nominated (and recallable at will) by their respective district and borough councils, and thus are only 'indirectly' rather than directly accountable. In each of the six metropolitan counties, three major services previously operated by the county councils – police, fire and civil defence, and passenger transport – are now the responsibility of joint boards. In London it is only fire and civil defence that is covered by a joint board – the GLC never having had any formal responsibility for the Metropolitan Police, and having lost its responsibility for passenger transport to a quango, London Regional Transport, in 1985. All these joint boards, as mentioned above, were precept-capped for the first three years of their existence – i.e. up to and including their 1988–9 budgets. In other words, their precept levels, and thus for all practical purposes their expenditure levels, are determined each year by central government. Applications for 'redetermination' of the permitted maximum precept are possible but, if successfully achieved, they involve conceding to central government the right to vet in detail the contents of the relevent joint board budgets – in just the same way as happens to rate-capped authorities who seek redetermination of their rate limits.

Policy choice is not, of course, *determined* by level of expenditure. But, with staffing costs constituting by far the largest element in revenue expenditure estimates, and with central government increasingly prepared to intervene on staffing levels, such choice can certainly be heavily constrained. Both precept-capping itself, therefore, and the application for redetermination limit the ability of joint boards to decide their own expenditure levels, and severely restrict their scope for policy choice – indirectly in the first case, directly in the second.

The policy choice of the new Passenger Transport Authority (PTA) joint boards has been restricted still further by the Transport Act 1985, which opened up the provision of public transport to private competition by the 'deregulation' of road service licensing. Prior to abolition and deregulation there was in effect an 'arm's length' relationship between the policy and financial responsibilities of the PTA – the metropolitan county's passenger transport committee or its equivalent – and the day-to-day management and operational responsibilities of the Passenger Transport Executive (PTE), composed of non-elected paid officials who were appointed, and dismissable, by the PTA. In the post-deregulation structure the commercial operators constitute a new third body – the Passenger Transport Companies (PTCs) – the effect of which is both to complicate relationships and to reduce the discretion of the PTA joint boards to determine passenger transport policy for their areas. Their current policy brief is thus limited mainly to an influence on the fares levels charged by the PTCs, the choice of routes requiring subsidy, concessionary fares, and the planning and operation of new schemes – for example the Light Rapid Transit proposals in Greater Manchester and the West Midlands.

Of more general significance, though, has been the depoliticizing impact of the very nature and structure of these joint boards. The 1981–6 Labour administrations in the GLC and MCCs had provided many examples of decisive and innovative political direction – in relation to employment and industry, transport, planning, women, ethnic minorities, the police, and the arts. There were the Enterprise Boards, most notably in Greater London, the West Midlands, West Yorkshire and Merseyside: limited companies to whom funds were allocated for investment in the local economy, in the saving or creation of jobs, and the regeneration of industrial wastelands (Green, 1987; Mackintosh and Wainwright, 1987). There were the 'cheap fares' policies for bus travel, pioneered in the 'Socialist Republic of South Yorkshire', but later taken up, to a greater or lesser extent, by the other MCCs and of course the GLC (Bridges *et al.*, 1987; Livingstone, 1987). In Greater Manchester and Merseyside the county councils' police committees were pepared to challenge forcefully the traditional pattern of deference to the Chief Constable, particularly in the aftermath of the inner city riots of 1981 in Moss Side and Toxteth.

While elements of these and many other metropolitan county initiatives have survived abolition, the political impetus behind them has been hard to sustain. This largely reflects the fragmented political networks of the various new joint boards and committees. Members of the MCC police and passenger transport committees, for example, tended to meet together regularly, both informally between scheduled meetings and also more formally in pre-committee party caucuses. By contrast, the joint boards, composed as they are of members from a range of different district councils (or London boroughs), meet only at or fairly briefly before the formal meetings of the board and its committees. In these circumstances it is much more difficult for an active and thriving political network to be maintained.

It follows that the interest, experience, personal commitment and political stance of the chairmen (and/or vice-chairmen) of the joint boards become correspondingly more important. To a much greater extent than in the former MCCs, these leading figures come to form the main channel of communication and influence between the joint board members and the relevant chief officers. Nor is it invariably the case that the potentially most effective member ends up in the chair – for in most of the MCC areas it has been agreed that the chairman be appointed from amongst the councillors from the 'lead authority' which has been selected to provide the administrative back-up for the service concerned.

Officer influence

A corollary of these developments is that the positions of the respective chief officers – chief constable, chief fire officer, PTE director-general, etc. – have been strengthened *vis-à-vis* elected members. In the case of the police, moreover, this trend has been reinforced by the growing influence of the statutory one-third of magistrate members on the joint boards. Whereas on a metropolitan county council, the majority party, irrespective of its political complexion, invariably ensured that it had a majority on its police committee, in four of the six joint boards the magistrates now hold, and are increasingly ready to exploit, the balance of power. When the relative inexperience of many of the new nominated board members is added in to the equation, it is hardly surprising that, as Loveday reports, most Chief Constables in the MCC areas now seem to be enjoying a somewhat less testing and conflictual relationship with their local politicians than was the case in the years immediately preceding abolition (Loveday, 1987, pp. 94–5). Likewise, PTEs appear, with only limited exceptions, to have experienced a lessening of the detailed control and strong political direction to which they were subject prior to 1986.

Inter-district networks

A more positive repercussion of abolition has been the way in which, in some MCC areas at least, the constituent districts have demonstrated a capacity to co-operate amongst themselves, in some instances on a cross-party basis. In South Yorkshire and in Tyne and Wear, of course, cross-party co-operation is hardly necessary, all districts being controlled by Labour. In the other four former MCC areas, the influence of the Militant Tendency in the Labour party machinery in Liverpool, Knowsley and St Helens continues to act as a deterrent to any extensive inter-district co-operation in Merseyside. But in Greater Manchester, West Midlands and West Yorkshire Labour, Conservative and hung authorities have demonstrated a capacity to work together to set up and operate joint services in a way which represents at least some transcendence of individual district interests – and which would not necessarily have been predicted beforehand. The joint studies initiated by the districts in Greater Manchester and the West Midlands to assess the need for large out-of-town shopping centres provide one such illustration; and another would be the all-party support for the complex machinery of AGMA – the Association of Greater Manchester Authorities – which operates now as a kind of mini-county council.

In summary, therefore, abolition has in general weakened the sense of local political assertiveness and innovation which was apparent especially during the latter years of the GLC and MCCs. Central government financial control, administrative intervention and regulation have increased, as has the influence of officers over elected members. At the same time, there has developed a measure of inter-district co-operation at the political level, which at least acknowledges the value of county-wide activities in some service areas by choosing to operate them.

The changing climate of local politics, 1986–8

There is one massive irony that hangs over the whole abolition saga, which is that the metropolitan county councils and particularly the GLC were never more popular than when they came to be abolished. In September 1984, just before the Brighton Conservative Conference, the GLC had been able to launch a poster campaign publicizing its Harris poll finding that '74% SAY NO' to the Council's abolition. Support for the continued existence of the MCCs was never quite as strong as this, but a MORI poll also conducted in that summer of 1984 showed an overall majority of metropolitan county respondents (52 per cent) disapproving of abolition, with a third (32 per cent) 'strongly disapproving' (Robb and Burns, 1986, p. 379). A year later, as the Abolition Bill was completing its progress through Parliament, public opinion was still firmly against the government. Table 41 summarizes the results of a MORI survey in June 1985, showing that clear overall majorities of respondents – particularly those in the affected metropolitan areas – disapproved of abolition. On balance, it looked like a policy that was much more likely to lose votes for the Conservatives than to gain them.

Questions:
1 'To what extent do you approve or disapprove of the
government's decision to abolish the Metropolitan County
Councils and the GLC?'
2 'Thinking about the proposal to abolish the Metropolitan
County Councils and the GLC, has this proposal made you
. . .?'

	All respondents %	MCC residents only %	GLC residents only %
1			
Strongly approve	12 ⎫22	13 ⎫23	13 ⎫27
Tend to approve	10 ⎭	10 ⎭	14 ⎭
Neither	14	9	11
Tend to disapprove	22 ⎫51	29 ⎫61	20 ⎫59
Strongly disapprove	29 ⎭	32 ⎭	39 ⎭
No opinion	13	7	3
Net 'approve'	−29	−38	−32
2			
More likely to vote Conservative	3 ⎫	4 ⎫	2 ⎫
A little more likely to vote Conservative	3 ⎬6	4 ⎬8	2 ⎬4
Made no difference	57	53	51
A little less likely to vote Conservative	8 ⎫	9 ⎫	8 ⎫
A lot less likely to vote Conservative	23 ⎬31	25 ⎬34	33 ⎬41
No opinion	5	4	2
Net 'more likely'	−25	−26	−37
Base	1066	420	123

Source: MORI, *Abolition of the GLC and the Metropolitan County Councils*, Research Study conducted for the Metropolitan County Councils (MORI, June 1985)

Table 41 *Approval of abolition and its effect on the Conservative vote (1985)*

The 1986 local elections

Had there been a general election during 1985 or 1986, it is quite possible that some of this antipathy might actually have translated itself into votes. It certainly seemed to do so in the parliamentary by-elections and the local elections that were held during this period. As Peter Jenkins records:

> Livingstone could not save the GLC, but he had found one last mobilizing issue. For a brief moment Labour was popular in London, superficially at least. Abolition helped it on its way to victory in the Fulham by-election that month [March 1986], which in turn helped Labour to gain seats in the borough council elections in May. (P. Jenkins, 1987, p. 244)

With the benefit of hindsight, it is now possible to see those 1986 local elections, both in the London boroughs and in the now county-less metropolitan districts, as representing something of a turning point for Labour local government. Admittedly, the seats being contested included many of those that had been won by the Conservatives in 1982, in the elections coinciding with the Falklands conflict. But in London in particular Labour undoubtedly did well, winning control in Brent, Ealing, Hammersmith & Fulham, and Waltham Forest, and gaining a 45–13 majority on the new directly-elected Inner London Education Authority (ILEA) – the first time since the abolition of school boards in 1902 that local residents had had the chance to elect directly the people to run public education in their area. The Labour-controlled Association of London Authorities (ALA) was strengthened sufficiently to enable it to dominate the Fire and Civil Defence joint board that had taken over the responsibility of the GLC. In Lambeth, where thirty-one Labour councillors had recently been surcharged and disqualified from office for their rate-making delay the previous year, a new set of Labour candidates fought on the old council's record and increased both the party's share of the vote and its majority. In neighbouring Wandsworth and also in Merton, two of the boroughs which had led the way in the contracting-out of council services, the Conservatives hung on to control by only the narrowest of margins. The only real setbacks for Labour

in the capital were the Alliance's winning of seats in Islington
and Southwark and, above all, its gaining control of Tower
Hamlets Council – the culmination of the inroads made by
the Liberals' 'community politics' in the earlier elections of
1978 and 1982.

Outside London, in the other former MCC areas, Labour
also made some notable gains. Bradford, Bury, Dudley,
Rochdale and Walsall were all won, and the Conservatives
were deprived of their former control in Sefton, Wirral and
Trafford. Out of the thirty-six metropolitan districts, the
Conservatives now had an overall majority in only one:
Solihull. In Liverpool, where Labour councillors were still
fighting their battle against disqualification in the Appeal
Court, the results were no better for the Conservatives,
though rather more equivocal for Labour. The party actually
increased its number of seats, and thus its overall council
majority, but in terms of share of the vote, it was outpolled
for the first time by the Alliance. Probably Labour's worst
big-city result in 1986, though, came outside the former MCC
areas altogether, in Leicester. Here, it seems, was a clear
example of the phenomenon referred to in Chapter 7: a local
election being fought, in part at least, on local issues. In this
instance the principal concerns were the recent large percentage increase in the district council's rate, and the publicity
engendered by the Labour council's support for various
controversial causes, including the renaming of a park after
Nelson Mandela. Interestingly, it was these two themes –
Labour council's reactions to increasing financial restrictions,
and what might be called the 'politics of gesture' – that were
to dominate local government debate for much of the year
up to the general election of June 1987.

Rate-capping and creative accountancy

In May 1986, of course, there was no way of knowing when
the next general election would be, or what the state of
national opinion would be like at the time. But, extrapolating
from those 1986 local election results, as many media pundits
did, it seemed at least conceivable that Labour might be able
to win a parliamentary majority. A hung parliament of some

description was rather more probable, but even that would be likely to prevent the return of a third Thatcher administration. Certainly that was the view taken by many of those recently elected London Labour councillors. Moreover, as Margaret Hodge, leader of Islington Council and of the Association of London Authorities, was later to admit, they came, quite literally, to bank on a Labour victory (Wolmar, 1987).

The 1985–6 rate-capping saga, referred to above, can best be seen as but one of many stages in what Michael Parkinson has termed 'the guerilla warfare that has been going on between central and local government in the 1980's (Parkinson, 1986, p. 32). The government had failed, to its own satisfaction, to restrain local government expenditure by means of its battery of guidelines, targets, penalties and grant reductions. Too many authorities had responded to their loss of grant not by cutting service expenditures, but by increasing their rates – as Leicester, rate-capped in 1985–6, was ironically permitted to do in 1986–7. Rate-capping was the device designed to prevent such increases – initially selectively and then, if it proved necessary, generally. It prompted in its turn the response of the ill-starred non-compliance campaign by the initially selected Labour councils.

The campaign was, as we have seen, an embarrassing failure for most of the Labour councils involved. But it would be wrong to conclude from that failure that rate-capping itself was a success, and that the government had finally hit on an effective way of restraining council expenditure. If anything, the reverse was true: a principal reason for the collapse of the campaign was that most of the councils knew, privately at least, that they could, if they chose, both set a legal rate *and* avoid excessive service cuts. The means by which to do so were the various 'creative accounting' measures made available to them over the preceding few years through the ingenuity and enterprise of their treasurers.

Creative accountancy has been described as one of the few areas of local government expansion during the 1980s. Among the most widely deployed measures are those referred to by Parkinson in his admirable explication of Liverpool's complex finances: capitalization, rescheduled debt repayments, the use of special funds, the sale of mortgages and deferred purchase agreements (Parkinson, 1986a). As they contemplated their prospective 1985-6 budgets, councillors in most of the rate-capped authorities had good reason to suppose that some combination of these and other measures would enable them to set legal rates – thus avoiding the frightening prospect of personal surcharge – without anything approaching the swingeing service cuts and redundancies that were being publicly quoted.

In the event, this is essentially what transpired. The bulk of Labour councillors – sometimes albeit after extremely protracted and personally acrimonious budget meetings – voted to set rates, stay in office, and thus comply with the advice of their party's leader, Neil Kinnock. At the height of the rate-capping battle, at the February 1985 Labour Party Local Government Conference in Birmingham, Kinnock had argued against the illegal non-compliance strategy: 'Better a dented shield than no shield at all. Better a Labour council doing its best to help than Government placemen extending the full force of Government policy. . . . Our basic concern is – and must remain – jobs, services and democracy' (Leapman, 1987, pp. 88–9).

The 'dented shield' metaphor is a vivid one, and the speech remains one of Kinnock's most significant. It was significant at the time because it served to emphasize the growing ideological division between the party's pragmatists and dogmatists, between its 'soft' and 'hard' left. It was of longer term significance too, through the implicit message which the pragmatists were able to read into it. Stay in office, they took Kinnock to be saying, and a future Labour government will help bail you out of the financial difficulties in which you may find yourselves as a result of the creative accounting techniques used to avoid cuts.

Whether a 1987 Kinnock government would have been either able or prepared actually to do any such thing will, of course, always remain a matter of conjecture. What is less conjectural is that the sum required to do so would have been at least £2 billion:

Rate-capping has reduced the income base of certain Labour councils. But, rather than cut spending, these councils chose to use financial devices to artificially and temporarily boost revenue income. They hoped that this temporary stop-gap would bridge the period of financial restraint until the re-election of a Labour government. As this did not happen, it could be argued that local government is in deficit to the tune of about £2 billion – the total of recent creative accounting used by many Labour councils and some others.   (Labour Co-ordinating Committee, 1988, p. 8)

That figure of £2 billion is both a testimony to the ingenuity of local government treasurers and a measure of the extent to which a relatively small number of Labour councils were prepared to mortgage their futures while optimistically hoping for the return of a sympathetic national government. The principal devices employed to avoid cuts were deferred purchase arrangements – a form of municipal hire purchase – and 'sale and lease back' schemes, in which council buildings (or even, in the case of Camden, its parking meters) were sold to financial institutions and then leased back for the council's continued use. In keeping with Parkinson's 'guerilla warfare' characterization of central-local relations, the government responded to these procedures by curtailing or outlawing them – but not before they had been extensively exploited by 'hard' and 'soft' left councils alike.

The 'loony left' campaign

Imprecise though they may sound, these labels – 'hard' and 'soft' left – do represent, and would be acknowledged to represent, a genuine ideological division within the present-day Labour party (Seyd, 1987, pp. 168–9). The label heard much more frequently, however, during the 1986–7 period was that of 'loony left'. As Jolyon Jenkins describes it:

1986 was the year when Loony Leftism climaxed: when the *Sun* announced that it was going to award a prize – a symbolic two-finger statuette – at the end of the year to the looniest council of them all . . . when the *Daily Mail* and *Mail on Sunday* sent teams of reporters chasing round London boroughs in search of good (if not true) stories; when even *The Times* used the term without apparent irony. Most importantly, it was the year when Environment Secretary Nicholas Ridley and Conservative Party Chairman Norman Tebbit decided this could be harnessed as a vote winner for the Tory Party. (J. Jenkins, 1987, p. 8)

The stimulus for the Conservative party campaign, if not for that of the tabloids, was the party's perceived failure, and Labour's relative success, in the May 1986 local elections. In the London boroughs especially those elections swept in a wave of new left-wing councillors – including increased numbers of blacks and women – changing not only the party balance in those authorities won from the Conservatives, but also the ideological balance on several of those already held by Labour. The financial results of these developments have already been touched upon. Rate-capped authorities explored further avenues of creative accountancy, while newly-elected Labour councils, in boroughs such as Ealing and Waltham Forest, agreed budgets designed to remedy what were identified as 'service gaps' created by previous Conservative administrations, but which brought with them rate increases of around 50 per cent or more.

It was not so much these mainstream spending policies, though, that attracted the 'loony left' tag from the tabloid press and Conservative Central Office. Rather, it was the councils' equal opportunities policies, their efforts positively to promote the interests of previously neglected sections of the anti-nuclear and anti-apartheid campaigns that came in for the greatest mockery. The London boroughs of Brent, Haringey, Lambeth, Southwark, Camden, Hackney, Islington and Ealing were probably the most popular targets, but others on a list issued by Norman Tebbit of 143 examples of 'crazy campaigns of Left-wing councils' included Manchester, Bristol, Sheffield, Derbyshire and Edinburgh.

In several of the most widely publicized instances – Hackney Council's alleged renaming of manholes as 'access chambers' in order to avoid sexism; Haringey's reported banning of black dustbin liners; and, perhaps most notoriously of all, the supposed banning of the nursery rhyme 'Baa, Baa, Black Sheep' – the stories proved quite unfounded and were eventually acknowledged as such (Goldsmith's Media Research Group, 1987; J. Jenkins, 1987). In other cases, ideas discussed, and quite possibly rejected, at Labour group or party meetings were written up as if they were official council policy.

James Curran of Goldsmith's Media Research Group has estimated that between 1981 and 1987 there were some 3000 of these 'loony left' stories in the national tabloids alone, a large proportion of which were partially or entirely fabricated, and all of which were aimed at swinging public and political opinion against a relatively small number of mainly inner London Labour councils. It was, as the results of the 1987 general election were to show, a signally successful campaign – much more far-reaching in its impact than anything the GLC had been able to achieve. The 'GLC effect', which had appeared to benefit the Labour Party's cause between 1984 and 1986, was by early 1987 being openly described by the party leadership as an electoral liability – a key reason being the opposition felt by increasing numbers of 'traditional' white Labour voters towards the 'crazy schemes' apparently being supported and financed by these 'loony' London authorities (Waller, 1987, Ch. 12).

It might be argued that Labour MPs ought to know better than to believe everything they read in the newspapers. Ordinary electors tend to believe that 'there's no smoke without fire', and they had no means by which to differentiate any substantially true stories from the entirely fictionalized. Some of the stories, indeed, were not fictionalized, and some of the 'gesturism' went to lengths which a non-tabloid and non-Conservative commentator like Peter Jenkins was able to describe as more 'sinister' than 'loony':

Parents were appalled at the idea of their children being instructed in homosexuality. They were outraged by some of the political propaganda that passed as teaching. Workers employed by some of the councils were reported by informers for making 'racist' jokes or remarks and were disciplined or sacked. In some case their unions refused to represent them. (P. Jenkins, 1987, p. 246)

Widdicombe issues

There were, therefore, verifiable examples among all the 'loony left' mythology of at least some of Goodson-Wickes' catalogue of 'disturbing trends' that, as we noted at the start of this chapter, had helped create the Widdicombe agenda. Other 'Widdicombe issues' surfaced too during this 1986–7 period: 'twin-tracking' or 'cross-employment'; 'political appointments'; and the treatment of 'in post' chief officers.

The phenomenon of twin-tracking – officers or employees of one local authority serving as elected members on another (see Chapter 2) – has for some years been much more prevalent in the London area, where there is much greater opportunity for it, than elsewhere in the country. The abolition of the GLC had reduced some of that opportunity, but the 1986 London borough elections produced a further crop of colourful examples – with the implication, if not the hard evidence, that twin-tracking was increasing in significance. 'Racket of Labour's twin-track councils' (*Sunday Times*, 22 November 1987) was a not atypical headline, accompanied by sarcastic references to 'jobs for the boys', 'moonlighting councillors', and the 'abuse of patronage'. Individuals mentioned included Dorman Long, leader of Brent Council and race adviser in Lambeth's housing department; Russell Profitt, Lewisham councillor and Brent's principal race relations adviser; Jessica Wanamaker, chair of Southwark's police committee and head of Hammersmith and Fulham's community and police unit; and, almost inevitably, Patrick Kodikara, who had been appointed as Camden's Director of Social Services while serving as a member of Hackney's social services committee. There were similarly quotable examples of allegedly 'political appointments': John McDonnell, ex-GLC deputy leader, as policy adviser to Camden's leader, Tony Dykes; Reg Race, former Labour MP and head of the GLC's programme office, as Chief Executive of Derbyshire County Council.

As we noted in Chapter 6 above, the concept of what constitutes a 'political appointment' is far from easy to define in practice. In a similar way, it is by no means clear whether the reported move or early retirement of a chief officer 'on mutually acceptable financial terms' is in fact a euphemism for dismissal at the hands of the majority party. There can be little doubt of the increasing pressures facing chief executives and other chief officers nowadays, on councils of all party political complexions; nor that there are cases where individuals have been 'encouraged' to leave and may have been only too glad to do so. Documented examples of chief officers actually being 'dismissed', however, are still something of a rarity.

The difficulty with all of these issues is that, in the absence of the kind of systematic research commissioned and considered by the Widdicombe Committee, the only available evidence tends to be partial, impressionistic and anecdotal. This was true of Goodson-Wickes' compilation of 'abuses' drawn from exclusively Labour authorities, and it is inevitably true of the kind of personalized media reporting referred to above. The Widdicombe Committee stressed how they 'considered it most important that our recommendations be based on a firm foundation of fact' (Report, p. 19). But, as the months passed without any official government response to the Report, that 'foundation of fact' became progressively less firm and more dated. Similarly, the Committee's detailed and research-related deliberations – and certainly its plea to have its recommendations considered 'as a whole, a balanced package' – became easier for the government to discount.

The third Thatcher administration

Following the June 1987 general election and the return of a third Thatcher government with a second successive three-figure parliamentary majority, the Widdicombe proposals still received no immediate attention. Meanwhile the psychological impact of the election result on local Labour administrations can hardly be exaggerated. So much that had been done by Labour councils during the 1985–7 period had been premised on the election of a government which would rescue them financially, remove the problems of rate-capping and contracting-out, and restore the GLC (and possibly even the metropolitan county councils). In the event, not only was no such response at hand, but the councils found themselves facing a massive and radical legislative programme, designed quite explicitly to emasculate local government and destroy all vestiges of 'municipal socialism'. The four main Bills introduced in the first session of the 1987 Parliament dealt with finance, competitive tendering, education, and housing. Their main provisions, as they impinge upon the present powers and responsibilities of local government, included:

1 the abolition of domestic rates and the introduction of the *flat-rate community charge* or poll tax, to be levied on all adults;

2 the replacement of local business rating with a nationally-set *uniform business rate*;

3 the requirement that councils put out to '*competitive tender*' six specified services: refuse collection, street cleaning, the cleaning of buildings, school meals, parks maintenance, and vehicle maintenance;

4 the introduction of *opting out for schools*, enabling schools, following a majority parental vote, to leave local authority control and become grant-maintained – independent of the local education authority and funded by central government;

5 the *abolition of the Inner London Education Authority*;

6 the establishment of a *national curriculum* of specified subjects for all primary and secondary schools, coupled with written tests for every child at the proposed ages of 7, 11, 14 and 16;

7 the establishment of *City Technology Colleges*, financed by a combination of government funding and business sponsorship;

8 the extension of *financial delegation* in schools, giving headteachers and governing bodies more control over school budgets and the appointment of staff;

9 the *independence of polytechnics and colleges of higher education* from local authority control;

10 the creation of government-appointed *Housing Action Trusts*, to take over and sell off run-down council estates;

11 the establishment of council tenants' right to '*pick a*

landlord' – to choose to transfer from their local authority landlord to a housing association, trust, co-operative or private landlord;

12   the continued encouragement of council tenants' '*right to buy*' their homes.

But the government's plans to cut down or by-pass elected local government are not confined to this legislative programme, wide-ranging though it clearly is. Perhaps the most forceful demonstration of its hostility, particularly to inner-city Labour authorities, is to be found in the Prime Minister's personal initiative to fight urban decay, *Action for Cities*. Promised on the night of her general election victory, it was unveiled at a Prime Ministerial press conference in early 1988, not in the form of a conventional White Paper, but as a glossy brochure. The inter-departmental package consists primarily of extensions to a number of existing activities, such as a new Urban Development Corporation for Sheffield, City Action Teams for Leeds and Nottingham, a simplified City Grant to support private sector development, and two new road schemes for London and the Black Country. What is conspicuously absent from the package is any mention at all of a role for local authorities, beyond the fact that they should be compelled to release more of their derelict and unused land for development by the private sector.

With creative accountancy having been exploited virtually to its limits, with real budget deficits beginning to emerge, and facing what they see as a legislative programme threatening their very existence, the outlook for Labour local councils looks bleak indeed. The mood of sober realism, noted first following the collapse of the anti-rate-capping campaign, has spread, in London as elsewhere. There is more talk of 'making the system work', 'making services better', and of the need to 'improve management and training, develop new financial procedures, introduce value for money audits, performance monitoring and review, and make some hard choices about increasing efficiency'. In short, 'local government has suddenly become a job for grown-ups' (Labour Coordinating Committee, 1988, pp. 49–50).

This is not, of course, the message that all Labour councillors and party members have wanted to hear. The pages of *London Labour Briefing* during the winter of 1987–8 made it clear that within many Labour-controlled London boroughs there were 'Fightback' factions committed to opposing any 'cuts in jobs and services' to the bitter end. But such factions were outvoted in borough after borough by combinations of traditional Labour councillors and former radicals who had become convinced of the need for a change in strategy. In the process, leaders were defeated (Council leader, Steve King, and deputy leader, Martha Osamor, in Haringey), stood down (Merle Amory in Brent), and, where they survived, were subjected to considerable criticism from the 'Fightback' campaign groups. There could be few more eloquent testimonies to the new cold climate confronting Labour councils than the reports of erstwhile radical leaders such as Merle Amory, Anne Matthews (Southwark), Linda Bellos (Lambeth) and Tony Dykes (Camden) being accused of 'selling out' and 'political defeatism' for 'pushing through cuts packages'.

The message for the government would seem to be clear: if local councils can be financially straitjacketed, stripped of many of their key powers and responsibilities, and persuaded to fight amongst themselves for good measure, there is less immediate need for any legislation to regulate their internal political operations. Widdicombe's prime importance to ministers derived, as we have seen, from its Interim Report on Local Authority Publicity, rather than from its 300-page final report and associated research volumes. Though initially hijacked by the House of Lords, the legislation restricting councils' publicity powers came into effect during 1988, effectively curtailing their right to campaign against the very Bills that will deprive them of many of their established functions. Legislation, piecemeal or comprehensive, on other Widdicombe topics may now follow, along the lines of the 1988 White Paper, but in ministerial eyes it can hardly seem the priority it once was.

9
Politicization re-visited

In our opening chapter we referred to the process of party politicization as 'a steady long-term trend', the course of which could be traced over the past 150 years. In subsequent chapters we examined the acceleration of that trend over recent years. In doing so it became apparent that quantitative changes in levels of party domination of local government were being accompanied by certain qualitative changes in the character of local politics, for example, in the relations between parties, between members and officers and between councils and the public. In many instances the qualitative changes that we have recorded have proved challenging but nevertheless manageable: in other cases the scale or the nature of the changes have been judged by some as being as at least problematic or at worst malign.

In the case of inter-party relations we spoke of changes in the direction of formalization, polarization and intensification. The need to formalize relations between party groups, notably on hung councils, has often stretched the ingenuity and mutual tolerance of those involved but on the other hand it has provided a useful clarification of what were previously uncertain or even largely non-existent conventions. Polarization and intensification have brought a sharper edge to political debate and a clear crystallization of policy choices; yet they have also on occasions promoted heightened levels of rancour and intolerance within the inter-party conflict.

Relations between councillors and officers have undergone clear changes in many authorities. Sometimes these changes have been assimilated, even welcomed, by all concerned: for example the need for officers to be more sensitive to political realities and the mutual benefits of allowing officers to give advice to group meetings are now more widely recognized. Yet in some authorities mutual trust and confidence between councillors and officers has been put under great strain. In November 1987 for example the ruling Conservative group at Westminster City Council discussed a report showing that forty-eight senior and middle-grade officers, including fourteen chief officers had left the council since 1983: one Conservative councillor feared that 'the morale of staff is at an all-time low' and another blamed the sitatuion on the 'abrasive style' of the council's leader, Lady Porter. In the nearby borough of Lambeth earlier in the year similar problems provoked a memorandum from the chief executive to the Labour leader Linda Bellos, in which he complained of councillor and trade union interference in officers' work and warned of consequent problems in recruiting and retaining staff.

Relations between councils and the public too have not been without their problems despite the attempts of some authorities to respond positively to a more demanding community through consultative and participatory initiatives. We have referred previously, in our opening chapter, to the commotions in various public galleries at London council meetings in April 1987. Similar events occurred at other such meetings later in the year and into 1988, provoking charges and counter-charges as to exactly who provoked whom to do what. For some, such occurrences provided evidence of an ugly escalation of political activism from demonstration and protest to intimidation and violence. For others they were a measure of the genuine desperation of those who feared that council policies would mean their own permanent exclusion from decent housing or adequate social care. In any event they certainly reflected a qualitative change in the nature of local politics.

As the foregoing examples indicate, the various qualitative changes experienced in recent years can sometimes be interpreted as representing problems as much as progress. Different people will no doubt make their own different interpretations of where the balance lies between problems and progress in the case of particular changes. What is clear however is the very real nature of those changes and also the differing reactions that they have evoked. In this final chapter we offer an account of the sources of those changes and of the reactions to them.

In accounting for the acceleration of the long-term trend towards greater party politicization we identified the role of certain key factors such as local government reorganization and the deliberate electoral strategy of the main political parties. However, while factors such as those help us to account for the quantitative changes, they are less helpful in enabling us to understand the various qualitative changes which have occurred. Nor do they help us to account for some of the reactions which those qualitative chnages have provoked, not least from the government of the day as well as from the media.

When local government began to experiment in the late 1960s and early 1970s with innovations such as corporate planning, area management and public participation it was, by and large, allowed to get on with it. There was a limited amount of media interest and the attitude of both Labour and Conservative governments was basically one of encouragement, but generally such innovations were regarded as the proper business of local government; outsiders might offer advice or even criticism but in the last analysis they did not presume to do local government's job for it.

This no longer seems to be the case. The changes which have been occurring in local government since the late 1970s have provoked a far more assertive response from those outside its ranks. Particular policies or practices have been widely publicized by the media and by national politicians either as bold experiments or as evidence of political depravity. Those with national influence or power have sought to elevate the experiences of a Westminster or a Lambeth as object lessons – good or bad – for us all. Talleyrand is said to have observed that 'war is much too serious a thing to be left to military men'. Nowadays it appears that local politics is much too serious a thing to be left to local politicians.

In trying to account for recent qualitative changes in local politics and for the reactions they have produced we shall place them in a wider context. In particular we shall relate them to the contemporaneous search in a variety of quarters for new models of democratic politics, a search which in turn reflects the impact of certain social changes on the post-war welfare state consensus.

The place of local politics

The subject of local politics in Britain was for long a rather neglected field of study and it is only since the mid-1970s that it has attracted serious attention whether in the form of empirical investigation or of theoretical analysis. Some studies have concentrated largely on specific localities, interpreting their political history in terms of the changing fortunes of particular individuals or groups: even so such essentially localist studies have often attempted to suggest ways in which locally based findings might be tested for wider application (for example Jones and Norton, 1978). At the opposite pole structuralist explanations have emphasized the role of underlying economic and social forces and the consequences for local politics of the workings of the capitalist system (for example Duncan and Goodwin, 1982).

Between purely structuralist and purely localist explanations of local politics lies that 'very simple middle range theory' (Saunders, 1983, p. 21) developed by Cawson and Saunders (1983) in the form of a dualistic theory of the state. They postulate a basic distinction between a 'politics of production' (related to decisions concerning private-sector profitability) and a 'politics of consumption' (related to provision of social consumption such as housing, education, etc.). They go on to suggest that production and consumption functions are located at different levels of the state, in particular that 'local government becomes associated with questions of social need while regional and central agencies become associated with private sector profitability' (Cawson and Saunders, 1983, p. 25). This mutual insulation of the imperatives of needs and profitability at different levels of government is also accompanied by a similar locational divorce between the two core elements of the dominant ideology within British society, between the rights of citizenship which prevail at the local level and the rights of property which prevail at the regional and central level.

The outcome of this approach is a distinction in ideal typical terms between (a) a politics of production mainly at central and regional level in which capital and labour are directly represented as classes which negotiate with the state in a relatively exclusive corporate sector of the polity and in which the prevailing ideology is that of private property rights in a market system and (b) a politics of consumption mainly at the local government level in which the plurality of consumption sectors mobilize as non-class-based interest groups, competing through electoral and pressure group activities and in which the dominant ideology is that of citizenship rights in a welfare system.

This dualistic theory does suggest what it is that may be specific in the nature of local politics, namely a plurality of non-class-based consumption sectors mobilizing within a competitive sphere of politics informed by an ideological concern for the rights of citizenship, and capable of analysis through theories stressing the relative openness of public agencies to local pressure and opinion rather than through theories of a structuralist nature.

The dual state theory has not been without its critics (for example Dunleavy, 1985), but, even if we were to assume for the moment its general validity, it might still be regarded as modelling a vanishing world, one in which the role of the state in the spheres of both production and consumption was generally accepted and where the dual state arrangement provided a practical way in which to perform that role. This vanishing world was that of the post-1945 welfare state consensus, in which both central and local governments, and both major parties, shared certain common assumptions. It was a world in which the respective demands of need and of profit, of citizenship and of property, seemed capable of being kept in some sort of balance within a mixed economy and in which some form of 'dual state equilibrium' could be maintained as part of an 'historic compromise' between the competing principles and interests of capital and labour.

The current instability in central-local government relations may be symptomatic of a breakdown in that dual state equilibrium, which along with ideological polarization and multi-party politics, may in turn reflect a major readjustment in, or replacement of, the previously dominant Keynesian welfare state paradigm of public policy (Marris, 1982; Mishra, 1984). The terms of the dual state thesis, if correct, may prove to have been not timeless but confined to a particular period of history.

The notion of the central and local levels of the state co-existing by virtue of a mutually agreed division of their respective functions is one which has parallels outside the literature of the dual state thesis; so too is the idea that such co-existence in equilibrium may from time to time be disturbed.

Bulpitt (1983, p. 3), for example, has talked in terms of an historic dual polity involving 'an operational separation of powers between the national institutions of government in London and a considerable amount of reciprocal autonomy for peripheral governments and interests'. Such an arrangement implied the existence of 'High Politics' with which the Centre wished to concern itself and a 'Low Politics' of lesser matters which it was content to leave in the hands of those whom Bulpitt calls 'local elite collaborators' (p. 3). The failure of Labour to develop any clear political strategies of its own for local government or to develop a territorial politics around geographical inequalities (Sharpe, 1982) led Labour to acquiesce in this patttern of centre-periphery relations despite its essentially Conservative inspiration. Under such an arrangement both central and peripheral governments achieved a relative autonomy from one another and there was a low degree of interpenetration between national and local politics. The system however depended upon 'a common culture at both the Centre and in the periphery' and on 'an elaborate system of compromise and mutal deference between political and administrative elites at the Centre and in the periphery' (pp. 223–4).

The first strains in the dual polity emerged in the 1960s

when the search for economic and institutional moderniza-
tion raised questions of efficiency, planning and participation. Although these were matters of High Politics, it was
impossible to address them without entering into the world of
Low Politics for they were seen to involve questions of
regionalism, local government reform and public accountability. Thus the Centre 'became interested in many aspects of
peripheral activity'; at that point however its interest did not
extend to disrupting the dual polity which 'survived the
troubles' of that era (Bulpitt, 1983, pp. 173, 238).

Much greater strains however have been imposed since
1979 with the advent of

... Thatcherism ... the most innovative feature of which was its
concern to increase the role of the ordinary citizens and private
enterprise in the local political process. Under the stress of
continuing economic problems, of 'hard times', this code was altered
to emphasise the Centre's ultimate responsibility for macro-
economic policies and hence the legitimacy of its attempts to
increase its control over local authority expenditure. (Bulpitt,
1983, p. 236)

The result of all this was that the 'system began to break
down' as the government began to insist on, and indeed to
exploit, the 'constitutional subordination of local authorities
to the central government' (Bulpitt, 1983, p. 224) in its efforts
to change the nature of the 'local political process'.

Bulpitt clearly approaches the issue of relations between
the central and local elements of the state in different terms
from Cawson and Saunders, drawing as he does on notions
of territorial politics and historic traditions of Court and
country. Yet in their different ways the dual polity and dual
state theses each recognize that it has been possible for the
two levels to co-exist in a workable arrangement over a
considerable period of time.

The upsetting of an arrangement which has long been
mutually agreeable to both parties is not normally undertaken lightly. Yet in the case of central and local government
their mutual relations have clearly changed for the worse in
recent years and the dualistic arrangements of an earlier
period have come under great strain. 'The long standing

insulation of national and local political elites' has ended, leaving ministers in 'face-to-face-confict with local leaders' (Rhodes, 1985, pp. 41, 45): dualism, it seems, has been replaced by duels. Bulpitt's references to High and Low Politics may help us to understand the sources of this new antagonism. High Politics he takes to involve matters central to the very existence of a regime, such as external security, internal law and order and the general economic and social welfare. However 'the lives of governments and the existence of regimes do not normally turn (in the West at least) on the continuous and close supervision by the Centre of elected local governments' (Bulpitt, 1983, p. 29); the work of local government was thus, in the normal order of the dual polity, a part of Low Politics. The implication of Bulpitt's account of the breakdown of the dual polity however is that suddenly local government has become High Politics. It is now seen to require that 'continuous and close supervision by the Centre' which it once avoided.

At first sight such a development may seem incongruous if not perverse for how could local government be seen as threatening the life or existence of the government of the day? Whatever the sub-revolutionary rhetoric of some of the government's far left opponents in local government, and despite their incursions into the High Politics of nuclear-free zones or Northern Ireland, no serious observer could have imagined that they have ever possessed the resources necessary to overthrow an elected government. Yet it may be the case that local government has nevertheless been seen as some sort of threat, or at least an obstacle, not to the government's existence but to its dominant strategy for securing the general economic and social welfare. If that were the case, then the translation of local government from Low Politics to High Policits would become explicable. Certainly the Thatcher government has made no secret of its desire to bring about a major transformation in the fields of economic and social policy, a transformation entailing a revival of the market economy as the key to national success. It is the relationship of local government to this strategy of market based transformation which holds the key to its heightened political salience.

Local government and social transformation

As Loughlin (1986, p. 167) has pointed out, most of the changes made by the government since 1979 to the financial regime of local authorities reflect a desire for 'the incorporation of market rationality into local services and local authority management structures'. He cites a number of specific instances of this incorporation of market rationality including asset sales (of land and buildings); direct competition with the private sector (as in transport deregulation); the promotion of economic pricing policies; the minimization of cross-subsidization (for example in transport and housing); the re-structuring of services as residual activities, rather than as substantial alternatives, to the private sector (for example transport and housing); the emphasis on 'value for money'; and the promotion of ratepayer and individual consumer influence. The general pattern, he argues, has been one of requiring local authorities 'to withdraw from *public provision* of services, to *reduce subsidies* and to *deregulate*' (Loughlin, 1986, p. 171, italics in original). Further evidence along these lines could be seen in the government's 1987 proposals for a new housing policy incorporating deregulation in the private rented sector, market rents for new housing association lettings and competition between landlords for existing council housing. In education, too, proposals for allowing schools to opt out from the local education authority seemed designed to encourage a quasi-market in school selection amongst parents. Combined with proposals for compulsory competitive tendering, these developments can all be seen as part of a concentrated attempt to impose market rationality upon local government.

Any such attempt is likely to require changes at the level of local authority management since it demands new attitudes and practices; and it may be that in councils with a low level of politicization these changes encounter no great political resistance. Elsewhere however the notion of market rationality as a touchstone of good local government is likely to be greeted with varying measures of doubt or hostility since it rests on a particular set of political values which are not universally shared. However the sources of potential conflict between market rationality and local government involve more than ideological differences between particular sets of politicians; for there are two ways in which local government has developed historically with the clear purpose of countering market rationality.

Thus one major function of local government has been that of regulating or avoiding what might otherwise be the consequences of unbridled market rationality, through such services as public health, consumer protection and town and country planning. However, from a market perspective it appears that 'too many people in . . . local government spend too much of their time regulating the activities of others' and that such 'constraints on enterprise . . . are not always justified by any real public benefit'. The White Paper *Lifting the Burden* (1985), in which these comments appeared, was followed by another titled *Building Business, Not Barriers* (1986). Both documents reflected a continuing theme of environmental deregulation also identifiable in such policy initiatives as enterprise zones, simplified planning zones and the creation of urban development corporations. Circulars and appeal decisions and changes to the Use Classes and General Development Orders have meanwhile steered development control policy towards a greater presumption in favour of development, less scope for aesthetic judgements and a greater responsiveness to market realities. The unease with which such moves have been greeted by many Conservative councillors, for example in the context of debates over the future of the Green Belt and surplus farming land, indicates the extent to which notions of market rationality go against the grain of local government as traditionally practiced.

Apart from its regulatory functions another major area of local authority activity has been in the field of redistributive services which in greater or lesser degree seek to modify what might otherwise have been the outcomes of market rationality. On one calculation such services have absorbed an increasingly large share of local authority spending over recent decades, from 43 per cent in 1935 to 65 per cent in 1975 (Loughlin, 1986, p. 6). Moreover they include those services towards whose funding and development Labour has been most favourably disposed (Sharpe and Newton, 1984). For the present government however such redistributive concerns are suspect. Thus Nicholas Ridley warned the 1987 Conservative local government conference that 'redistributive taxation must be a matter for one taxing authority only – central government' and accused some councils of 'testing the redistributive rating system to its limits and driving out businesses and enterprises as a result'. He returned to the topic at the party's annual conference later in the year, warning of the danger of 'damage to the local economy' if Labour councils tried 'to bribe minority groups so that they vote for them again'; redistributive taxation he insisted must be a matter 'for the Chancellor of the Exchequer . . . not, thank goodness, for the councillors of Brent, Lambeth or Liverpool'.

Given the conflict between promoting market rationality and the established practices of regulation and redistribution it is hardly surprising that the government should have encountered opposition to its aims from local government. The tone of some of this opposition has however been sharpened by the fact that whilst the government was coming to view local councils as obstacles to its project of social transformation the Labour left was seeing them as possible vehicles for their own very different and competing project.

Except when major policy issues were crystallized by some local dispute as at Poplar or Clay Cross the Labour left had traditionally tended to ignore local government or to dismiss it as being of little real significance. Thus Ken Livingstone (1987, p. 18) records that his first candidature for the council in Lambeth in 1971 met with the reaction from one Militant supporter that 'local government was a complete dead end'. In the 1980s however increasing attention came to be paid to local government as a fruitful area for a new and more radical politics of local socialism.

The nature of this attention embraced two main elements. One was the idea of using 'the local state . . . as an example of what we could do as a Socialist government at national level', thereby creating local models of socialism with an emphasis on a 'Socialism [which] is going to mean something to people at the grassroots' (Blunkett, 1981a, p. 102). The other was the notion of local government as an arena for campaigning against public sector cut-backs. The statement of aims of the journal *Local Socialism*, launched jointly in 1980 by the Labour Co-ordinating Committee and the Socialist Environment and Resources Association, made explicit the need 'to link current campaigns against the cuts with debate about long-term ideas on the reform of local government, decentralisation and news of constructive action on economic and environmental issues'. Linking the two elements of local models of socialism and campaigns against the cuts was the concept of mobilization, of the need 'to mobilise the community in defence of itself and positively in favour of the new way forward' (Blunkett, 1981b) and 'to abandon its preoccupation with electoralism and adopt a campaigning perspective, mobilising outside the conventional political system, in the community and the work place' (Hain, p. 202).

Such a strategy soon brought left-wing councils into conflict with the government, not merely by virtue of its opposition to Conservative policy on public spending but also because of its promotion of what Norman Tebbit described to the Greater London Conservatives in March 1984 as 'this new, modern divisive version of socialism'. Left Labour councils were providing not merely opposition but also an alternative to the market-oriented policies of the government, involving experiments with decentralization, equal opportunities, local economic planning and municipal enterprise.

The mutual incompatibility of the two approaches was described starkly by Nicholas Ridley in a BBC Radio 4 *Analysis* programme on the inner cities in September 1987:

You cannot have a free market government using public spending for doing what is properly within the public domain and at the same time municipal socialism with its ideology that there should be public ownership of land, of enterprise, houses and other buildings, because the two are in conflict. So if they insist on pursuing municipal socialism we will redirect our resources away from local authorities.

A right-wing Conservative government thus faced a traditional local government establishment doubtful about, resentful of, or hostile to much of its market-rationality project, and left-wing Labour councils who claimed to have an alternative project pre-figuring a decentralized and campaigning socialism. Given the government's determination to proceed with its own project as an essential prerequisite for the nation's economic and social health and given also the respective reluctance and hostility of its traditionalist and leftist opponents the elevation of these matters into the realms of High Politics becomes understandable.

Despite the very different prospectuses for social transformation offered in the name of the free market and of local socialism the two ventures shared two significant characteristics. One was the determination of their adherents to secure the fullest possible implementation of their policies. At the local level this led to a much more intensely ideological and interventionist style of political management with major implications for councillor-officer relations and local authority decision-making, as we saw in Chapters 4 and 6. Perhaps inevitably the government tended to see these developments as more problematic when they occurred amongst its opponents than amongst its supporters.

The second shared characteristic was a sense that local government could not continue as before. This was clearly explicit in the case of the government's successive initiatives aimed at opening up local government to market forces. It was also however implicit and sometimes explicit amongst the proponents of local socialism whose search for more accessible and accountable forms of service delivery stemmed in part from the recognition that 'no one will easily defend a socialist principle (like for example direct labour) if it is encapsulated in a service (like council housing repairs) which is paternalistic, authoritarian or plain inefficient' (Blunkett and Green, 1984, p. 2). In both camps there was thus disquiet about many of the assumptions which had underlain established patterns of local service delivery, about bureaucratic structures and about the claims of professionalism. There was a corresponding consciousness, shared also with the proponents of the grass-roots populism of Liberal community politics, of a more active and assertive local public. The projects of social transformation in which local government had become embroiled reflected an awareness of accumulated social changes which had altered the character of local politics.

Local politics and social change

An American, Stephen Elkin, observed that London's local politicians in the early 1960s operated in a wholly different political environment from their opposite numbers in the United States. American politicians saw 'a heterogeneous electorate most of whose major social and economic differences are politically relevant' whereas councillors in London 'saw an electorate which was relatively homogeneous with only one important political cleavage' (Elkin, 1974, p. 78). That cleavage was class, expressed through a two-party system of local politics; cleavages based on ethnicity, neighbourhood, issues and organized interest groups were conspicuously absent compared with their presence in American cities. Because of their more simply structured environment.

Councillors in London were not political entrepreneurs. They did not have to engage in a continuous dialogue with their market, the public, to see what would sell, and compared to their American counterparts, had little incentive to invest any significant amount of resources in trying to monitor and mould citizen opinion. (Elkin, 1974, p. 114)

Yet by the time Elkin wrote up his research in 1973 he was conscious that changes were under way. He was conscious of a citizenry growing more knowledgeable of and involved with local government decision making; he observed 'higher levels of conflict both in and outside of government' and 'a changing political culture, manifested in an increase in citizen organisation'; and he identified a growing tension arising from 'the juxtaposition of a citizenry becoming more concerned with issues and more active in local politics with a set of institutional arrangements and political patterns appropriate to a more hierarchical politics' (Elkin, 1974, p. x).

We can now see that the form of local politics which Elkin was witnessing in the early 1960s was about to be displaced by something rather different as a result of certain fundamental changes within British society at large from the mid-1960s onwards. British political culture, for example, with its traditional assumptions of respect for, and trust in, public bodies and of deference towards established authority was beginning to embrace much more questioning, sceptical and assertive attitudes. Consumers began increasingly to assert their rights against providers of goods and services and new Commissioners or 'Ombudsmen' were set up to handle public complaints over maladministration in local and central government and the health service. The onset of economic decline began to mean that questions of how resources should be distributed became much more hotly contested now that prizes could no longer be made available for everybody.

Those changes had their impact on local politics. Pressure for more public participation, for example, led to the setting up of the Skeffington Inquiry into Public Participation in Planning which reported in 1969. Amenity societies, residents' associations, tenants' associations and community action groups began to flourish throughout the late 1960s and into the 1970s. Accompanying the new degree of public assertiveness was a loss of confidence in professional experts amongst the public. The professional claims of planners, architects, road engineers, social workers and teachers were increasingly called into question by a sceptical public informed by a combination of more widespread educational opportunity, investigative journalism and – sometimes the most crucial – their own lay experience of professional solutions.

Between them the rise of local pressure groups and the decining trust in professionalism called into question some of the traditional modes of local authority operations. Councillors in their committees and officers in their departments were not necessarily assumed to be well-informed and well-intentioned; they were sometimes seen as remote and out of touch, pursuing their own party and professional goals at the expense of individuals or localities. In response to this critique some local councils attempted to change their style of operation, to consult more widely and to listen more carefully, adopting the various strategies which we discussed in Chapter 7.

The increasing need for local authorities to operate in a more open and responsive fashion was also fuelled by certain social trends leading away from a largely homogeneous mass society towards one that is not only more assertive but also more diversified. Within politics itself such trends became apparent in the rise of single-issue politics, focused around campaigns for quite particularized goals in such areas as pollution and the environment, sexual behaviour, media policy, animal welfare, homelessness, transport policy, energy policy and disarmament and defence. This form of politics does not rely on party politics and representative democracy to secure its aims but pressures, lobbies and campaigns for quite specific goals which often cut across traditional political alignments or are simply not reflected within them. More generally, in the context of the state of public opinion on key political issues, Young (1985, p. 31) has identified 'a country of distinct publics and diverse opinions . . . a great diversity of sub-cultures'.

In terms of social structures, changing patterns of employment, the return and apparent persistence of unemployment, the growing number of working women and the expansion of the informal economy has complicated the traditional relations between work, class and life-style. The existence in some areas of substantial ethnic minorities has added a further element of complexity. Among these minorities meanwhile the concern of an older generation for integration and assimilation has been challenged by attempts to assert specific minority rights. In some cases this has taken the form of political activism within the established party system; in other cases it is expressed in the form of more separatist strategies entailing own language teaching, religious schools and bans on transracial adoption. Religion, meanwhile, has shown an increasing diversity with a rapid growth of differing sects and cults both within and outside the Christian tradition and with mosques replacing chapels and synagogues in some areas. Economically, the increasing diversity of society is reflected in the growth of specialist shops, of direct-mail targeting and of moves towards customized production rather than standarization, whilst in the media special interest magazines proliferate. In the field of welfare the voluntary sector expands and diversifies: self-help and mutual-aid groups arise to cater for specific problems, disabilities and disadvantages amongst particular sections of the community.

Taken together these changes amount to a move away from a homogeneous mass society with a large degree of consensus on interests and values, and towards a more diverse and fragmented society within which there are asserted a plurality of sectional interests and values. This is not to imply that the nature and the degree of diversity is everywhere the same; nor that each of the contending interests and values necessarily commands the same degree of resources and respect. It does however imply that politics faces the test of brokering, facilitating and arbitrating among such diverse interests and values rather than of summoning up some universal 'general will'. The political problems of a society increasingly characterized by such diversity have been summarized by Toffler (1981, p. 420):

On all sides, countless new constituencies, fluidly organized, demand simultaneous attention to real but narrow and unfamiliar needs . . . . In a mass industrial society, when people and their needs were fairly uniform and basic, consensus was an attainable goal. In a de-massified society . . . the diversity in any congressional district or parliamentary constituency . . . is so great that its 'representative' cannot legitimately claim to speak for consensus . . . . What then happens to the very notion of 'representative democracy'?

The history of local government over the past two decades has been, in part, one of attempts to supplement not only the established institutions of representative democracy in the face of social diversity but also those of professional service departments in the face of public assertiveness. Public participation, area management, neighbourhood and community councils, consultation and co-option, all these ventures which have now gradually accumulated over the past twenty years or so, have shared one common perception.

They have seen the traditional institutions of representative democracy and professional service departments as being insufficiently fine grained to respond to the variety of interests being expressed at the local level. The simply structured local politics of a relatively homogeneous electorate which Elkin found in London in the early 1960s has been gradually displaced both there and elsewhere by one much closer to that with which Elkin was familiar in America, one in which politicians needed to 'engage in a continuous dialogue' with the public, to 'monitor and mould citizen opinion' and to act increasingly as 'political entrepreneurs' rather than as wholly authoritative decision-makers. However for political radicals of right and left these ventures were not wholly convincing. For them the challenges presented by a more assertive and more diverse public required more radical solutions than those with which local authorities experimented in the 1960s and 1970s.

Variants of democracy

To radicals of both right and left demands for more responsive and accountable government came as no great surprise. To those on the right such demands confirmed their suspicions that institutions of government inevitably failed to deliver and that local government had shown itself to be both 'expensive and incompetent in the absence of competition or any valid means of assessing and responding to consumer preferences' (Forsyth, 1981, p. 15). Their counterparts on the left meanwhile saw local government as plagued by a heavy-handed paternalism dominated by middle-class professionals and authoritarian political leaders who were out of touch with the problems of working-class communities (cf. Baine, 1975). However, although they agreed that something was amiss right- and left-wing radicals did not agree on the appropriate remedies.

Market democracy

For the radical right the quest for greater responsiveness and accountability certainly did not lie in an extension of political activity, such as through the actions of pressure groups. In their eyes a major weakness of government was that it 'yields to organised and vested interests rather than to the dispersed unarticulated opinions of the public in general' (Seldon, 1982, p. 6) and there were thus no gounds for encouraging even more such activity. Indeed the attitudes of the new Conservative government after 1979 were welcomed on the grounds that 'Gone will be the days when councils are considered as gift-horses to every tin-pot pressure group prepared to shout, harass and blackmail for money' (Conservative Party *Local Government Brief*, October 1980).

To some degree this hostility reflected suspicion about the actual nature of certain specific pressure groups and fears that they were 'extreme pressure organisations with little or no public support' eager 'to launch their weird and way-out policies with local monies' (*Local Government Brief*, February 1981). It also though reflected a more general hostility, common on the New Right, towards pressure group politics and indeed to politics itself as a mode of resource allocation. 'While organised interests are able to articulate their demands for a larger share of the goods available through the agencies of the state, groups which are not able to organise receive correspondingly less attention from government' (Kukathas, 1985, pp. 65–6). Since 'the benefits are concentrated among a relatively few while the costs are spread over the many but only a little on each' (Ashford, 1985, p. 407) the correspondingly low incentive to count the general costs rather than the specific benefits of group action would encourage pursuance of the latter in any individual case. Moreover it was conversely the case that 'benefits from restraint in the use of group power are . . . thinly diffused among the whole population, while the costs are incurred by the group which exercises restraint' (Brittan, 1975a, p. 112). The total outcome was thus a mass of sectional demands whose complete fulfilment would be incompatible with the general interest.

From the New Right perspective moreover such an outcome was not merely an aspect of inter-group politics but was an intrinsic weakness of politics itself in which there was no incentive for actors to count the true economic costs of their granting, or being granted, specific demands, for 'there is no real equivalent to loss and bankruptcy in political action' (Barry, 1987, p. 39). Thus, far from politics being seen as a benign activity by the New Right, it is seen as one which deflects attention away from a long-term public concern over the general production of wealth to short-term sectional concern over its particular distribution. Accordingly any demands for greater responsiveness and accountability in the sphere of local government ought not to be met by expanding the area of political action, through a livelier pressure-group system or other participatory devices. The mechanisms of the economic market place are offered instead.

. . . independent providers . . . are nearer to public demand than local authorities can ever be . . . their perpetual search for profitability . . . stimulates them to discover and produce what the consumer wants. . . . In this sense the market sector is more genuinely democratic than the public sector, involving the decisions of far more individuals and at much more frequent intervals. (Adam Smith Institute, 1983, p. 3)

Moreover the market is seen as especially suitable not only for meeting demands for democratic accountability but also for catering for diversity:

. . . the economic market is superior to the ballot box in its ability to cater sensitively for minorities on an exact measure of proportional representation. Small groups of consumers with unusual needs or preferences can invariably find a supplier to meet their distinctive requirements at a price.   (Harris and Seldon, 1979, p. 68)

Seen in this light the drive for a greater element of market rationality in local government does not merely represent part of an attempt to impose a particular financial discipline on the public sector. It is also part of a wider political project to promote a particular concept of market-based democracy. At one point it seemed possible to speak, in the local context at least, of the promotion of what might be termed 'ratepayer democracy' (Gyford, 1986, p. 128). Michael Heseltine, as Secretary of State for the Environment, declared himself in 1979 to be the minister not only for the rate collectors and spenders but 'in the last resort for the ratepayers as well' (Gyford and James, 1983, p. 173). Such initiatives as the abortive plan for rates referenda, the introduction of rate-capping and the arrangements for consultations with non-domestic ratepayers gave a new urgency to traditional Conservative defences of the ratepayer interest.

However the subsequent proposals for replacing domestic rates by a community charge or poll tax cast a new light on this strategy. All adults would now be paying a local tax, at a flat rate. Moreover there would be a 'gearing effect' built into the system since something like 75 per cent of council income would now be under central government control through the grant system and the uniform business rate. As a result a given percentage increase in council spending would require a much exaggerated percentage increase in the level of community charge, thus imposing a high marginal cost on those responsible for paying it. By this means everybody might be brought to act like economic man and something akin to market rationality might thereby enter into the voting process at election time. The early attempts at ratepayer democracy can thus now be seen as one step on the way to the wider goal of a market democracy in which political activity would be both tempered by market discipline and diminished by transferring more decisions into the market place.

Participatory democracy

To the radical left, in contrast, the appropriate remedy for unresponsive and unaccountable local government was to widen the scope for political activity rather than to discipline it or displace it by market mechanims. This did not mean however that they were satisfied with the formal machinery of consultation and participation established during the late 1960s and the 1970s. Experience of this machinery in operation produced fears on the left that 'those in authority see participation as a means of neutralising dissent or mobilising support for their policies' so that it was 'being officially sponsored in order to secure popular legitimacy for government programmes' (Hain, 1980, pp. 8, 170). Advocates of a more radical approach based on self-organizing community action feared that conventional modes of public participation were concerned 'to optimise the efficiency of feedback systems in the decision-making process' whilst simultaneously 'incorporating the protests of the powerless'; they were not an appropriate means for 'the development of the collective organisation of the powerless' in order 'to challenge the interests of the status quo' (Lees and Mayo, 1984, p. 29).

The community action strategy developed alongside, and sought to challenge, the conventional arrangements for participation from the late 1960s onwards. There were however limits to what could be achieved by individual campaigns and locally based activism and by the late 1970s some of those most closely involved were moving towards an accommodation with an increasingly left-wing Labour party (Gyford, 1985, p. 33–6). It was this eventual rapprochement between the Labour left and community action which provided one of the elements of the new local socialism of the late 1980s, for it was seen as a possible creator of 'prefigurative forms of alternative models of participative "socialist democracy"' (Lees and Mayo, 1984, p. 29). From this source flowed a concern for the decentralization and democratization of service delivery, for the promotion of co-operative ventures, for greater client or user control of facilities and for the encouragement of self-organization and self-management in a more generously funded voluntary sector.

Liberals too had seen a need to go beyond the limits of statutory participation and to promote community-based activism. Their own brand of community politics considerably pre-dated the emergence of Labour's local socialism, although for many years it was more an electoral strategy based on attention to local problems than a prescription for service delivery or council management. Increasing electoral success however placed Liberals in a position where they could implement certain experiments of their own in authorities such as Richmond-on-Thames and Tower Hamlets. The latter case seemed also to indicate the ways in which Liberal and Labour approaches to decentralization might differ. In Tower Hamlets the Liberal council, committed to the idea of electoral reform, made provision for proportional representation in elections to the new neighbourhood committees. Meanwhile, in Islington, the Labour council, committed to the idea of equal opportunities, made provision for reserved seats for ethnic minorities in election to the new neighbourhood forums.

Despite such divergent perceptions of desirable electoral procedure both Labour's local socialism and the Liberals' community politics have each in their differing ways tried to put a positive value on the extension of local politics and on creating a more participative democracy. They have sought to build on, and to go beyond, the various consultative and co-operative arrangements which have flourished in local government since the late 1960s rather than to deflect the quest for accountability into non-political market-based directions. In doing so they have reflected a recognition of the need to respond to a more diverse and assertive society; they represent a shift towards a more participatory democracy and away from the more limited ambitions of representative democracy.

Such developments however are not without their problems for the traditional workings of local government, based as the latter are on the principles of representative democracy. The problem posed by moves in the direction of participatory democracy lies in their uneasy relationship with the implicit assumption of representative democracy, namely that it can ultimately identify a general community of interest, that a representatively elected body can operate as an assembly 'of the whole – where not local prejudices ought to guide, but the general good, as resulting from the general reason of the whole' as Edmund Burke explained it to the electors of Bristol. They also sit uneasily with the other Burkean concept of representation, according to which the representative relies upon 'his mature judgement, his enlightened conscience' rather than upon the electors' opinion of their own interests. Institutions founded upon such presuppositions are clearly liable to undergo considerable strain in situations where social consensus is challenged by the emergence of diversity and sectionalism, with competing groups conscious of their own particular identities, promoting their own particular claims and passionately asserting their particular rights – tenants' rights, the right to buy, parents' rights, claimants' rights, patients' rights, minority rights, the rights of the disabled, etc. In responding to such pressures participatory democracy presents as much of a challenge to local government as does market democracy: each in its own way claims to offer a remedy for the shortcomings of a local democracy based upon traditional notions of representation.

Delegate democracy

A further challenge to the sway of representative democracy is also identifiable in the form of delegate democracy which attempts to weld together the representative and the participatory forms. Here elected officer holders, such as councillors, are seen as delegates who are expected to reflect the express wishes of their constituents and are held accountable by the latter's direct participation in the formulation of their instructions and in the judgement of their performance. Delegate democracy lays great stress on the acceptance of majority decisions, on the mandating of delegates and on their reporting back to those who confer the mandate upon them. It may be arguable that representative democracy began to move in the direction of delegate democracy once politics became synonmyous with party politics, with its notions of the caucus, party discipline and the mandate. It has however been particularly associated with Labour movement politics as a consequence of the latter's desire to avoid the fragmentation or dilution of collective strength by the waywardness of individuals or minorities.

Whereas market democracy identifies the 'people' with individual 'economic men' seeking private gain, the delegate democracy of the Labour movement identifies the 'people' with a working class seeking collective advancement, with diversity and sectionalism being transcended by unity and solidarity. It tends to see the institutions of the Labour party as having a crucial role as the mechanism whereby popular aspirations are given practical effect. Thus if the voters elect a Labour council to power on the basis of a specific manifesto then the local Labour party becomes the guardian of that voters' mandate and on behalf of the voters the party must ensure that councillors keep faith with their election pledges. Labour's experiments in local socialism have often attempted to combine elements of delegate democracy alongside those of participatory democracy in a way which clearly distinguishes them from Liberal ventures in community politics, which make no such attempts. Combining the two variants of democracy has not always proved easy. The former chair of the GLC Womens' Committee, for example, realized that in trying to increase women's participation it was necessary to recognize that 'large numbers of women are unorganised, so the normal delegate meetings you have in the labour movement would not be appropriate' (Wainwright, 1987, pp. 110–11).

The problems of trying to combine delegate and participatory democracy may not be confined solely to the area of women's issues. In the course of reviewing the Labour left's impact on local government, Patrick Seyd (1987, p. 154) points out a more general difficulty: 'Election manifestos and electoral mandates provide a clear basis for action whereas "grass-roots" decision-making will tend to modify such clarity of direction.' The prospect of any such 'modification' might not be too appealing to the more rigorous proponents of delegate democracy.

The nearest approach to a working model of party based delegate democracy at local level in recent years was that of Liverpool during the period 1983–6. There an extremely active local Labour party continuously reported back to the electorate on its council activities via frequent newsletters, doorstep campaigning and numerous public meetings at workplace, ward and city level. The party insisted however that its own institutions were the only appropriate forums for any debates on city issues and its concept of politics was one of mobilizing people around an agreed party line rather than opening up a wider public debate (Gyford, 1985, pp. 91–3). At the same time the party, as guardian of the voters' mandate, maintained effective control over the majority Labour group, whose policies and officers it selected. No other authority has displayed the full range of features of delegate democracy that were exhibited in Liverpool. However, in one or two cases there have been debates as to how far, for example, a councillor should accept a mandate from a local ward branch when voting in group or in council and one local Labour party in London described its GLC councillor as 'an elected delegate of this party' (Livingstone, 1987, p. 334). Some party activists have accused councillors of betraying their mandate by a failure to keep to the letter of the manifesto and some Labour councillors themselves have resigned from their council rather than break faith with the terms of the manifesto against the wishes of those who had mandated them.

This last practice highlights one particular conflict between delegate democracy and the conventional workings of local government under representative democracy. This conflict was explored in the case of *Regina v. London Borough of Waltham Forest* in which six Labour councillors were alleged to have voted in council in support of a 62 per cent increase in the domestic rate for 1986–7 contrary to their personal views which had led them to oppose the increase at the prior Labour group meeting. Mention was made in Chapter 1 of the hostility the rate increase generated among some rate-payers, even to the point of a death threat against the leader of the council. A less drastic remedy however was canvassed by a Ratepayers' Action Group which sought a judicial review of the rate increase decision. The Queen's Bench Divisional Court dismissed the application for review and the Action Group then appealed.

A key point at issue before the Court of Appeal was the question posed in his eventual judgement by the Master of the Rolls, Sir John Donaldson, namely whether 'the Council-lors fettered their discretion by regarding themselves as bound by the terms of their election manifesto'. Sir John was quite clear that each councillor had a 'personal and indi-vidual duty to consider the issues involved and to reach his own decision' – the very model of Burkean representative democracy. If any councillor had allowed his discretion to be fettered to the extent of regarding himself 'as a mere delegate of the majority group as a whole' who 'either votes with the majority or . . . resigns from the Council' then 'he would be failing in his duty'.

The judgement of the court was that there was a fine but

'very real' line to be drawn between 'giving weight to the views of colleagues and to party policy . . . and voting blindly in support of party policy'. In this instance the councillors' conduct was judged to fall on the acceptable side of that fine line and the Action Group's appeal was dismissed. The case had however exposed some of the tensions between the differing imperatives of delegate and representative democracy in the conduct of local government.

Democracy and political management

Local politics today is thus the scene of four contending variants of democracy: representative democracy, market democracy, participatory democracy and delegate democracy. These four variants of democracy are not wholly unrelated to one another in certain respects. Market democracy and participatory democracy for example are particularly concerned with defending particular rights whether of economic individuals or of sectional groups: conversely representative and delegate democracy are less concerned with particular rights and more concerned with securing general agreement either by articulating some 'general will' or by securing the acceptance of a majority decision. Delegate democracy and participatory democracy both place a stress on high levels of political activism; conversely representative and market democracy are more passive variants with the former prepared to place much trust in elected representatives and the latter seeing participation in the market place rather than political activity as the best guarantee of accountability.

One issue on which the four schools of thought differ is the question of how they define the interests they promote. Representative democracy adheres to a notion of the public interest; delegate democracy, operating on a class-based model of politics, seeks to promote the class interest of what is seen as a working-class majority in society; participatory democracy facilitates the expression of a range of sectional interests; and market democracy is concerned with promoting the individual interest. All these varying views and relationships can be shown in diagrammatic form, as in Figure 2.

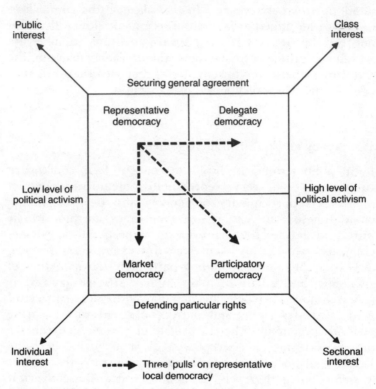

Source: Modified from Gyford (1986) in Widdicombe Community Research, Vol. IV.

Figure 2   *Four variants of democracy*

Each variant of democracy has its own implications for the place of local authorities in relation to the wider community and for the ways in which politicians and officers manage those authorities. The established form of local government based on the idea of representative democracy has placed power and responsibility firmly in the hands of councillors and their professional advisers subject only to the checks of the ballot box. Councillors have been seen as guardians of the public interest, frequently ill-defined, with responsibility for policy decisions and for the welfare of their constituents. Officers have been seen as the source of reliable professional solutions to the problems of the locality and as responsible for policy implementation and departmental management. The inter-action of the two sets of actors is seen as the crucible of authoritative decision-making for the community. The other three variants of democracy however call into question this form of political management.

Delegate democracy sees local authority decision-making as part of a chain of decisions which begins outside the authority itself, in the conveying of a mandate and in the (party based) procedures necessary for monitoring and securing the implemention of that mandate. Councillors are seen as the driving force in achieving that implementation with officers and their departments expected to subordinate themselves to that end. A clear political executive – a one-party policy committee or a group executive – and some political appointments may be seen as a necessity to ensure clear political control of the authority. Professional attitudes are judged largely according to whether or not they assist or obstruct the achievement of political goals. Participatory democracy accepts the notion that some decisions can be made outside the formal structure of local authority commit-tees and departments and that the role of councillors is as much that of broker and facilitator as of authoritative decision-maker. The traditional departmental structures of officer working may have to yield to more generic, commun-ity or client-focused arrangements as far as service delivery and management is concerned, and lay opinion may no longer be devalued or dismissed by professional expertise. Finally, market democracy seeks to divest councils of many decision-making powers by returning them to individual consumers and tax payers and to focus officers' attention away from a bureaucratic professionalism towards a com-mercial entrepreneurialism. As for those powers that do remain, an increasingly arms-length relationship may emerge between council decision-makers and the private contractors or in-house cost centres upon whom service provision is devolved.

Figure 2 suggest that the traditionally dominant representative form of local democracy is now being pulled simultaneously in three different directions by adherents of the other three variants. In particular the government has been attempting to pull it towards a greater element of market democracy whilst its opponents have been concerned either to defend representative democracy or to promote alternatives of the delegate or participatory variety.

The conflicts attendant upon this venture have naturally had consequences for the inner workings of local authorities as they are pulled one way or another by local enthusiasts for, or opponents of, market democracy. The conflicts have moreover been particularly sharp in those urban areas where serious economic and social problems have compounded the problems of promoting or resisting the market project. However this project is not simply an isolated attempt to tinker with the workings of local government for its own sake. It represents part of a broader attempt at social transformation in the wake of social changes which are seen as undermining the basis of the post-war welfare state consensus. As such it produces a clear break with the easy-going dual polity arrangements of earlier years: local government is now placed firmly on the agenda of High Politics with its nature and purpose undergoing radical reappraisal. In that new and exposed position the workings of local politics are inevitably subjected to greater strains and to a greater scrutiny than for a long time past.

Bibliography

Adam Smith Institute (1983) *The Omega File: Local Government Policy*, Adam Smith Institute.

Alexander, A. (1979) *Borough Government and Politics: Reading 1835–1985*, Basil Blackwell.

—— (1982) *Local Government in Britain since Reorganisation*, George Allen & Unwin.

—— (1984) 'Darkness visible: selecting chief executives', *Local Government Studies*, vol. 10. no. 1. pp 1-5.

Allison, G.T. (1971) *Essence of Decision: Explaining the Cuban Missile Crisis*, Boston: Little, Brown, 1971.

Anwar, M. (1986) *Race and Politics*, Tavistock.

Ashford, N. (1985) 'The Bankruptcy of collectivism', in A. Seldon (ed.), *The New Right Englightenment*, Economic and Literary Books, pp. 34–45.

Association of Councillors (1982) *Support Services for Councillors*, The Thomas Report, Association of Councillors.

    (1987) Support Services for Councillors: Recommendations for the improvement of support services provided for elected members in local authorities, Charles Knight.

Association of Liberal Councillors (n.d.) *Standing Orders for Liberal Groups*, Association of Liberal Councillors.

Bachrach, P. and Baratz, M.S. (1970) *Power and Poverty: Theory and Practice*, New York: Oxford University Press.

Baddeley, S. and James, K. (1987) 'From political neutrality to political wisdom', *Politics*, vol. 7. no. 2 pp 35–40.

Baine, S. (1975) *Community Action and Local Government*, Occasional Papers on Social Administration no. 59, London School of Economics.

Bains, M. (Chairman) (1972) *The New Local Authorities: Management and Structure*, HMSO.

Barrett, S. and Fudge, C. (1987) *Policy and Action*, Methuen.

Barron, J., Crawley, G. and Wood, T. (1987) *Married to the Council? The Private Costs of Public Service*, Bristol Polytechnic.

Barry, N. (1987) *The New Right*, Croom Helm.

Beloff, M. (1975) 'Introduction', in G. Peele and C. Cook (eds), *The Politics of Re-appraisal 1918–1939*, Macmillan.

Behrens, R. (1980) *The Conservative Party from Heath to Thatcher*, Saxon House.

Blondel, J. *Voters, Parties and Leaders*, Penguin, 1963.

Blunkett, D. (1981a) 'Towards a socialist social policy', *Local Government Policy Making*, Vol. 8. no. 1. pp. 95–103.

   (1981b) 'Struggle for democracy', *New Socialist*, 1981b no. 1. p. 33.

   (1986) 'Pressures on members and officers', *Local Government Studies*, vol. 12. no. 1. pp. 9–12.

   and Green, G. (1984) *Building from the Bottom*, Fabian Tract 491, Fabian Society.

   and Jackson, K. (1987) *Democracy in Crisis: The Town Halls Respond* The Hogarth Press.

Boaden, N. (1971) *Urban Policy-Making*, Cambridge University Press, 1971.

Boaden, N., Goldsmith, M., Hampton. W. and Stringer, P. (1982) *Public Participation in Local Services*, Longmans.

Boddy, M. and Fudge, C. (1984) *Local Socialism?*, Macmillan.

Boyle, Sir Lawrence (1986) 'In recommendation of Widdicombe', *Local Government Studies*, vol. 12, no. 6, pp. 33–9.

Bridges, L., Game, C., Lomas, O., McBride, J. and Ranson, S. (1987) *Legality and Local Politics*, Avebury.

Briggs, A. (1968) *Victorian Cities*, Penguin.

Bristol, S., Kermode, D. and Mannin, M. (eds) (1984) *The Redundant Counties?*, Hesketh.

Bristow, S. (1978) 'Local politics after reorganisation – the homogenisation of local government in England and Wales', *Public Administration Bulletin*, December, no. 28. pp. 17–33.

Brittan, S. (1975a) 'The economic consequences of democracy', in A. King (ed.), *Why is Britain becoming harder to govern?*, BBC Publications, pp. 96–137.

   (1975b) *Participation without Politics*, Institute of Economic Affairs.

Brooke, R. (1982) 'Keeping the officer out of politics', *Local Government Administrator*, January, vol. 1 no. 1 pp. 3–6.

(1986) 'Management aspects of Widdicombe', *Local Government Studies*, vol. 12. no. 6. pp. 40–9.

Brown, A.F.J. (1980) *Colchester, 1815–1914*, Essex Record Office.

Bulpitt, J. (1983) *Territory and Power in the United Kingdom*, Manchester University Press.

Butler, E. (1985) 'Contracting out municipal services: fading official interest, growing public concern', *Local Government Studies*, vol. 11, no. 6. pp. 5–8.

Byrne, T. (1986) *Local Government in Britain*, Penguin, 4th edn.

Carvel, J. (1984) *Citizen Ken*, Chatto and Windus.

Cawson, A. and Saunders, P. (1983) 'Corporatism, competitive politics and class struggle', in R. King (ed.), *Capital and Politics*, Routledge & Kegan Paul, pp. 8–27.

Clarke, A. (1987) *The Rise and Fall of the Socialist Republic: A History of South Yorkshire County Council*, Sheffield: Sheaf Publications.

Cockburn, C. (1977) *The Local State*, Pluto Press.

Cole, G.D.H. (1948) *A Short History of the British Working Class Movement*, Allen & Unwin.

(1957) *History of Socialist Thought: Volume II – Marxism and Anarchism 1850–1890*, Macmillan.

Conservative Party (1979) 'Why have politics in local government?', in *Local Government Lead In*, Conservative Central Office.

Cooke, B. (1984) 'The appointment of Justices of the Peace – the Advisory committee system', *The Magistrate*, vol. 40. no. 5. pp. 69–72.

Cook, C. (1975) 'Liberals, Labour and local elections', in G. Peele and C. Cook (eds), *The Politics of Re-appraisal 1918–1939*, Macmillan.

Cox, W. H. and Laver, M. (1979) 'Local and national voting in Britain', *Parliamentary Affairs*, vol. 32, pp. 383–93.

Crewe, I. (1985) 'MPs and their constituents in Britain: how strong are the links?, in V. Bogdanor (ed.), *Representatives of the People?* Gower, pp. 44–65.

Davies, J. G. (1972) *The Evangelistic Bureaucrat*, Tavistock Publications.

Deakin, N. (1987) *The Politics of Welfare*, Methuen.

Dearlove, J. (1973) *The Politics of Policy in Local Government*, Cambridge University Press.

Dennis, N. (1970) *People and Planning: The Sociology of Housing in Sunderland*, Faber & Faber.

(1972) *Public Participation and Planner's Blight*, Faber & Faber.

Department of the Environment (1977) *Policy for the Inner Cities*, HMSO, Cmnd 6845.

(1983) *Streamlining the Cities*, HMSO, Cmnd 9063.

Doig, A. *Corruption and Misconduct in Contemporary British Politics*, Penguin, 1984.

Donoughue, B. and Jones, G.W. (1973) *Herbert Morrison, Portrait of a Politician*, Weidenfeld & Nicolson.

Duncan, S. S. and Goodwin, M. (1982) 'The local state and restructuring social relations: theory and practice', *International Journal of Urban and Regional Research*, vol. 6. no. 2., pp. 157–86.

Dunleavy, P. (1981) *The Politics of Mass Housing in Britain 1945–1975*, Clarendon Press.

(1987) 'The limits to local government', in M. Boddy and C. Fudge (eds), *Local Socialism?*, Macmillan, pp. 49–81.

Elkin, S. (1974) *Politics and Land Use Planning*, Cambridge University Press.

Elliott, M. (1983) 'Constitutional continuity and the position of local government', in K. Young (ed.), *National Interests and Local Government*, Heinemann.

England, J. (1986) 'The characteristics and attitudes of councillors', in *The Local Government Councillor, Research Volume II, Committee of Inquiry into the Conduct of Local Authority Business*, HMSO, pp. 9–123.

Flynn, N., Leach, S. and Vielba, C. (1985) *Abolition or Reform? The GLC and the Metropolitan County Councils*, Allen & Unwin.

Forrester, A., Lansley, S. and Pauley, R. (1985) *Beyond Our Ken: A Guide to the Battle for London*, 4th Estate.

Forsyth, M. (1981) *Re-servicing Britain*, Adam Smith Institute.

Fowler, A. (1986) *Notes on Local Government Staffing Structures*, Institute of Local Government Studies, University of Birmingham.

Franklin, B. (1986) 'Public relations, the local press and the coverage of local government', *Local Government Studies*, vol. 12. no. 4., pp. 25–33.

Fraser, D. (1976) *Urban Politics in Victorian England*, Macmillan.

(1979) *Power and Authority in the Victorian City*, Basil Blackwell.

Game, C. (1981) 'Local elections', *Local Government Studies*, vol. 7. no. 2., pp. 63–68.

—— (1986) 'In poll position', *Public Service and Local Government (PSLG)*, November, pp. 33–4.

(1987a) 'Spending approval', *Public Service and Local Government (PSLG)*, January 1987a, pp. 33–4.

(1987b) 'Local voters', *Public Service and Local Government (PSLG)*, May, pp. 30–1.

(1987c) 'The council count', *Public Service and Local Government*

(PSLG), June, p. 21.

(1987d) 'Public attitudes to the abolition of the Mets', *Local Government Studies*, vol. 13. no. 5., pp. 12–30.

(1987e) 'Widdicombe: Some considered responses', *Local Government Policy Making*, vol. 13. no. 3., pp. 3–28.

and Skelcher, C. (1983) 'Manifestos and other manifestations of local party politics', *Local Government Studies*, vol. 9. no. 4., pp. 29–33.

Goldsmith, M. and Newton, K. (1984) 'Central-local government relations: the irresistible rise of centralised power', in H. Berrington (ed.), *Change in British Politics*, Cass, pp. 216–33.

Goldsmith's Media Research Group (1987) *Media Coverage of London Councils – Interim Report*, Goldsmiths College, May.

Goodson-Wickes, C. (1984) *The New Corruption*, Centre for Policy Studies.

Goss, S. (1986) *Local Labour and Local Government*, unpublished D.Phil. thesis, University of Sussex.

Grant, W. (1977) *Independent Local Politics in England and Wales*, Farnborough: Saxon House.

Green, G. (1987) 'The new municipal socialism', in M. Loney (ed.), *The State or the Market: Politics and Welfare in Contemporary Britain*, Open University, pp. 203–21.

Greenwood, R. (1983) 'Changing patterns of budgeting in English local government', *Public Administration*, vol. 61., pp. 149–68.

Hinings, C. R., Ranson, S. and Walsh, K. (1976) *In Pursuit of Corporate Rationality*, Institute of Local Government Studies, University of Birmingham.

and Warner, A. (1985) *Local Authority Structures 1984–1985*, Institute of Local Government Studies, University of Birmingham.

Grigsby, J. (1985) ' "Jobs for the boys" move delayed', *Daily Telegraph*, 1 November.

Gyford, J. (1985) *The Politics of Local Socialism*, Allen & Unwin.

—— (1986) 'Diversity, sectionalism and local democracy', in *Aspects of Local Democracy, Research Volume IV, Committee of Inquiry into the Conduct of Local Authority Business*, HMSO, pp. 106–31.

and James, M. (1983) *National Parties and Local Politics*, Allen & Unwin.

Hain, P. (1980) *Neighbourhood Participation*, Temple Smith.

Harris, R. and Seldon, A. (1979) *Over-ruled on Welfare*, Institute of Economic Affairs.

Hasluck, E. (1948) *Local Government in England*, Cambridge University Press.

354   *The Changing Politics of Local Government*

Haynes, R. (1980) *Organisation Theory and Local Government*, Allen & Unwin.

Hayton, H. (1985) 'Let the people know!', *Local Government Studies*, vol. 11. no. 6., pp. 24–7.

Heald, G. and Wybrow, R. (1986) *The Gallup Survey of Britain*, Croom Helm.

Hinings, C. R., Greenwood, R. and Ranson, S. (1975) 'Contingency theory and the organisation of local authorities: Part II. Contingencies and structure', *Public Administration*, vol. 53., pp. 169–90.

Greenwood, R., Ranson, S. and Walsh, K. (1980) *Management Systems in Local Government*, Institute of Local Government Studies, University of Birmingham.

Hoggett, P. and Hambleton, R. (eds) (1987) *Decentralisation and Democracy: Localising Public Services*, School for Advanced Urban Studies, University of Bristol.

Hollis, P. (1987) *Ladies Elect*, Oxford University Press.

Institute of Public Relations (1986) *Public Relations in Local Government*, Institute of Public Relations.

Jenkins, J. (1987) 'The green sheep in "Colonel Gadaffi Drive"', *New Statesman*, 9 January, pp. 8–10.

Jenkins, P. (1987) *Mrs Thatcher's Revolution: The Ending of the Socialist Era*, Jonathan Cape.

Johnson, R. W. (1972) 'The nationalisation of English rural politics: Norfolk South-west 1945–1970', *Parliamentary Affairs*, vol. 26. no. 1., pp. 8–55.

Jones, G. W. (1969) *Borough Politics*, Macmillan.

(1975) 'Varieties of local politics', *Local Government Studies*, vol. 1. no. 2., pp. 17–32.

and Norton, A. (eds) (1978) *Political Leadership in Local Authorities*, Institute of Local Government Studies, University of Birmingham.

Karran, T. J. and Bochel, H. M. (1986) *County Elections in England and Wales, 1985: Results and Statistics*, University of Dundee.

Keith-Lucas, B. and Richards, P. G. (1978) *A History of Local Government in the Twentieth Century*, Allen & Unwin.

King, M. and May, C. (1985) *Black Magistrates*, Cobden Trust.

Kline, R. and Mallaber, J. (1986) *Whose Value? Whose Money?* Local Government Information Unit.

Kukathas, C. (1985) 'Competition as a voyage of discovery', in A. Seldon (ed.), *The New Right Enlightenment*, Economic and Literary Books, pp. 57–69.

Labour Co-ordinating Committee (1988) *Labour Councils in the Cold: A Blueprint for Survival*, LCC, January.

Laffin, M. and Young, K. (1985) 'The changing roles and responsibilities of local authority chief officers', *Public Administration*, vol. 63., pp. 41–59.

Leach, S. (1986) 'The Widdicombe Report – a perspective', *Local Government Studies*, vol. 12. no. 6., pp. 64–79.

— (1987) 'The transfer of power from Metropolitan Counties to Districts: An Analysis', *Local Government Studies*, vol. 13. no. 2., pp. 31–48.

— (1987) 'The treatment of joint activities in local election manifestos (April 1987) in the metropolitan districts', *Working Paper on Research into the Future of Metropolitan Government*, Institute of Local Government Studies, University of Birmingham.

— (1987) Coulson, A., Davis, H., Game, C., Skelcher, C. and Watt, P., *The Impact of Abolition on Metropolitan Government*, Institute of Local Government Studies, University of Birmingham.

— (1986) Game, C., Gyford, J. and Midwinter, A. *The Political Organisation of Local Authorities, Research Volume I, Report of the Committee of Inquiry into the Conduct of Local Authority Business*, HMSO.

— and Stewart, J. (1987) *The Changing Patterns of Hung Authorities: A Report of a New Survey*, LGTB.

Leapman, M. (1987) *Kinnock*, Unwin Hyman.

Leftwich, A. (ed.) (1984) *What is Politics?*, Blackwell.

Lipsey, D. (1982) 'Labour's new (non-manual) breed of councillor', *The Sunday Times*, 19 September.

Livingstone, K. (1987) *If Voting Changed Anything, They'd Abolish It*, Collins.

Loughlin, M. (1986) *Local Government in the Modern State*, Sweet & Maxwell.

— (1987) 'The conduct of local authority business', *The Modern Law Review*, January.

Loveday, B. (1987) 'Joint boards for police in the metropolitan areas – a preliminary assessment', *Local Government Studies*, vol. 13. no. 3., pp. 85–101.

Lynn, J. and Jay, A. (1988) 'Power to the people', *Yes, Prime Minister*, BBC 2, 7 January.

Mackintosh, M. and Wainwright, H. (eds) (1987) *A Taste of Power: The Politics of Local Economics*, Verso.

Madgwick, P. J. (1978) 'Councillor H. H. Roberts, Cardiganshire and Dyfed: a modern leader in rural Wales', in G. W. Jones and A. Norton (eds), *Political Leadership in Local Authorities*, Institute of Local Government Studies, University of Birmingham, pp. 51–69.

Marris, P. (1982) *Community Planning and Conceptions of Change*, Routledge & Kegan Paul.

Martlew, C., Forrester, C. and Buchanan, G. (1985) 'Activism and office: women and local government in Scotland', *Local Government studies*, March/April, vol. II. no. 2., pp. 47–65.

Maud, Sir John (later Lord Redcliffe-Maud) (Chairman) (1967) *Management of Local Government:* vol. 1, *Report*; vol. 2, *The Local Government Councillor*; vol. 3, *The Local Government Elector*; vol. 4, *Local Government Administration Abroad;* vol. 5, *Local Government Administration in England and Wales*, HMSO.

Miller, W. L. (1986) 'Local electoral behaviour', in *The Local Government Elector, Research Volume III, Report of the Committee of Inquiry into the Conduct of Local Authority Business*, HMSO, pp. 101–72.

Mishra, R. (1984) *The Welfare State in Crisis*, Wheatsheaf, 1984.

MORI (Market and Opinion Research International) (1985) *Abolition of the GLC and the Metropolitan County Councils*, MORI, June.

(1985) *Attitudes Towards Local Government*, Research Study conducted for the Association of Metropolitan Authorities (AMA), MORI, October.

(1986) *Attitudes to Local Authorities and their Services*, Research Study conducted for the Audit Commission, MORI, May.

Moss, L. (1980) *Some Attitudes Towards Government*, mimeo, Birkbeck College.

Muchnick, D. (1970) *Urban Renewal in Liverpool*, Bell.

Murphy, D. (1976) *The Silent Watchdog: The Press in Local Politics*, Constable.

National Consumer Council (1986) *Measuring Up: Consumer Assessment of Local Authority Services*, National Consumer Council.

Newton, K. (1976) *Second City Politics*, Oxford: Oxford University Press.

Norton, A. (1978) 'The evidence considered', in G. W. Jones and A. Norton (eds), *Political Leadership in Local Authorities*, Institute of Local Government Studies, University of Birmingham, pp. 206–31.

O'Leary, B. (1987) 'Why was the GLC abolished?', *International Journal of Urban and Regional Research*, vol. II. no. 2.

Parkinson, M. (1985) *Liverpool on the Brink*, Policy Journals.

(1986a) 'Creative accounting and financial ingenuity in local government: the case of Liverpool', *Public Money*, March, vol. 5. no. 4. pp. 27–32.

(1986b) 'Decision-making by Liverpool City Council: setting the rate 1985–86', in *Aspects of Local Democracy, Research Volume IV, Committee of Inquiry into the Conduct of Local Authority Business*, HMSO, pp. 36–80.

Pinto-Duschinsky, M. (1972) 'Central office and "power" in the Conservative party', *Political Studies*, vol. 20. no. 1., pp. 1–16.

Potter, J. (1986) *Measuring Up: A Background Note*, mimeo, National Consumer Council.

Prashar, U. and Nicholas, S. (1986) *Routes or Roadblocks? Consulting Minority Communities in London Boroughs*, Runnymede Trust.

Rallings, C. and Thrasher, M. (1981) 'Disillusion, age and frustration – why councillors are calling it a day', *Local Government Chronicle*, 9 October, no. 5970., pp. 1041–2.

and Thrasher, M. (1987) *The 1987 Metropolitan Borough Council Election Results: A Statistical Report*, Centre for the Study of Local Elections, Plymouth Polytechnic.

Ramsdale, P. and Capon, S. (1986) 'Members' Allowances', in *The Local Government Councillor, Research Volume II, Report of the Committee of Inquiry into the Conduct of Local Authority Business*, HMSO, pp. 124–57.

and Capon, S. (1986) 'An analysis of local authority discretionary expenditure in 1984–85', in *Aspects of Local Democracy, Research Volume IV, Report of the Committee of Inquiry into the Conduct of Local Authority Business* HMSO, pp. 11–35.

Ravetz, A. (1974) *Model Estate*, Croom Helm.

Rhodes, R. A. W. (1985) 'Intergovernmental relations in the post-war period', *Local Government Studies*, vol. 11. no. 6., pp. 35–57.

(1986) *The National World of Local Government*, Allen & Unwin.

(1987a) 'The reform of local government – revival of an industry', *Public Administration*, vol. 65. no. 2., pp. 193–207.

(1987b) 'Developing the public service orientation', *Local Government Studies*, vol. 13. no. 3., pp. 63–73.

Robb, D. and Burns, T. (1986) 'Advancing the science of advocacy polling: the case of the Greater London Council', in ESOMAR, *Seminar on Opinion Polls*, Strasburg, France, November, pp. 371–89.

Robinson, D. (Chairman) (1977) *Remuneration of Councillors:* vol. I, *Report*, vol. II, *The Surveys of Councillors and Local Authorities*, HMSO.

Saunders, P. (1983) *The 'Regional State': A Review of the Literature and Agenda for Research*, Urban and Regional Studies Working Paper 35, University of Sussex.

Schofield, M. (1977) 'The "nationalisation" of local politics', *New Society*, 28 April, pp. 165–6.

Seldon, A. (1982) 'Preface' in D. Green, *Welfare State: For Rich or For Poor?*, Occasional Paper 63, Institute of Economic Afairs.

Seyd, p. (1987) *The Rise and Fall of the Labour Left*, Macmillan.

Sharpe, L. J. (1978) 'Reforming the grass roots', in A. H. Halsey and D. E. Butler (eds), *Policy and Politics*, Macmillan.

(1982) 'The Labour party and the geography of inequality: a puzzle', in D. Kavanagh (ed.), *The Politics of the Labour Party*, Allen & Unwin, pp. 135–70.

and Newton, K. (1984) *Does Politics Matter?*, Oxford University Press.

Shaw, G. B. S. (1908) *The Common Sense of Municipal Trading*, Fabian Socialist Series No. 5, Fabian Society.

Smith, J. and Chanan, G. (1986) *Public Service and Community Development*, Community Projects Foundation.

SOLACE (1986) *Response to the Report of the Widdicombe Committee*, SOLACE.

Soldon, N. (1974) 'Laissez-faire as dogma: the Liberty and Property Defence League, 1882–1914', in K. D. Brown (ed.), *Essays in Anti-Labour History*, Macmillan, pp. 208–33.

Stanyer, J. (1976) *Understanding Local Government*, Fontana.

Stevenson, J. (1984) *British Society 1914–45*, Penguin.

Stewart, J. (1986) *The Many Roles of the Chief Executive*, Institute of Local Government Studies, University of Birmingham.

(1988) *The Role of Councillors in the Management of Local Authorities*, Audit Commission.

and Clarke, M. (1987) 'The public service orientation: issues and dilemmas', *Public Administration*, vol. 65. no. 2., pp. 161–77.

Stoker, G. (1987) 'Decentralisation and local government', *Social Policy and Administration*, vol. 21. no. 2., pp. 157–70.

(1988) *The Politics of Local Government*, Macmillan.

and Wilson, D. (1986) 'Intra-organisation politics in local authorities: towards a new approach, *Public Administration*, vol. 64. no. 3., pp. 285–302.

Taylor, J. (1986) *Public Involvement in Council/Committee Meetings*, Community Rights Project and Community Advisory Group.

Tennant, B. (1985) 'Rates consultation – a guide for the future?', *Local Government Studies*, vol. 11, no. 6., pp. 27–30.

Toffler, A. (1981) *The Third Wave*, Pan Books.

Tyme, J. (1978) *Motorways versus Democracy*, Macmillan.

Vallely, P. (1987) 'Voices in the wilderness', *The Times*, 4 May.

Wainwright, H. (1987) *Labour: A Tale of Two Parties*, The Hogarth Press.

Walden, B. (1987) 'Apply the brakes to our local politicians', *Sunday Times*, 26 July.

Walker, D. (1983) *Municipal Empire*, Temple Smith.

Waller, R. (1980) 'The 1979 local and general elections in England and Wales: is there a local/national differential?', *Political Studies*, vol. 28. no. 3. pp. 443–50.

—— (1987) *Moulding Public Opinion*, Croom Helm.

Webb, B. (1983) *The Diary of Beatrice Webb. Volume 2: 1892–1905, All the Good Things of Life*, N. and J. Mackenzie (eds), Virago Press.

Wheatley, Lord (Chairman) (1969) *Report of the Royal Commission of Local Government in Scotland, 1966–1969*, HMSO.

Widdicombe, D. (Chairman) (1986) *Local Authority Publicity – Interim Report of the Committee of Inquiry into the Conduct of Local Authority Business*, HMSO.

Wolmar, C. (1987) 'The fresh face of the capital's politics', *New Statesman*, 18 September, pp. 10–11.

Young, K. (1975) *Local Politics and the Rise of Party*, Leicester University Press.

—— (1985) 'Shades of opinion', in R. Jowell and S. Witherspoon (eds), *British Social Attitudes: the 1985 Report*, Gower Press, pp. 1–32.

—— (1986a) 'Attitudes to local government', in *The Local Government Elector, Research Volume III, Report of the Committee of Inquiry into the Conduct of Local Authority Business*, HMSO, pp. 9–100.

—— (1986b) 'Party politics in local government: an historical perspective', in *Aspects of Local Democracy, Research Volume IV, Report of the Committee of Inquiry into the Conduct of Local Authority Business*, HMSO, pp. 81–105.

—— (1986c) 'Widdicombe from the researcher's angle', *Local Government Studies*, vol. 12. no. 6., pp. 27–32.

—— (1987a) *Politicians and Professionals: The Changing Management of Local Government*, Local Government Training Board.

—— (1987b) 'An outsider looking in', Paper 8 in *Political Will and Professional Skill*, Thomas Telford Ltd.

Index